# HIGHER EDUCATION SYSTEMS 3.0

SUNY SERIES, CRITICAL ISSUES IN HIGHER EDUCATION
Jason E. Lane and D. Bruce Johnstone, editors

# Higher Education Systems 3.0

## HARNESSING SYSTEMNESS, DELIVERING PERFORMANCE

Edited by
Jason E. Lane and D. Bruce Johnstone

For information, contact State University of New York Press, Albany, NY
www.sunypress.edu

Production by Ryan Morris
Marketing by Michael Campochiaro

**Library of Congress Cataloging-in-Publication Data**

Higher education systems 3.0 : harnessing systemness, delivering performance / edited by Jason E. Lane and D. Bruce Johnstone.
    pages cm. — (SUNY series, critical issues in higher education)
  Includes bibliographical references and index.
   ISBN 978-1-4384-4977-7 (hardcover : alk. paper)
   ISBN 978-1-4384-4978-4 (pbk. : alk. paper) 1. Higher education and state—United States—States. 2. Education, Higher—United States—States. 3. Education, Higher—United States—States—Administration. 4. Education, Higher—United States—Finance. I. Lane, Jason E. II. Johnstone, D. Bruce (Donald Bruce), 1941–
  LC173.H544 2013
  379.1'21—dc23
                         2013008103

10 9 8 7 6 5 4 3 2 1

# CONTENTS

List of Illustrations                                                    vii

Acknowledgments                                                           ix

## Part I.
### The History and Definition of Systemness

Chapter 1. Higher Education System 3.0: Adding Value to States
and Institutions
JASON E. LANE                                                             3

Chapter 2. Systemness: Unpacking the Value of Higher
Education Systems
NANCY L. ZIMPHER                                                          27

Chapter 3. The History and Evolution of Higher Education
Systems in the United States
AIMS C. MCGUINNESS JR.                                                    45

## Part II.
### Challenges to System Innovation: Unpacking the Tensions

Chapter 4. Higher Educational Autonomy and the
Apportionment of Authority among State Governments, Public
Multi-Campus Systems, and Member Colleges and Universities
D. BRUCE JOHNSTONE                                                        75

Chapter 5. The Changing Role of Higher Education Systems
in Finance
JANE V. WELLMAN                                                           101

Chapter 6. Reorganizing Higher Education Systems: By Drift or Design?
KATHARINE C. LYALL                                               127

Chapter 7. Board Governance of Public University Systems: Balancing Institutional Independence and System Coordination
C. JUDSON KING                                                  149

Chapter 8. Systems, Ecosystems, and Change in State-Level Public Higher Education
MARIO MARTINEZ AND BRANDY SMITH                                 169

Chapter 9. Serving Public Purposes: Challenges for Systems in Changing State Context
AIMS C. MCGUINESS JR.                                           193

### Part III. Emerging Roles for Systems

Chapter 10. The Changing Role of Systems in Academic Affairs
JAN M. IGNASH                                                   215

Chapter 11. Workforce Development at Community Colleges: Can Systems Make a Difference?
DAVID F. SHAFFER                                                237

Chapter 12. The Systemness of Internationalization Strategies: How Higher Education Systems Are Aiding Institutions with Globalization
JASON E. LANE                                                   261

Chapter 13. Higher Education Systems in an Era of Public Engagement: An Organizational Learning Perspective
DAVID J. WEERTS                                                 283

Contributors                                                    311

Index                                                           317

# ILLUSTRATIONS

| | | |
|---|---|---:|
| Figure 1.1 | States with Public Multi-Campus Systems | 9 |
| Table 3.1 | Shifts in State Higher Education Policy | 57 |
| Table 5.1 | System Central Office Fiscal Functions, Ranked by Percentage of Systems Reporting Function to Be a "Major Role" | 103 |
| Table 5.2 | Nationwide Enrollment Growth in U.S. Education, 1980–2010 | 106 |
| Table 5.3 | 2000–2010 Change in Revenue Sources for Public Higher Education, Per Capita, in CPI Adjusted Constant Dollars | 107 |
| Figure 5.1 | State Expenditures by Major Functional Area, FY1987–FY2011 | 108 |
| Figure 5.2 | Distribution of State Expenditures, FY1987, FY1991, FY2001, and FY2011 | 109 |
| Figure 5.3 | Annual Percent Change in Higher Education Appropriations, FY1960–FY2012 | 111 |
| Table 5.4 | Budget Models by Colleges and Universities, FY2007–2008 and 2010–2011. | 117 |
| Table 5.5 | Perceived Effectiveness of Budget Models | 118 |
| Figure 8.1 | Public Higher Education Ecosystem | 173 |
| Table 9.1 | Arguments for and against Campus-Level Boards in Wisconsin | 205 |

Table 12.1  Sample of System-Level International Offices
and Selected Functions                              267

Table 13.1  Evolving Model for Higher Education Systems    296

Table 13.2  Advancing Community Engagement in Florida:
Two Perspectives                                    301

# ACKNOWLEDGMENTS

Public higher education is confronting unprecedented challenges and demands. There is an ongoing and significant change in the demographics of the students being served. How education is being delivered to students is transforming in the wake of massive technological advancements. Employers are looking for graduates with better critical thinking skills and more specialized knowledge. Governments are increasingly recognizing the criticality of educating students and producing cutting-edge research for enhancing a state's or nation's economic competitiveness. In the midst of all of this, there has been a significant change in the higher education sector's revenue models and regulatory environment, creating new opportunities and constraints.

The SUNY series Critical Issues in Higher Education was developed in 2011 to support and encourage broad-based engagement by scholars, academic leaders, and policy makers to explore issues of critical importance to higher education and to society. As one of the largest public systems of higher education in the United States, the State University of New York (SUNY) believes that it is important for it to take a leadership role in facilitating critical conversations and research that will help public colleges and universities confront the many challenges that they are facing.

Each year, the SUNY series Critical Issues in Higher Education supports an academic conference and a corresponding edited volume on an issue of importance to the higher education community. In the first volume, the series focused on the topic of higher education's contributions to economic development. In its second year, the focus shifted to the future of higher education systems. The conference, which was held in November 2012 in New York City, was entitled Harnessing Systemness, Delivering Performance. More than 400 individuals gathered for a day and half to discuss the current status of higher education systems and what future role they could play to add value to the state they serve and the campuses of which they are comprised. This volume, which was developed alongside the conference, allows for both experienced system heads and scholars to engage in more depth the topics discussed at the conference.

We are indebted to many people for their hard work, thoughts, suggestions, and support in developing the volume. As with any attempt to give thanks to specific individuals, we surely will omit some that were instrumental in bringing this volume to fruition, and for this we apologize in advance. But we want to make sure we do our best to acknowledge those who deserve our thanks. In addition to writing a chapter, Jane Wellman helped conceptualize the scope of the volume and recruit some of the authors. Patrick Ziegler, a doctoral student at the University at Albany and Jason's graduate assistant, aided with research and administrative support. Sarah Fuller Klyberg is one of the most amazing copyeditors we've worked with. Her knowledge of writing style and the study of higher education made this a much stronger contribution to the literature. Kaitlin Gambrill and Johanna Kendrick-Holmes were our compatriots in developing the conference and volume. We spent countless hours on the phone together. Heather Trela, Michael Cooper, and Michelle Charbonneau of the Rockefeller Institute helped with the finishing touches. The entire team at SUNY Press has been great to work with—and special thanks go to Beth Bouloukos, Donna Dixon, Fran Keneston, James Peltz, and Ryan Morris for their support and leadership in developing the Critical Issues in Higher Education book series, bringing these volumes quickly to production, and promoting them broadly. To all of the contributors, who worked under short deadlines and a multifaceted editorial process, we give our heartfelt thanks—this volume is the product of their expertise, knowledge, and passion for understanding higher education systems. Finally, we give our great appreciation to SUNY Chancellor Nancy Zimpher for her vision in creating this series and recognizing the importance of supporting research and writing on public higher education.

Editing books is an intellectually stimulating process as well as a time-consuming one. So, we give thanks to our colleagues and family for their support of such activities. In particular we thank our wives, Gail Johnstone and Kari Lane, for their endearing love and support.

Jason E. Lane
Albany, N.Y.

D. Bruce Johnstone
Buffalo, N.Y.

# Part I

## THE HISTORY AND DEFINITION OF SYSTEMNESS

# 1

## HIGHER EDUCATION SYSTEM 3.0

### Adding Value to States and Institutions

JASON E. LANE

ABSTRACT

Multi-campus higher education systems in the U.S. developed during the 20th century. They began as a way for states to oversee their several public colleges and universities. By the middle of the last century, they started to develop prominent roles as coordinators, regulators, and allocators. However, the structures and roles of the past are not necessarily the best way to contend with current demands and environmental constraints on public higher education. Some systems have begun to explore ways to steer their constituent campuses to advance the needs of their state and to identify new ways to support and serve the campuses—that is, add value to internal and external stakeholders. This concept of adding value is a core dimension of higher education system 3.0. This chapter provides a broad overview of the development and current status of multi-campus higher education systems, briefly examines the literature on the topic, and provides readers with an orientation to the structure of the volume.

In November 2012 a very unusual weather pattern formed off the east coast of the United States. Superstorm Sandy, a super-charged hurricane, traveled up the eastern seaboard, making a sudden turn inland around New York City, bringing high-powered winds, dramatic water surges, and significant amounts of rain. It proved to be one of the most destructive natural disasters in the region's history, with estimates as high as $42 billion in damages for New York State alone. The widespread damage caused by the storm proved that New York's physical and administrative infrastructure needed significant investment to better mitigate the impact of similar catastrophic events in the future.

In the following weeks, New York governor Andrew Cuomo created the NYS 2100 Commission to assess the resilience and strength of the state's infrastructure and identify ways to enhance that infrastructure to deal with natural disasters and other emergencies. The commission was co-chaired by the head of the Rockefeller Foundation, which provided financial and administrative support to the commission. However, despite the wide range of expertise brought by the varied commissioners and the Rockefeller Foundation, the governor's staff recognized that for any effort of this nature to have a meaningful impact, the engagement of cutting-edge scientists and researchers would be required. Identifying the right individuals was a daunting task, because a natural disaster such as Sandy crossed many areas of study, including engineering, environmental studies, energy, finance, insurance, and public policy.

To find these experts, the governor's office turned to its state university system. The State University of New York's (SUNY) vice chancellor of research worked with administrators at the constituent campuses[1] to identify experts across the system. Ultimately, they developed a team of experts of more than 20 scientists and researchers from five of the system's campuses. These experts worked collaboratively with the commission's subcommittees to provide information about cutting-edge research and helped to develop the recommendations that formed the final report that would guide New York's natural disaster preparedness.

The situation described here demonstrates the value that higher education systems can add to states, as well as to their constituent campuses and faculties. The state was in need of research-based expertise to help it devise a plan to secure the health, well-being, and prosperity of its citizens in the future. The state could have sent out a general call for assistance or reached out to one or two institutions in the hope that they could provide some assistance. However, those staffing the NYS 2100 Commission had limited time and knowledge, making it difficult for them to find the right people in the short time they had. Thus, they reached out to SUNY, which was able to quickly mobilize faculty members from across the system to provide the required assistance.

From a campus and faculty perspective, there is also value in this scenario to being a part of the system. If no system existed, or had the state reached out to individual campuses on its own, it is likely that some members of the team would have still been identified to engage in the work of the commission. However, assistance from the system office likely created a stronger team of experts as it drew on expertise across the entire system. Thus, individual campuses and faculty members were given the opportunity to use their knowledge and resources in a way that could have significant real-world impact. The exercise proved successful enough that the team of experts began looking for ways to continue their collaboration beyond their work for the commission.

This enhanced collaboration, or *systemness* as SUNY chancellor Nancy L. Zimpher refers to it in chapter 2, is the key aspect of version 3.0 of higher education systems. That is, to be successful in the future, higher education systems need to move beyond their roles as allocators, coordinators, and regulators. They need to exert leadership in moving higher education institutions toward greater impact in their societies. They need to identify and pursue ways that add value to the states they serve and the campuses of which they are comprised. In moving toward systemness, higher education systems need to find ways to (1) promote the vibrancy of individual institutions by supporting their unique missions; (2) focus on smart growth by coordinating the work of campuses to improve access, control costs, and enhance productivity across the system; and (3) leverage the collective strengths of institutions to benefit the states and communities served by the system.

However, it is also important to be realistic about the environment in which systems exist. They face several challenges to harnessing systemness. Tensions often exist between "flagship" institutions and other colleges and universities within the system. Systems need to balance the needs of disparate institution types and geographically dispersed campuses. System governing boards are charged with protecting the interests of the state and ensuring the financial stability and academic quality of the institutions in their care. Sustained reduction in public funding over the recent years has caused systems and their constituent campuses to identify other sources of revenue to maintain their quality. Finally, the Great Recession has forced systems to reconsider a host of operational issues as they have sought to address issues of access, cost, and productivity.

This chapter sets the stage for the rest of this volume. The chapter begins with a brief discussion of the environmental factors affecting higher education and why now is an opportune time for higher education systems to reform themselves in ways that will provide enhanced value to their states and constituent campuses. Subsequently, I examine the reach of higher education systems in the United States, including the fact that they exist in a majority of states and serve a large proportion of the nation's college students. Next, the inherent tensions of higher education systems are discussed, along with new ways in which systems can create value for their various stakeholders. The chapter concludes by outlining a research agenda for the future study of higher education systems.

## IN SEARCH OF HIGHER EDUCATION SYSTEM 3.0

This volume focuses on the remaking of the governance, administration, and mission of higher education systems in an era of expectations for increased accountability, greater calls for productivity, and intensifying fiscal austerity. Higher education systems were first created as a means for facilitating state oversight of vastly decentralized public higher education sectors. In the 1960s and 1970s, systems began to focus also on ensuring effective use of state resources, such as controlling the duplication of academic programs. More recently, however, there has been a concerted effort by system heads to identify ways to harness the collective contributions of their various institutions to benefit the students, communities, and other stakeholders whom they serve. *Higher Education Systems 3.0* explores some of the recent dynamics of higher education systems, focusing particularly on how systems are now working to improve their effectiveness in educating students and improving communities, while also identifying new means for operating more efficiently.

In the 21st century, public higher education is confronting a number of challenges. The funding provided by many states has stagnated or is diminishing. Demand for access to higher education is expanding, particularly among populations that have not typically pursued formal education beyond the high school diploma. Many students are now swirling through the postsecondary experience, taking courses from a wide variety of institutions (McCormick, 2003). Online educational provision has achieved widespread legitimacy, with even Ivy League institutions making significant investments in these endeavors and broadening their reach to thousands of new students (Lewin, 2012; Pappano, 2012). Finally, the world has flattened, necessitating that colleges and universities explore new ways to become internationally engaged and to prepare their students to be competitive in a global marketplace (Friedman, 2005).

Moreover, state governments are increasingly questioning the return on their investment in higher education. On one hand, they are having to find ways to balance state budgets—a difficult task given the skyrocketing costs for the health care and prison systems and, for most states, declining revenues following the Great Recession of 2008 (Zumeta & Kinne, 2011). On the other hand, states have had to respond to their constituents, who are decrying the rapidly rising cost of postsecondary education. Thus, higher education officials have had to be more active in evidencing the value that their institutions bring to their students and the communities in which they exist.

The environment in which higher education institutions now operate necessitates a reexamination of the structures that guide and govern their activities. For most public colleges and universities, this means focusing on the systems in which they operate. In the United States, responsibility for education falls to the state, meaning that there is no central education ministry or department that controls education across the nation.[2] As such, each state needed to develop a way to govern and administer its public colleges and universities. At first, many states followed the model of private institutions and developed lay governing boards for each of their public institutions (Duryea, 2000). However, in the 20th century, concerns began to arise about the lack of coordination among public institutions, the undue political influence some elected officials were trying to exert over individual institutions, and the increasing competition for resources (i.e., requests for state appropriations) from individual institutions (see chapter 3).

To alleviate these concerns, many states created higher education systems, overseen by comprehensive governance and administrative structures that were situated between the institutions and the state government. To be clear, in this book the focus is mostly on the multi-campus system. One of the more common definitions has been developed by the National Association of System Heads (NASH, 2011):

> A public higher education system [is] a group of two or more colleges or universities, each having substantial autonomy and headed by a chief executive or operating officer, all under a single governing board which is served by a system chief executive officer who is not also the chief executive officer of any of the system's institutions.

Such systems are different from a university structure wherein there is one flagship campus and a number of branch campuses.[3] It also does not refer to a coordinating board structure, where there is a state agency with some authority over higher education, but each institution is governed by its own governing board.[4] However, the tensions, visions, and new directions discussed in this volume are not limited to multi-campus systems. Many of the lessons from the varied contributions are relevant to other configurations where multiple campuses work together.

Multi-campus higher education systems are a primary component of the higher education landscape in the United States. At the time of this writing, the National Association of System Heads (2011) reported that there existed 51 multi-campus systems in the United States, spread across 38 states (see figure 1.1).[5] In academic year 2011, they collectively served more than six million students–approximately 30% of all postsecondary students in the United States and more than 40% of all students studying in public higher education.[6] Moreover, many of the leading public research universities are part of these higher education systems.

There are generally two types of multi-campus systems: segmented and comprehensive. The 23-campus California State University (CSU) system, created in 1961, is considered a segmented style system as all the campuses are similar in terms of mission and academic degrees offered (Gerth, 2010). The CSU system was created to provide broad access to higher education for the citizens of California and

Figure 1.1. States (in gray) with Public Multi-Campus Systems

# State Systems in U.S.

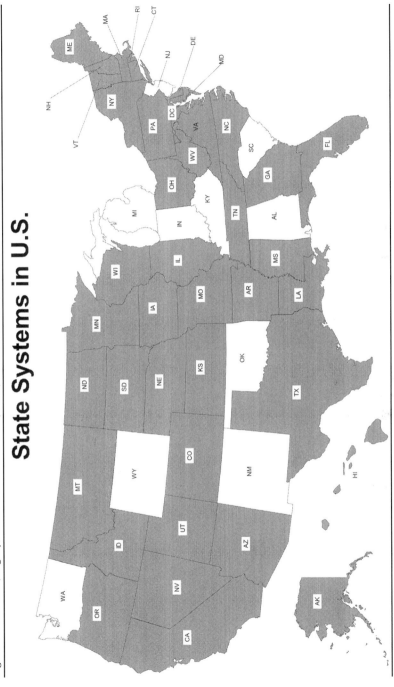

*Source*: National Association of System Heads (2011)

currently enrolls more than 400,000 students per year. The SUNY system, founded in 1948, is comprised of 64 campuses and serves more than 450,000 students annually (Leslie, Clark, & O'Brien, 2012). It is considered a comprehensive system, as it includes different institutional types, including community colleges, comprehensive colleges, research universities, and several special focus institutions.

The role of these systems has historically been to provide a level of coordination among the campuses, allocate funding from the state to the campuses, enact and enforce regulations, serve as a common voice for higher education to the state government, and communicate the needs of the state to the campuses (Lee & Bowen, 1971; Millett, 1984). However, while the existence of systems was acknowledged, many institutional leaders and scholars of higher education governance continued to emphasize the importance of individual institutions and the criticality of institutional autonomy (Corson, 1975; Millett, 1984).

This view was often reinforced as system structures evolved as a type of organization different from an institution. Specifically, they often are perceived as more bureaucratic than academic. They do not have students, faculty, or alumni—those affiliations are with the constituent campuses. Systems are not directly responsible for teaching courses or engaging in research; those functions fall to the campuses.

However, in an era of increasing competition and greater demand for demonstrating societal benefit, there exists an opportunity for systems to take a leadership role. The title of this book, *Higher Education Systems 3.0*, is intended to prompt consideration of what higher education systems can be in the future. That is, how can they reinvent themselves so that they add greater value to their states and campuses?

## WHY FOCUS ON SYSTEMS?

Multi-campus higher education systems are one of the most common ways for states to organize and govern their public colleges and universities in the United States. Despite their expansive presence in the higher education landscape, they receive very little attention from scholars. Myriad studies have examined the impacts of more or less centralized governance structures (e.g., McLendon, 2003; Toma, 1990; Lowry, 2001a, 2001b; Zumeta, 1996), but the study of higher education systems as entities has been sparse and sporadic. The lack of scholarship in this area does not, however, diminish how significant these entities are to the operations of higher education.

The traditional roles of higher education systems are that of allocators, coordinators, and regulators. That is, they most frequently serve as a means for disbursing state appropriations to institutions; coordinating the activities and programs of campuses, primarily with an eye toward minimizing unnecessary duplication; and enacting and enforcing broad policies affecting public higher education. The extent to which any given system engages in these roles will vary based on system and state, but each to an extent will have some involvement in these areas. In many ways, systems have become very functional but not very strategic. They have become bureaucracies, not leaders; conduits of communication, not agenda setters.

This observation is not to suggest that systems are unimportant. By their very size and scope, they have become a core component within the U.S. higher education arena. They serve as a bridge between higher education institutions and their state government— serving to the extent that they can as advocates for institutions to the state government and representatives of the state government to institutions. Organizational theorists may refer to systems as "boundary spanners" (Scott & Davis, 2007). They exist in that nether region between the institution and the government, a leg in each, but never considered fully a part of either.

Higher education systems are complicated entities. A Blue Ribbon Commission (Rhode Island, 1987) focusing on the future of higher education in Rhode Island observed:

> There is no preferred model or perfect system of public higher education governance. The governing system in each state must reflect unique historical, economic, social, political and geographic conditions. However, what is clear is that the governing of state public higher education systems is perhaps one of the most complex balancing acts in the field of public administration. Conflicting goals, objectives and interests are a reality. Systemwide interests are not always the same

> as institutional priorities, and despite claims to the contrary, systemwide interests are not necessarily the sum of the interests of each state institution. (p. 20)

Moreover, state systems have a responsibility for identifying and helping to address the needs of the state. In most states, the public sector of higher education was created because there was a widespread belief that higher education was a public good. The notion of what comprises the public good varies based on the state. For example, in New York, SUNY was created to provide broad-based access to higher education, a role not being served by the state's private colleges (see chapter 2). In Wisconsin, one of the driving principles has been to provide service to the state in the way that the Wisconsin Idea has guided the development of the University of Wisconsin System.[7] The University of California system was developed with a primary mission of advancing research, knowledge, and innovation. Ultimately, it often falls to the system to support institutions and ensure that the public mission of higher education continues to be met. Sometimes this public mission is heavily grounded in the past such as with the Wisconsin Idea, but it is also very much linked to the future, with new calls for higher education to contribute to the state's economic prosperity (Lane & Johnstone, 2012).

Too often, however, the discussion about the appropriate role for higher education systems becomes bogged down in discussion of authority and autonomy, and centralization and decentralization (see chapter 4). These discussions are not unimportant, and several chapters in this volume address them. Rather than only focusing on the degree of authority divided between systems and their member institutions, it is critical to reexamine the role of systems in the future. Beyond being merely allocators, coordinators, and regulators, how can higher education systems bring greater value to their states and campuses? This is the question we pose in the search of higher education system 3.0.

## ADVANCING KNOWLEDGE ABOUT SYSTEMS

Any exploration of the future of systems requires an assessment of their current condition. As important as higher education systems

have become in the United States, they have been remarkably un-
derstudied. As McGuinness chronicles in chapter 3, higher education systems came of age in the decades following World War II. In
fact, by the early 1970s most states had implemented some type of
coordinating structure to help manage the state's public colleges and
universities. Some states had adopted a multi-campus system model
or several systems. Other states created coordinating boards, which
were not intended to govern institutional activity but rather to provide a level of oversight and coordination of academic offerings and
the state budgetary processes. One of the main differences between
these two models was that systems centralized governing and coordination authority in one shared board, while coordinating models left
much of the governing authority to campus-level boards.

A quick scan of the governance structures operating across the
United States reveals a great deal of variability. For example, in states
such as California, New York, and Texas, multiple multi-campus
systems manage different aspects of the postsecondary landscape. In
California, the systems are segmented with institutions grouped by
similarity of mission. In New York and Texas, the systems are more
geographically distinct, although some overlap exists. States such as
North Dakota and South Dakota both operate statewide systems,
where all of the four-year public campuses are governed by one system. Missouri combines both coordinating and system structures.
The four-campus University of Missouri is a multi-campus system,
while the comprehensive universities each retain their own governing
board. The entirety of the public higher education sector is coordinated by Missouri's Coordinating Board of Higher Education, which
has authority over institutional mission, academic program approval, and state budgetary requests. Michigan, as an alternative, is on
the far extreme, in that there is no formal centralized governance or
coordination, and each institution operates of its own accord.

Despite their emergence as a prominent means for organizing
public higher education, scholarly inquiry into the development, operation, and leadership of systems has remained scant. Even in some
of the more prominent histories about the development of U.S. higher
education, systems receive very little attention. For example, Thelin
(2004) dedicated only a couple of pages to chronicling the development of the higher education systems in California, particularly in
light of the implementation of the state's 1960 Master Plan for higher

education (Master Plan Survey Team, 1960). He made only passing reference to similar such developments in a handful of other states. In *The Shaping of American Higher Education*, Cohen (1998) observed that there was a general trend toward greater statewide coordinating in the middle of the 20th century, noting that Section 1202 of the 1965 Higher Education Act accelerated the trend toward more coordination by requiring states to identify ways to achieve greater efficiencies in the use of government funding of higher education.

Brubacher and Rudy (2002) actually argued that one of the distinguishing features of higher education in the United States was its "unsystematized diversity" (p. 427). There is little doubt that institutions of higher education in the United States are incredibly diverse, largely due to the lack of any central coordination at the national level and very little at the state level, at least until the middle of the last century. Even the use of the term *unsystematized* could be overlooked in this context had there been some substantive discussion of the actual existence of systems or other coordinating structures existing in the United States, but such a discussion does not occur.

Much of the literature that does exist on multi-campus systems is subsumed under the theme of state coordination of higher education and dates back to the 1970s and 1980s. The literature on state coordination tends to focus on two primary areas. The first area centers on issues of disbursement of authority and autonomy in different types of governance structures (e.g., Berdahl, 1972; Corson, 1975; Millett, 1984). For example, Millett (1984) discussed statewide system governance structures in great depth, often as one form of how states organize higher education. For Millett, the multi-campus system represented a statewide governing structure with direct control over institutions, which contrasted with coordinating boards that have limited authority and advisory boards that have almost no authority.

The second area of focus concerns the academic review, planning, financing, and auditing functions of systems and how coordinating structures impact institutional operations (e.g., Callan & Jonsen, 1980; Glenny & Schmidtlein, 1983; Millard, 1980). Much of this work has approached the analysis of systems from an institutional perspective, lumping the multi-campus system structure with other forms of statewide coordination activities and viewing them as a state agency rather than as a new organizational form to govern higher education. Because of this broad lumping, in many cases analysis tended to assess how the actions of the system affected institutional operations rather than how the system fulfilled its mission of serving the state. In fact, the tension between system and institutional missions, discussed throughout this book, seemed not to be widely considered in this earlier era of analysis. In many cases, the institutional mission was simply prioritized over the system mission. Consequently, systems tended to be marginalized as bureaucratic structures, and very little attention was given to how they could add value to their states and campuses.

Much of what has been written explicitly about multi-campus higher education systems exists as policy reports, commentary, and unpublished papers (e.g., Callan, 1994a, 1994b; Johnstone, 1991, 1992, 1993; Langenberg, 1994; Lyall, 2011; McGuinness, 1991; Millett, 1982; Pettit, 1989; Yudof, 2008). However, there exists a handful of more scholarly inquiry into this area. A very small number of studies have engaged in a comprehensive examination of system structures. Some scholars have examined specific aspects of the multi-campus system, such as the role of the chief executive officer (Kauffman, 1980), decision-making processes (Timberlake, 2004), planning (Womack & Podemski, 1985), lobbying (Pettit, 1987), and accountability mechanisms (Rothchild, 2011). In each of these writings, the authors explored these specific aspects of the system, weighing the system's role and its relationship between the state and constituent campuses.

The first systematic study of multi-campus systems was completed in the early 1970s by Lee and Bowen (1971, 1975), who investigated the operations of 11 multi-campus systems, each of which was governed by a system-wide executive who did not also have responsibility for an individual campus. A decade later, Cresswell, Roskens, and Henry (1985) developed a typology of multi-campus systems, examining characteristics such as geographic breadth, composition of institutional types, administrative structure, and whether the system was public or private. Almost another 10 years later, Gade (1993) examined four multi-campus structures, identifying specific policies and good practices.

More recently, two edited volumes have examined higher education leadership and governance in the context of multi-campus systems. Gaither (1999) produced what is probably the most comprehensive examination of these entities since the work of Lee and Bowen in the 1970s. The volume, subtitled "perspectives on practice and prospects," gathered contributors with extensive experience in system administration to reflect on their areas of expertise and to discuss what they saw as the future of higher education systems. Schuman (2009) took a slightly different approach from most others writing about higher education systems by examining them from the perspective of those who help lead branch campuses. Not all the contributors of these two volumes worked at campuses that are part of multi-campus systems as they have been defined here, but the perspective of the academic leader who operates as part of a larger system is an important one, critical for understanding multi-campus systems.

What is interesting about both volumes (Gaither, 1999; Schuman, 2009) is that very little attention was given to the complex tensions that exist because of the different missions of systems and institutions, particularly in relation to serving the needs of the state. Most of the discussion assumed that the activities of public colleges and universities enhance the public good, but there was very little examination of what the needs of the state are and how systems and campuses might help to fulfill those goals. More to the point, there was almost no recognition that it is possible for the goals of an institution not to align with the needs of the state. In this era of fiscal austerity and greater demands of public accountability, the role of systems in steering higher education to meet the needs of the state while also protecting the institutional diversity and academic autonomy of institutions seems ever more important.

Nearly 20 years ago, McGuinness (1996) predicted:

> Despite all the challenges and a few successful, radical changes, multicampus systems are likely to be even more a characteristic of American public higher education in 2015 than they are in 1995. What will change most dramatically is what constitutes a "system"; changes will be made in how systems are led and how they function, both internally and in relationships to multiple external stakeholders. (p. 222)

This volume is based on the premises that systems exist in era of dramatic change, and that many are examining how they function in relation to both internal and external stakeholders. The focus, therefore, is not explicitly or exclusively on how to improve institutional effectiveness. Rather, the authors examine the tensions that arise when trying to balance the needs of both the state and the campuses and explore how systems can add value to each.

This volume is organized into three parts. The first part provides a history and definition of systemness. In chapter 2, Nancy Zimpher, SUNY chancellor, describes how systems can move toward a value-added orientation, drawing extensively on examples from SUNY. Aims McGuinness, senior fellow with the National Center for Higher Education Management Systems (NCHEMS), traces the historical development of systems through six distinct periods. While the first part of this book (chapters 1–3) establishes the context for the volume, the second part (chapters 4–9) examines the existing tensions within higher education systems. Part three (chapters 10–13) looks into the future, examining new ways in which systems can add value to their states and campuses.

*Challenges to System Innovation: Unpacking the Tensions*

At the core of any discussion of system tensions are the issues of authority and autonomy. In the context of public higher education, autonomy is fundamentally the freedom from state authority. This authority is multifaceted, however. The state delegates a certain level of authority to the system, which then delegates a portion to the individual campuses. How much authority is apportioned to any one level within this hierarchy will have a significant impact on the mission and activities of the campuses. These issues are explored by Bruce Johnstone, a former system head and campus president, in chapter 4.

As with many relationships, the tensions between campuses and systems often lie in the financial arrangements between them. In chapter 5, Jane Wellman, the executive director of NASH, reports findings from a 2012 survey of system finances sponsored by NASH and NCHEMS. The survey data suggested that there is a continuum of degrees of control over funds, ranging from some systems' having significant control over the disbursement of state appropriations, to others' serving only as pass-through agents that disburse funds as allocated by the state, to others' having almost no role at all as the government allocates funds directly to the campuses. The nature of the relationship between the system and its campuses is changing in many states as funding decreases, tuition dependency increases, and performance funding mandates emerge.

The issues of authority and autonomy have propagated a number of proposed system revisions in the wake of the Great Recession. Some of the more extreme proposals have been made by leaders of flagship institutions, who tend to argue that their institutions could be more successful if not shackled with system bureaucracy and that they should be set free or granted increased levels of autonomy. Critics of such proposals assert that what may be good for individual institutions may not be best for their state, and with such freedom institutions may pursue interests that might not align with the needs of the state, such as enrolling more out-of-state students (as opposed to in-state students) as a way of increasing revenue via higher tuition rates.

Katharine Lyall, former head of the University of Wisconsin System, starts the exploration of several of these proposals in chapter 6. She argues that changing political and financial environments and shifting student markets are requiring higher education systems to modify how they operate. In addition, she asserts that if they opt not to pursue change by their own design, change will come in a chaotic manner by which they will drift among new demands.

In chapter 7, Judson King, former provost at the University of California, Berkeley, and current head of Berkeley's Center for Studies in Higher Education, explores the need to balance institution independence against system coordination. He argues that the ongoing environmental changes confronting higher education warrant more institutional autonomy so that institutions can respond quickly and confidently to these changing environments. He presents a number of alternatives to system-level governance and explores the possibility of creating campus-level boards within a system structure.

Of course, changes to higher education systems do not occur in a vacuum. Rather, they are subsumed in a larger political ecosystem comprised of many different people, processes, and structures. In chapter 8, Mario Martinez, a professor at the University of Nevada, Las Vegas (UNLV), and Brandy Smith, a doctoral student at UNLV, present a model of the public higher education ecosystem, in which the work of higher education systems is compressed between pressures and expectations rising up from the campuses and pushing down from the state's public policy activity. The model is intended to help readers understand the contextual issues that exist when trying to foster change in higher education systems.

The section concludes with chapter 9, in which Aims McGuinness, senior fellow at NCHEMS, offers an analysis of how the pressures from the Great Recession and the 2010 elections are forcing a rethinking of what an effective system is. He describes proposed changes to systems in California, Oregon, and Wisconsin. The chapter includes an assessment of the positive and negative aspects of creating campus boards within systems and concludes with the potential actions that a system could take to redefine its mission and core functions to meet the challenges of the coming decades.

*Emerging Roles for Systems*

The pursuit of higher education systems 3.0 is about identifying new roles for systems, particularly new ways in which such entities can add value to campuses and states. Chapter 1 began with an example of how SUNY worked to bring the collective knowledge of its faculty to support New York State in preparing for future natural disasters. However, the future of systems does not lie only in pulling together researchers. It is about enhancing collaboration to find cost savings that can be reinvested into core activities such as teaching and learning, and expanding access. It is about supporting the work of campuses to have direct impact on the quality of life and economic prosperity of those who live in the state and beyond. It is about improving the educational pipeline so that students can take advantage of courses and academic programs at multiple campuses. It is about fulfilling the mission of systems to harness the power of higher education to improve the states where they are located.

In the third part of this book, authors explore some of the ways in which systems have begun to find new ways to support campuses in achieving the goals of their state. The section starts in chapter 10 with an examination by Jan Ignash, the chief academic officer of the State University System of Florida, of the changing role of systems in academic affairs. Historically, systems have focused on academic program approval, ensuring that new programs are viable and do not create unneeded duplication. However, in an area of increased accountability and enhanced awareness of the need for creating partnerships across multiple stakeholders, systems have begun to take leadership in building and maintaining connections among K–12 education, public and private colleges and universities, government, foundations, and business and industry. In this way, systems have begun to take on new roles in bringing together relevant constituencies to improve the educational pipelines and ensure the development of an educated citizenry and competitive workforce.

Many of the new roles of systems lie outside of the areas traditionally considered their core functions. For example, another new area of engagement for systems is in economic development. Many systems have begun to identify ways for harnessing economic development activities across the system. For example, the University of Wisconsin System employs a vice president of economic development, and SUNY's latest strategic plan, *The Power of SUNY*,[8] has a central focus on developing the economic potential of New York State. In chapter 11, David Shaffer, a senior fellow at the Rockefeller Institute of Government, explores how several community college systems are creating system-wide initiatives to confront the predicted skills gap between the nation's workforce and projected job openings.

In addition to taking leadership in developing relatively new roles for higher education, such as economic development, systems can also provide support for functions traditionally viewed as primarily under institutional authority. Jason Lane, deputy director for research at Rockefeller Institute of Government, reports in chapter 12 on part of a study on the growing involvement of systems and government in the internationalization of higher education. He finds that there are both reputational advantages and economies of scale that can be achieved by systems, which are not possible for many institutions. However, system involvement in these areas, which have traditionally been an institutional responsibility, can create tensions, and serious consideration needs to be given to what extent new programs or services are mandated or optional for campuses. Too much direction from the system level could quash the grassroots initiatives that tend to drive much internationalization at the campus level.

Finally, the volume concludes with an exploration by David Weerts, a professor at the University of Minnesota, of how systems can support the public engagement of their campuses. As discussed previously in this chapter, the University of Wisconsin System has been driven by the Wisconsin Idea, which views the entire state as the campus of the state's public higher education sector and is grounded on the idea that public higher education should work to improve the quality of life for the state's citizens. Weerts argues in chapter 12 that there is now a renewed desire among systems to re-envision the civic roles and responsibilities of colleges and universities.

The discussions presented here are only a snapshot of the new directions that higher education systems might pursue in the future. The topics of these chapters were selected to evidence the development of higher education systems 3.0, but there are still many more options to be explored.

## AN EYE TOWARD THE FUTURE

One of the few certainties of the governance of public higher education is that it is ever changing. It seems that every year at least one state is evaluating, if not changing, the composition of its higher education system governance structures. Such changes seem to go through evolutions of more or less centralization of authority, although it is very unlikely that states—at least the vast majority that now have it—will completely eliminate central coordination. In fact, McGuinness appears to be correct that systems are more important now than they were 20 years ago, and they are likely to grow in importance in the coming decade.

Even though states now pay a lower share of the overall operating costs of public higher education than they have in the past, they still expect that public colleges and universities contribute to the overall well-being of the state and its citizens. This expectation means that the role of systems will likely expand beyond being administrative bureaucracies. Their value will be found in their ability to communicate the contributions of campuses to state leaders, enable campuses to pursue their missions, and steer campuses to meet the needs of the state.

## NOTES

1. The terms *campuses* and *institutions* are often used interchangeably in the volume in reference to the academic entities of which systems are comprised.
2. There is a U.S. Department of Education, which is headed by a member of the president's cabinet. This entity is responsible for overseeing the federal financial aid system and a host of other

federally funded programs for higher education. It also implements federal regulations for higher education, but it does not have any direct control over the nation's colleges and universities. See Hendrickson, Lane, Harris, and Dorman (2012) for more information about federal engagement in postsecondary education.

3. An example of this type of system is the Pennsylvania State University, which has 24 campuses. The flagship campus is located at University Park, and the president of that campus also serves as the head of the entire university.

4. Missouri's Coordinating Board for Higher Education has some limited budgetary and academic approval authority over all public colleges and universities in the state. However, the governing authority of each institution is vested in separate governing boards. One of those institutions, the University of Missouri, is an example of a multi-campus system as it has four campuses, each with its own chancellor. A single president oversees the entire system.

5. In the fall of 2012, the Louisiana State University System was undergoing structural changes that may result in the system becoming a single institution with multiple branch campuses and no longer fitting the NASH definition for a multi-campus system.

6. These numbers are calculated by dividing the total headcount for all multi-campus systems in academic year 2011 by the total number of students in the United States.

7. The Wisconsin Idea is the belief that the state's university system should provide benefit "to the government in the forms of serving in office, offering advice about public policy, providing information and exercising technical skill, and to the citizens in the forms of doing research directed at solving problems that are important to the state and conducting outreach activities" (Stark, 1995, p. 20).

8. More about *The Power of SUNY* and how the system is measuring its impact can be found at http://www.suny.edu/powerofsuny/.

## REFERENCES

Berdahl, R. O. (1971). *Statewide coordination of higher education.* Washington, DC: American Council on Education.

Brubacher, J. S., & Rudy, W. (2002). *Higher education in transition:*

*A history of American colleges and universities* (4th ed). Piscataway, NJ: Transaction Publishers.

Callan, P. M. (1994a, May/June). The gauntlet for multicampus systems. *Trusteeship*, 2(3), 16–19.

Callan, P. M. (1994b). *Multicampus systems: Questions for the 1990s*. Unpublished manuscript, California Higher Education Policy Center.

Callan, P. M., & Jonsen, R. W. (1980). Trends in statewide planning and coordination. *Educational Record*, 61(3), 50–53.

Cohen, A. R. (1998). *The shaping of American higher education: Emergence and growth of the contemporary system*. San Francisco, CA: Jossey-Bass.

Corson, J. J. (1975). *The governance of colleges and universities*. New York, NY: McGraw-Hill.

Creswell, J. W., Roskens, R. W., & Henry, T. C. (1985). A typology of multicampus systems. *The Journal of Higher Education*, 56(1), 26–37.

Duryea, E. D. (2000). *The academic corporation: A history of college and university governing boards*. New York: Falmer Press.

Friedman, T. L. (2005). *The world is flat: A brief history of the twenty-first century*. New York, NY: Farrar, Straus and Giroux.

Gade, M. L. (1993). *Four multicampus systems: Some policies and practices that work*. Washington, DC: Association of Governing Boards of Colleges and Universities.

Gaither, G. H. (Ed.). (1999). *The multicampus system: Perspectives on practice and prospects*. Sterling, WV: Stylus Press.

Gerth, D. R. (2010). *The people's university: A history of the California State University*. Berkeley, CA: Berkeley Public Policy Press.

Glenny, L., & Schmidtlein, F. (1983). The role of the state governance of higher education. *Educational Evaluation and Policy Analysis*, 5(2), 133–153.

Hendrickson, R. M., Lane, J. E., Harris, J. T., & Dorman, R. H. (2013). *Academic leadership and governance of higher education: A guide for trustees, leaders, and aspiring leaders of two- and four-year institutions*. Henderson, VA: Stylus Press.

Higher Education Act of 1965, Pub. L. No. 89-329 (1965).

Johnstone, D. B. (1991). Budget operations for SUNY in face of additional major cuts in general fund appropriations. In *Studies in Public Higher Education* (Vol. 2). Albany: State University of New York Press.

Johnstone, D. B. (1992). *Central administration of public multi-campus college and university systems.* Albany: State University of New York Press.

Johnstone, D. B. (1993). *Public multi-campus college and university systems: Structure, functions, and rationale.* Washington, DC: The National Association of System Heads.

Kauffman, J. (1980). Presidents and chancellors in multicampus systems. In *At the pleasure of board: The service of the college and university president.* Washington, DC: American Council on Education.

Lane, J. E., & Johnstone, D. B. (Eds.). (2012). *Colleges and universities as economic drivers: Measuring higher education's contributions to economic development.* Albany: State University of New York Press.

Langenberg, D. (1994, March/April). Why a system? Understanding the costs and benefits of joining together. *Change, 26*(2), 8–9.

Lee, E. C., & Bowen, F. M. (1971). *The multicampus university: A study of academic governance.* New York, NY: McGraw-Hill.

Lee, E.C., & Bowen, F. M. (1975). *Managing multicampus systems: Effective administration in an unsteady state.* San Francisco, CA: Jossey-Bass.

Leslie, W. B., Clark, J. B., & O'Brien, K. P. (2012). *SUNY at sixty: The promise of the State University of New York.* Albany: State University of New York Press.

Lewin, T. (2012, March 4). Instruction for masses knocks down campus walls. *New York Times,* A11.

Lowry, R. C. (2001a). Governmental structure, trustee selection, and public university prices and spending: Multiple means to similar ends. *American Journal of Political Science, 45*(4), 845–861.

Lowry, R. C. (2001b). The effects of state political interests and campus outputs on public university revenues. *Economics of Education Review, 20,* 105–119.

Lyall, K. (2011). *Seeking sustainable public universities: The legacy of the Great Recession.* (Research and Occasional Paper No. CSHE.10.11). Berkeley: Center for Studies in Higher Education, University of California. Retrieved from http://cshe.berkeley.edu/publications/publications.php?id=384.

Master Plan Survey Team. (1960). *A master plan for higher education in California, 1960–1975.* Sacramento: California State

Department of Education. Retrieved from http://www.ucop.edu/acadinit/mastplan/MasterPlan1960.pdf.

McCormick, A. C. (2003). Swirling and double-dipping: New patterns of student attendance and their implications for higher education. In J. E. King, E. L. Anderson, & M. E. Corrigan (Eds.), *Changing attendance patterns: Challenges for policy and practice* (pp. 13–24). San Francisco, CA: Jossey-Bass.

McGuinness, A. C., Jr. (1991). *Perspective on the current status of and emerging issues for public multicampus higher education systems* (AGB Occasional Paper No. 3). Washington, DC: Association of Governing Boards of Colleges and Universities.

McGuinness, A. C., Jr. (1996). A model for successful restructuring. In T. J. MacTaggart (Ed.), *Restructuring higher education: What works and what doesn't in reorganizing governing systems* (pp. 203–229). San Francisco, CA: Jossey Bass.

McLendon, M. K. (2003). State governance reform of higher education: Patterns, trends, and theories of the public policy process. In J. Smart (Ed.), *Higher education: Handbook of theory and research* (Vol. 18, pp. 98–120). Dordrecht, Netherlands: Kluwer.

Millard, R. M. (1980). Power of state coordinating agencies. In P. Jedamus & M. W. Peterson (Eds.), *Improving academic management: A handbook of planning and institutional research* (pp. 62–95). San Francisco, CA: Jossey-Bass.

Millett, J. D. (1982). Multicampus governance in the 1980s. *AGB Reports, 24*, 22–27.

Millett, J. D. (1984). *Conflict in higher education: State government coordination versus institutional independence.* San Francisco, CA: Jossey–Bass.

National Association of System Heads. (2011). *About NASH.* Retrieved from http://www.nashonline.org/about–nash.

Pappano, L. (2012, November 2). The year of the MOOC. *New York Times*, ED26.

Pettit, L. K. (1987). Ambiguities in the administration of public university systems. In L. E. Goodell (Ed.), *When colleges lobby states: The higher education/state government connection.* Washington, DC: American Association of State Colleges and Universities.

Pettit, L. K. (1989). *Old problems and new responsibilities for university system heads.* (Monograph Series No. 1). Normal, IL: National Association of System Heads.

Rhode Island. (1987). *Final report of the Blue Ribbon Commission to Study the Funding of Public Higher Education in Rhode Island Including Compensation of Faculty*. Providence, RI: The Commission.

Rothchild, M. T. (2011). *Accountability mechanisms in public multi-campus systems of higher education*. (Doctoral dissertation, University of Minnesota). Retrieved from http://purl.umn.edu/104605.

Schuman, S. (2009). *Leading America's branch campuses*. Lanham, MD: Rowman & Littlefield Education.

Scott, W. R., & Davis, G. F. (2007). *Organizations and organizing: Rational, natural, and open systems perspectives*. Upper Saddle River, NJ: Pearson Prentice Hall.

Stark, J. (1995). The Wisconsin Idea: The University's service to the state. In *1995–1996 Wisconsin blue book*. Retrieved from State of Wisconsin Legislative Reference Bureau website: http://legis.wisconsin.gov/lrb/pubs/feature/wisidea.pdf.

Thelin, J. R. (2004). *A history of American higher education*. Baltimore, MD: Johns Hopkins University Press.

Timberlake, G. R. (2004). Decision-making in multi-campus higher education institutions. *The Community College Enterprise*, *10*(2), 91–99.

Toma, E. F. (1990). Board of trustees, agency problems, and university output. *Public Choice*, *67*, 1–9.

Womack, F. W., & Podemski, R. S. (1985). Criteria for effective planning in multi-campus systems. *Planning for Higher Education*, *13*, 1–4.

Yudof, M. C. (2008, February 15). Are university systems a good idea? *The Chronicle of Higher Education*, *54*(27), A37.

Zumeta, W. (1996). Meeting the demand for higher education without breaking the bank: A framework for the design of state higher education policies for an era of increasing demand. *Journal of Higher Education*, *67*(4), 367–425.

Zumeta, W., & Kinne, A. (2011). The recession is not over for higher education. In *The NEA 2011 almanac of higher education* (pp. 29–42). Washington, DC: National Education Association.

# 2

## SYSTEMNESS

*Unpacking the Value of Higher
Education Systems*

NANCY L. ZIMPHER

ABSTRACT

Higher education is confronting many challenges and the value of
systems is increasingly being questioned by states and institutions.
The purpose of this chapter is to describe how a system can add
value to both states and their constituent campuses by harnessing
its *systemness*. Systemness is the ability of a system to coordinate
the activities of its constituent campuses so that, on the whole, the
system behaves in a way that is more powerful and impactful than
what can be achieved by individual campuses acting alone. Ideally,
systemness permits systems to channel institutional activity and resources in order to improve the economic status of the state in which
it operates and enhance the quality of life its citizens possess. This
chapter draws on the current efforts of the State University of New
York to illustrate how systemness can operate in practice and how a
system can harness the efforts of campuses to bring enhanced benefit
to the communities it serves.

Higher education is undergoing significant transformations.
Among them is the nature of the relationships between state governments, higher education systems, and public colleges and universities. Systems were designed to serve as an intermediary between the
state government and institutions, as a means to enact state policies,

coordinate the efforts of multiple institutions, and buffer institutions from undue political maneuvering. This role has often left systems stuck in limbo, many times seen by institutions as an enforcer of state regulations and budget decisions and by state officials as a biased advocate for institutions. This situation left very little room for systems to take a leadership role in harnessing the collective efforts of the constituent campuses and steering them toward meeting the needs of their state.

Higher education is increasingly becoming recognized as a valuable source of economic and social development (Lane & Johnstone, 2012). At the same time, states have become more demanding, expecting that higher education institutions evidence their contributions to the state—a requirement that has provided an opportunity for higher education systems to take a leadership role in aligning the efforts of colleges and universities to meet state needs. This opportunity is our *systemness*.

Higher education systems have an advantage over individual institutions in that they can harness the collective efforts of multiple institutions and channel those efforts to specific communities through a broad array of institutions and other outlets. Systemness is the ability of a system of higher education to coordinate the activities of its constituent campuses so that, on the whole, the system behaves in a way that is more powerful and impactful than what can be achieved by individual campuses acting alone. Ideally, systemness permits systems to channel institutional activity and resources in order to improve the economic status of the state in which it operates and enhance the quality of life its citizens possess.

At the time of this writing, *systemness* cannot be found in any printed dictionary, but the current unofficial status does not diminish its power, especially in higher education, where it describes the core strength of today's public university systems and how they are promising and delivering far more than our educational forebears could have ever imagined. Higher education systemness is proving to be a powerful game-changer in how communities—and entire states—are redefining and rebuilding themselves in today's challenging economy. Contributing to the impact of systemness is the fact that many universities are beginning to embrace their roles as "anchor institutions"—enterprises that are not likely to pick up and move away because of their large size and deep roots in the community (Rubin,

2000). They are, in effect, anchored in place, serving as reliable and powerful forces for economic development and natural contributors to the local quality of life.

In 1948, for example, New York created the State University of New York (SUNY) to provide for the expanding educational needs of the state and its increasingly diverse population. As I have written elsewhere, however,

> [A]t its founding, SUNY was decidedly not meant to be any kind of educational powerhouse. Rather, if anything, it was explicitly intended to be something of a catchall, a supplement to work in cooperation with the state's "priceless private colleges and universities," as was explained by Governor Thomas E. Dewey. (Zimpher & Neidl, 2012, p. 207)

The 1958 election of Nelson A. Rockefeller as governor of New York set SUNY on a new course and provided the first glimpse of SUNY's systemness. Under Rockefeller's leadership, state teachers colleges became comprehensive colleges and university research centers, community colleges rapidly expanded, and students began supporting the system directly by paying tuition for the first time. Importantly, SUNY faculty undertook significant scholarly research at four university centers in the major geographic regions of the state: in the east at Albany, in the west at Buffalo, along the Southern Tier at Binghamton, and on Long Island at Stony Brook.

Rockefeller's vision for SUNY was strikingly parallel to that of President Abraham Lincoln and Senator Justin Morrill for the nation's higher education sector as set forth in the Morrill Land-Grant Act of 1862. They both saw the potential of university systems to, in some way, offer all things to all people. In fact, it was their visionary legislation that first introduced the idea of colleges and universities as the driving forces that could make the American Dream a reality for all citizens. Senator Morrill summarized the aim of the act:

> The fundamental idea was to offer an opportunity in every state for a liberal and larger education to larger numbers, not merely to those destined for secondary professions, but to those much needing higher instruction for the world's business, for the industrial pursuits and professions of life.

(Trustees of the University of Vermont and State Agricultural College, 1890, p. 11)

However, the institutions established and funded under the provisions of the Morrill act did not—and do not—operate together as a system or network. Between and among these institutions, there is no universal or agreed-upon curriculum, and rarely is there a clear transfer pipeline for students or assurances of articulation between institutions. While there may be some semblance of an administrative umbrella provided by a state system, there has been little attempt by systems to purposefully add value to the work of constituent campuses or steer activities to meet the needs of the state.

## THE LAND-GRANT OF THE 21ST CENTURY

While the Land-Grant Act of 1862 was critical for developing many of the nation's leading research universities, what is needed today is a way to capture the collective efforts of the myriad educational institutions in the United States and direct these efforts to improve communities and economies across the nation. Systems are an important tool for aligning higher education with societal needs, as systems have the ability to coordinate institutions and to look across the state to see a panoply of needs and opportunities.

If the Morrill act were reintroduced today, one need only look to SUNY for its 21st-century model. SUNY is the largest comprehensive system of public higher education in America. It is comprised of 64 campuses—from community colleges to research universities—spread throughout New York State. With its 64 campuses, three hospitals, a veterans' home, and hundreds of research centers, SUNY is located within 30 miles of every New Yorker and touches the lives of hundreds of thousands of New Yorkers daily. In many cases, SUNY campuses are their region's largest employer and a critical anchor for their communities (Rockefeller Institute of Government and University at Buffalo Regional Institute, 2011).

One of the guiding principles of SUNY is to be responsive to the needs of the state and its communities. Higher education institutions often attempt to drive the policy agenda and argue for how the state can better serve its public colleges and universities. How-ever capable, SUNY resists the temptation to try to shape New York, and instead, we allow New York to shape us. SUNY has, since its founding, evolved to meet the changing needs of the state's students, communities, and workforce. In an era of decreasing state funding and increasing accountability, it is important for all higher education institutions and systems to find ways to be more responsive to the needs of their state.

## SYSTEMNESS REQUIRES COMPREHENSIVE VISION

Any system or institution that desires to be competitive in the 21st century needs to be mission driven. It should also have a well-articu-lated identity, a vision for the future, and a plan for moving forward. In New York, SUNY has made a priority of understanding itself as well as the needs of the state.

A vision, as embodied in a strategic plan, is best derived through the collaboration of many, reflecting the ideas, ambitions, and deter-mination of all stakeholders and a broad base of contributors. The plan that SUNY is utilizing now, *The Power of SUNY*,[1] for example, was launched in 2010, following my own 100-day statewide tour of all 64 campuses. At each stop, a town-hall-style meeting was held for students, faculty, and interested members of the community so that they could hear and speak about what they wanted from SUNY.

It was from these events and subsequent meetings and stakehold-er input that SUNY devised what would become the six "Big Ideas" or driving tenets of our strategic plan: SUNY and the Entrepreneurial Century, SUNY and the Seamless Education Pipeline, SUNY and a Healthier New York, SUNY and an Energy-Smart New York, SUNY and the Vibrant Community, and SUNY and the World. This plan is SUNY's roadmap, driving our service to students, faculty, employ-ers, and all of New York for the next decade. SUNY is responding to the needs of New York within each of these tenets: working to reduce the system's carbon footprint; supporting research, innova-tion, and new ideas; providing students and faculty with global ac-cess; preparing students in high-need careers; training doctors and nurses to address a shortage of healthcare workers; partnering with schools and communities to seal the leaks in the education pipeline; and contributing to the vibrancy of New York's communities at every opportunity.

In an overarching way, SUNY's goal with its strategic plan is to exceed its reach as an educator in the traditional sense and fulfill its role as an anchor institution in the largest sense—bolstering economic vibrancy and improving the quality of life throughout the entire state, campus by campus, community by community, region by region.

## SYSTEMNESS REQUIRES DISCIPLINE

Public universities are one of the United States' most significant engines for human capital production and research and innovation. Without such entities, observes Fogel (2012), its postwar prosperity and power would have been unthinkable and unattainable. Without question, the challenges faced in the early decades of the 21st century are what headlines are made of: steeply declining state appropriations, wavering federal investment in research, an aging physical plant, upward pressure on tuition, and alternative instructional delivery systems demanded by a new generation of digital natives.

Today and repeatedly, the federal government has increasingly called for reduced college cost, increased productivity in all that higher education does, and a stronger commitment to degree completion for college students and adult workers. This "iron triangle" of challenges must be bent in the direction of reducing our administrative and operational costs so that more of our funds can be invested in student success by shortening the time to degree, increasing availability of required courses, and heightening focus on expanding enrollments in fields that our workforce needs. Higher education needs to be more nimble, more accessible, more transparent, and above all, more efficient.

Critics often condemn the efficiency mentality as an attribute of business, one not appropriate for higher learning. However, the focus should not be on efficiency but rather on what makes an organization great. As Collins (2005) has stated:

> We must reject the idea—well-intentioned, but dead wrong—
> that the primary path to greatness in the social sector is to be-
> come "more like a business." Most businesses—like most of
> anything else in life— . . . have a desperate need for discipline
> . . . , disciplined people who engage in disciplined thought
> and who take disciplined actions. . . . A culture of discipline
> is not a principle of business; it is a principle of greatness.
> (pp. 1–2)

Higher education has historically embraced this principle: to think
and act in a strictly disciplined manner. It is my assertion that this
way of thinking—and of doing business—should shape the university systems of the 21st century.

## SYSTEMNESS IN ACTION

Higher education's greatest benefits for society are improving the
quality of life among all citizens; increasing access to and the distribution of a standard of living that closes, once and for all, the
immense economic divide in this country; and ensuring that the best
and brightest ideas get translated into a better economy and a better
quality of life for people in the United States and around the world.
That is exactly the character and climate of the 1860s that undoubt-
edly drove Lincoln to advocate for the Morrill act, and it character-
izes, even today, this dilemma: If we are the most preeminent higher
education system in the world, producing more knowledge and innovation, and educating more of our population than institutions in
other countries, sought after by parents and students from literally
all around the globe, why is the United States still facing so many
seemingly daunting and unsolvable problems? In short, what is the
relationship between our magnificence and the problems of the world
in which we live?

   To begin to respond to this dilemma, one must ask, "How can
U.S. higher education put its imprint on the most challenging problems of our day?" What follows are a few examples from SUNY that I
believe help characterize the magnitude of our collective opportunity.

*Resource Allocation to Support Innovation*

Resources are not inexhaustible. This fact makes thoughtful, innovative allocation of resources critical to the effective support of a system and its many working parts. New resource allocation methodologies are developing to help improve efficiency and reduce costs by empowering a system's individual institutions to manage more of their academic and financial affairs directly. In New York, difficult fiscal circumstances and the desire to reflect the priorities of the strategic plan prompted a review of SUNY's own resource allocation model. Following this review, it was determined that SUNY's methods were outdated and not in sync with our overall goals for the system.

After years of planning, including extensive debate, input, and discussion with stakeholders from across the system, SUNY moved from the planning phase into implementation of a new resource allocation plan. Included in this process was a review of our various state-funded, campus-specific programs and initiatives, many of which had been in place for years with little review or adjustment and had therefore become outdated. To remedy this situation, some allocations were eliminated or decreased, allowing SUNY to redistribute funding from those programs to priority areas such as diversity programs, student scholarship and grant programs, and initiatives that support the strategic plan. As a result, funding for our high-needs programs is enhanced and a new method for regularly reviewing program needs and distributing appropriate funding is at work.

*Shared Services*

One of the benefits of systemness in large university systems of higher education is that there is opportunity to share services and promote efficiency so that administrative costs on campuses are reduced and more resources can be channeled to academics and student support services. Here again, with an eye toward efficiency, SUNY's systemness allows for directing funds to support system priorities and SUNY's contributions to the state of New York.

SUNY's shared services initiative was adopted by the Board of Trustees in June 2011, when the board called on the system's campuses "to collaboratively develop and implement strategies to improve efficiency, generate cost savings, build capacity, and increase resources available to the core academic and student service missions of campuses."[2] The intent was to redirect resources generated through cost-saving measures toward the system's academic and strategic missions and most importantly, in direct support of students—in alignment with the SUNY strategic planning process and the system's core values of collaboration and student centeredness.

Devising shared services plans requires that institutions within a system work cooperatively to examine their operations for potential savings and develop plans to implement those savings. These plans can include different approaches, such as institutions partnering on a regional or mission basis to identify and implement shared administrative or business functions now performed individually by each campus. It can also mean fine-tuning efforts to enhance procurement effectiveness and expansion of system-wide contracting opportunities. Reviewing academic programs and course offerings, and realigning them where possible to improve academic quality and administrative efficiency is also part of this effort.

The value added can perhaps most clearly be seen in the benefits that being a part of a system provides to each of its component campuses. This value is especially the case for the smaller institutions under a system's umbrella, which not only gain prestige by operating as part of a larger system, but are afforded room to grow as they collaborate with larger, more established, and better-known institutions that have more resources at their disposal.

The University at Buffalo, for example, is gradually renegotiating its procurement contracts to incorporate some of SUNY's smaller western New York campuses. Therefore, community colleges in the region are gaining access to the favorable pricing that UB receives from their trademark and licensing firm as well as the company that makes their athletic uniforms and other apparel. The result is that SUNY campuses participating in this arrangement benefit from cost savings without making a larger investment.

In just one year, SUNY's shared services initiatives have redirected more than $6 million to academic instruction and student services through the elimination of duplicative administrative services and collaboration among campuses for business, finance, and procurement operations (SUNY, 2012). Increased opportunities for campuses to share best practices have also led to enhanced program offerings, academic advances, and the hiring of more full-time faculty in every region of New York.

### Student Mobility

A higher education system is only as strong as the students whom it educates and the success that they enjoy as a result of the education that they have received. We want to bring students in, nurture their interests, help them anticipate and overcome obstacles they may face along the way, and see that they reach their full potential: earning meaningful degrees to secure their place in the workforce and becoming active citizens who contribute to the vibrancy of their communities. To ensure that students graduate, and to promote efficient time to degree, fluid and easy mobility within the system is critical. All colleges and campuses within a higher education system must work together to ensure ease of transfer—to see that credits are accepted across the system and that coursework and programs are as relevant and portable as possible between and among institutions.

To this end, and as a result of SUNY's decade-long commitment to student mobility, New York is now the only state in which any associate's degree recipient can transfer as a true junior, if they take the guaranteed transfer courses in general education and their major. No other state has a defined core accepted at all two- and four-year campuses, making New York a leader in providing clear guidance for students and advisors. SUNY is also putting in place a system-wide electronic database to help advisers counsel students on degree and transfer options within SUNY, outlining for them the most advantageous opportunities they have throughout the system to complete their degree. In addition, SUNY has installed state-of-the-art software at all campuses that will identify students currently enrolled at one of our four-year institutions, who had previously transferred from a community college without completing their associate's degree, and enabling them to "reverse-transfer" their credits back to the community college and be awarded the associate's degree from the sending campus.

The ability to engage and serve students at every stage by offering thoughtful articulation and transfer mechanisms within the system is a major advantage of systemness. By working collaboratively, it is possible to shorten time to degree, save students money, and get them into the workforce quickly following graduation, where they can contribute to the local economy and enhance their own quality of life as well as the community in which they live.

## Strategic Enrollment Management

Working hand-in-glove with resource allocation and student mobility, systems can engage in greater strategic enrollment management. Universities can take into account the types of degrees and programs campuses offer as well as the jobs and training needed locally, providing necessary support for those programs that graduate students in high-demand careers in their region. SUNY, for example, plans to invest in helping campuses to start or expand programs that serve high-need areas for the state.[3]

Strategic enrollment management is a continual process, one that must be revisited and consistently tracked as new data emerge and are collected. Doing so should be the duty of any and all university systems, as having access to this vital information is essential to ensuring that programs and majors are applicable and relevant to the current job market. It also speaks to a large higher education system's understanding of itself as a potential anchor institution that stands to serve not only students and communities but entire regions and states.

## Community Colleges as Pathways to Success

In the past several decades, community colleges have played an increasingly important role in higher education, workforce training, and, in particular, the promotion of student mobility. Driven by developing technologies and the commensurate requirement for a highly specialized, knowledge-driven workforce, community colleges have evolved to meet new needs, all while maintaining their original mission to provide universal access to higher education by removing economic, social, and geographic barriers. They offer opportunities beyond the traditional liberal arts and business offerings, including degree and certificate programs in the widest possible range of practical disciplines.

More and more often, the path to a four-year degree starts at a community college. Generally more affordable than four-year colleges, often situated more conveniently for commuting students, and offering flexible class schedules that accommodate employment and open admissions, community colleges have seen consistent enrollment increases. In the 1960s alone, the number of community colleges in the United States doubled, from 412 to 909 (Dubb, 2007). As of 2012, they enrolled 44% of all college students in the United States (American Association of Community Colleges, 2012). At SUNY, more than half of the 468,000 students are enrolled in 30 community colleges.

## Research and Innovation

In addition to meeting existing workforce demands, higher education needs to be constantly focused on where the knowledge economy is headed. As epicenters for ground-breaking research and incubators of new ideas, innovations, and businesses, college campuses are also meeting the workforce demands of the future. Building upon what SUNY calls "innovation ecosystems"—campus hubs of innovation and existing partnerships with business and industry—higher education is a driving force behind the development of new technologies and in helping those technologies succeed in the marketplace. It is on college campuses that faculty inventions are created and validated by partners in the public and private sectors on the path to commercialization, and where our students and faculty alike adopt an entrepreneurial spirit. The value of developing research and new knowledge cannot be overstated. They bring in external funding and federal dollars, create new jobs, strengthen infrastructure, and generate the discoveries of the next generation.

## Going Global

The United States' public sector of higher education was founded to provide everyone with the opportunity to pursue an education and build a better life. This assurance must remain at the core of everything that higher education does. The key to upholding this mission is accessibility—making it easier for students from all backgrounds to apply to college, be accepted, and once enrolled, have access to a world of opportunities. This access can come from our faculty conducting research overseas, our students studying abroad, or our administrators partnering with their counterparts in foreign countries to deliver a more universal education. It can also come from increasing the number of international students and faculty who study and work on campuses.

Further, our student population should mirror that of the world, where students from all cultures and ethnic backgrounds are learning together and learning from one another, both here in the United States and at partner universities worldwide. In just the last couple of years, for example, SUNY's Office of International Programs has evolved into SUNY Global, a genuine global powerhouse that has expanded partnerships with China, Turkey, and Russia, among others. SUNY has also opened a campus in South Korea and worked with leadership in Malaysia to bring cradle-to-career education to the communities within that nation.

### Cradle-to-Career Education

Finally, higher education must embrace its capacity—or more accurately, its outright responsibility—to reach beyond college campuses in the opposite direction. That is, it must become immersed in schools and communities and aid education reform pre-college. We must partner with our K–12 schools, local businesses, and civic groups to play a role in every child's education from cradle to career. Then, and only then, will we build the more educated society that is the foundation of economic prosperity in every community, every state, and across the country.

The truth is that we do not yet have a system of education in this country. We have silos in which various forms and stages of education take place: preschool programs that introduce children to the alphabet and numbers; kindergarten and elementary school classrooms where kids begin reading on their own and learning basic English, math, and science skills that we help them advance in high school. Then there are the nation's colleges and universities, where—we hope—our students are prepared for sustainable, productive careers in the U.S. workforce. At each step, more students leave the educational pipeline.

This leaking education pipeline is at the core of all our challenges. As a nation, we have yet to connect the dots between the various stages of a student's education. Consequently, nearly half of children nationwide are underprepared for kindergarten. These same students are pushed through the system, and by the time they reach college—if they make it that far—they are saddled with remedial coursework that costs us all money and, in most cases, does not culminate in student success. The full potential of systemness will be best realized once schools, colleges, businesses, parents, elected officials, and civic organizations in every region agree to educate more children, educate them better, and educate them together.

## COLLECTIVE IMPACT

Initiatives and programs such as those illustrated in this chapter will move university systems forward with a vengeance in many respects, but I have to go back to this vexing dilemma: If higher education is so good and so disciplined, why are more of our societal problems not being solved? I propose that we remain in this dilemma because we are not approaching problem solving with the same discipline required to move this country from good to great, or more accurately, from great to premier. It is because we have not engaged in a strategy reported by FSG, a nonprofit consulting firm, called "collective impact"—the idea that genuine change, real improvement on any social issue, requires a cross-sector commitment from a group of passionate and dedicated leaders who are willing to set aside their individual agendas and work together to solve a specific social problem in which they all share an interest (Kania & Kramer, 2011).

While the Morrill Land-Grant Act was conceived of as a decentralized set of institutional efforts, our commitment to some degree of intentional "systemness," that the whole should be greater than the sum of its parts, is a better guide for our future. Examples of successful collective impact at work are popping up all over the country (Kania & Kramer, 2011). In Massachusetts, Shape Up Somerville has decreased childhood obesity. In Virginia, 1,000 acres of watershed on the Elizabeth River have been conserved or restored. Opportunity

Chicago has placed thousands of public housing residents into new jobs. Memphis Fast Forward reduced violent crime and created 14,000 new jobs in the city. Finally, the success of the Strive Partnership in Cincinnati has compelled nearly 100 communities across the country to replicate its framework for improving student success, from cradle to career.[4]

It is easy to see why collective impact is gaining popularity with reformers, policy makers, and advocates on Capitol Hill and in communities across the country. Since Kania and Kramer (2011) called attention to it last year, hundreds of individuals and organizations across the globe—including the White House—have started to explore collective impact as a means to solve the most complex social problems of our time. Higher education systems have the capacity to have a greater collective impact than any organization in the United States because there is no greater opportunity for this approach than in reforming the way we deliver education in this country.

## CONCLUSION

As the United States strives to offer the world's most formidable higher education enterprise in the 21st century, higher education systems need only to embrace their potential for collective impact. Friedman (2005) defined the flat world in which we live today. He later added:

> We have a huge natural advantage to compete in this kind of world, if we just get our act together. In a world where the biggest returns go to those who imagine and design a product, there is no higher imagination-enabling society than America. In a world where talent is the most important competitive advantage, there is no country that historically welcomed talented immigrants more than America. In a world in which protection for intellectual property and secure capital markets is highly prized by innovators and investors alike, there is no country safer than America. In a world in which the returns on innovation are staggering, our government funding of bioscience, new technology and clean energy is a great advantage. In a world where logistics will be the source of a huge number of middle-class jobs, we have FedEx and

UPS. If only—if only—we would come together on a national strategy to enhance and expand all our natural advantages: more immigration, more post-secondary education, better infrastructure, more government research, smart incentives for spurring millions of start-ups—and a long-term plan to really fix our long-term debt problems—nobody could touch us. We're that close. (Friedman, 2012)

Just as the land-grant universities established through the Morrill Act were designed to strengthen our nation's agricultural and engineering industries, the public university systems of today must promote the increasingly specialized, technical industries of the 21st century. As over the last several decades the population has grown and workforce demands have become increasingly complex, it makes sense that university systems have developed as they have. The most advanced systems answer the constant call for progress by driving forward while simultaneously rising to meet the intellectual, scientific, and social demands that same progress creates.

Every great city needs a great university. Great universities prepare students for careers and build the workforce of tomorrow. They provide a wide range of jobs in and of themselves, from faculty members and administrators to support staff and community liaisons, and they support existing jobs both locally and nationally. Great universities educate students, drive economic development, and bolster vibrancy in their communities—all aspects that great university systems can take to grand scale when there is effective, coordinated systemness in place.

## NOTES

Adapted from the opening address delivered at the Harnessing Systemness, Delivering Performance conference hosted by the State University of New York in New York City, November 8–9, 2012.

1. More about *The Power of SUNY* and how the system is measuring its impact can be found at http://www.suny.edu/powerofsuny/.
2. Language is from the resolution, Effective Resource Alignment through Shared Services, approved by the SUNY Board of Trustees June 15, 2011. Retrieved from http://www.suny.edu/

Board_of_Trustees/webcastdocs/SharedServices-June15.txt.
3. The system has already begun this analysis in the report issued by the Rockefeller Institute of Government and University at Buffalo Regional Institute (2011).
4. More information about these examples can be found in Kania and Kramer (2011).

## REFERENCES

American Association of Community Colleges. (2012). *2012 community college fact sheet.* Retrieved from http://www.aacc.nche.edu/AboutCC/Documents/FactSheet2012.pdf.

Collins, J. (2005). *Good to great in the social sector: Why business thinking is not the answer.* New York: HarperCollins.

Dubb, S. (2007). *Linking colleges to communities: Engaging the university for community development.* College Park, MD: The Democracy Collaborative.

Fogel, D. M. (2012). Introduction. In D. M. Fogel & E. Malson Huddle (Eds.), *Precipice or crossroads? Where America's great public universities stand and where they are going midway through their second century* (pp. xix–xlii). Albany: State University of New York Press.

Friedman, T. L. (2005). *The world is flat: A brief history of the twenty-first century.* New York, NY: Farrar, Straus, and Giroux.

Friedman, T. L. (2012, January 29). Made in the world. *New York Times.* Retrieved from http://www.nytimes.com/2012/01/29/opinion/sunday/friedman-made-in-the-world.html.

Kania, J., & Kramer, M. (2011, Winter). Collective impact. *Stanford Social Innovation Review.* Retrieved from http://www.ssireview.org/images/articles/2011_WI_Feature_Kania.pdf.

Lane, J. E., & Johnstone, D. B. (Eds.). (2012). *Colleges and universities as economic drivers: Measuring higher education's contributions to economic development.* Albany: State University of New York Press.

Rockefeller Institute of Government and University at Buffalo Regional Institute. (2011). *How SUNY matters: Economic impacts of the State University of New York.* Retrieved from University at Buffalo Regional Institute website: http://regional-institute.

buffalo.edu/Includes/UserDownloads/HowSUNYMatters_Final-Report.pdf.

Rubin, V. (2000). Evaluating university-community partnerships: An examination of evolution of questions and approaches. *Cityscape: A Journal of Policy Development and Research*, 5(1), 219–230.

SUNY. (2012). Zimpher: More than $6 million redirected to students in first year of shared services initiative [Press Release]. Retrieved from http://www.suny.edu/sunynews/News.cfm?filname=9.18.12RedirectedFundsinFirstYearofSharedServices.htm.

Trustees of the University of Vermont and State Agricultural College. (1890). Report. In *Vermont State Officers' Reports for 1889–1890*. Rutland, VT: The Tuttle Company, Official Printers.

Zimpher, N. L., & Neidl, J. F. (2012). Statewide university system: Taking the land-grant concept to scale in the twenty-first century. In D. M. Fogel & E. Malson Huddle (Eds.), *Precipice or crossroads? Where America's great public universities stand and where they are going midway through their second century* (pp. 197–220). Albany: State University of New York Press.

# 3

## THE HISTORY AND EVOLUTION OF HIGHER EDUCATION SYSTEMS IN THE UNITED STATES

AIMS C. MCGUINNESS JR.

ABSTRACT

States formed public systems of higher education over the past century in response to specific state issues and within the political, economic, and social context of a particular point in time. This chapter focuses on a particular kind of system, a *consolidated* system formed by the amalgamation of several public institutions or preexisting systems. It elaborates on the variations among different consolidated systems that reflect the contexts in which they were established. It then traces the evolution of consolidated systems through six historical periods from 1889 and the Progressive Era through the Great Recession of 2008–2010. Despite political and other pressures over the past century, systems have proved to be remarkably stable entities—many have been restructured, but very few have been abolished. The question remains, however, whether systems will have the capacity to adapt even further to the rapidly changing demands of the 21st century and beyond.

A fundamental question facing states across the United States is whether public higher education systems[1] are prepared for the challenges of the next decade and beyond. Systems are the dominant form of governance in public higher education in the nation. The capacity of the higher education enterprise to contribute to the nation's global competitiveness depends fundamentally on the capacity and commitment of systems to change and adapt to new demands and conditions. Many states formed public systems of higher education over the past century in response to specific state issues and within the political, economic, and social context of a particular point in time. However, the needs and contexts in most states have changed, and while some systems have been able to adapt to new demands over time, they remain mired in the past. This chapter examines the origins of state systems and discusses how these factors continue to affect the operation of many systems today.

## PATTERNS OF SYSTEM DEVELOPMENT

Several efforts have been made with limited success to construct simplified classifications for higher education systems (Johnstone, 2005). Most of these typologies are static; that is, they describe the landscape of systems at a particular point in time and focus on differences in the distribution of functions and powers between the system and the constituent units. Less attention has been given to differences in the social, economic, and political context in which the systems were established and evolved over time. While states established systems for educational purposes, they also established them to address noneducational problems of a particular time and specific state circumstance. For example, several systems were established ostensibly to contain competition and unnecessary duplication among state colleges and universities, but the underlying issue was competition for political power and influence between declining rural and expanding urban areas. Pressures for new campuses and programs were often a proxy for noneducational issues. Regional business and civic leaders pressed for a university presence (preferably a campus designated as a land-grant university) because of the prestige and economic benefits that it would bring to their community.

Similarly, several systems were established as a means for the state to manage or contain the centrifugal forces created by a significant political imbalance among the state's various regions as the population and economic power shifted from one region to another. In many respects, the ability of elected leaders to make policy decisions and reach consensus regarding the allocation of public resources among competing regions depends on a degree of political balance among competing forces—what Dahl (2005) described as "dispersed inequalities." With political power distributed so that no one region (or institution) could dominate the state political process, regions (and institutions) have a reason to work collaboratively to reach consensus through the state policy-making process. Lacking the ability to reach agreement vis-à-vis higher education, states with significant imbalance and shifting power turned to systems to achieve a degree of rationality in the allocation of state resources and manage significant transitions such as the development of new campuses in emerging urban areas. While systems proved successful in dealing with these challenges, the question remains whether such structures are relevant to the challenges of today and the future.

Yet, despite the different contextual factors affecting the consolidation of higher education, states generally used one of two different approaches to create a formal system structure. These two approaches were first identified by Lee and Bowen (1971):

*Consolidated systems* result from the aggregation under a new central administration and governing board of previously existing campuses;

*Flagship systems* resulted from the extension of an established campus in a system either by the creation of new campuses or the absorption of old ones.

They classified the California State Colleges (subsequently renamed the California State University) as a consolidated system because the 1960 California Master Plan legislation brought together under a single board and chancellor several colleges that had been functioning as relatively independent institutions under the jurisdiction of the state Board of Education. The University of California was considered a flagship system because it evolved from branches and specialized institutions of the University of California, Berkeley, and did not evolve into a system headed by a president with decentralized campuses headed by chancellors until the 1950s.[2]

Several of the systems within the scope of the NASH definition evolved from flagship universities with most if not all the development being through expansion from the original university. However, the more common developmental patterns over the past century have been one of consolidation. Patterns of consolidation include:

- Transfer of formerly separate normal schools and state colleges regulated by a state board of education to the jurisdiction of a new consolidated system under a single board and executive.
- Consolidation of separately governed colleges and universities with flagship systems or, as in the case of Maine, Maryland, and North Carolina, the consolidation of existing flagship and consolidated systems.

## EVOLUTION OF CONSOLIDATED SYSTEMS

The process of consolidation took place primarily from the late 19th century through the 1970s, with various shifts toward more or less consolidation occurring in the following decades. This history can be broken down into six fairly distinguishable periods, many of which coincide with significant economic transitions in the United States. For the most part, there is no clearly identifiable starting or beginning point for each period, and there is overlap among them. However, each period has discernible characteristics, and recognizing these differences can help one understand the context in which systems were created and, later, adapted. The periods are: (1) Progressive Era (late 1880s to World War I); (2) Consolidation Era (World War I to World War II); (3) Capacity Building, Expansion, and Standardization (World War II to 1970s); (4) Decentralization Era (1980s and early 1990s); (5) Era of Restructuring and Changing State Role (1990s through 2003); and (6) Responses to Recession and Slow Economic Recovery (2003 through the present). The following summarizes developments in each of these periods.

## PERIOD 1: PROGRESSIVE ERA
## (LATE 1880s TO WORLD WAR I)

Consolidation of higher education began as states enacted laws that sought to eliminate corruption and modernize—and often centralize—state government. The goal of such legislation was to counter the centrifugal forces of local and regional politics. Montana established a consolidated system in its first state constitution in 1889. At its constitutional convention, Montana considered creating a board of regents to oversee the University of Montana, following the example of the University of California. The convention rejected that model and instead consolidated responsibility for all public education, including higher education, under a single state board of education. This structure remained in place until a 1972 constitutional amendment established a separate Board of Regents of the Montana University System (McClure, 1999).

Several others (e.g., Idaho, Iowa, Kansas, and South Dakota) consolidated independently governed public institutions under a single statewide governing board several years after their first state constitutions (University of Iowa Libraries, 2012). The expressed intent of consolidation was to curb what was perceived as counterproductive lobbying of the state legislature for state funding, unnecessary duplication of academic programs and activities, and in some cases, political intrusion and corruption.

The 1889 South Dakota State Constitution placed all public institutions under a Board of Regents for Education appointed by the governor and confirmed by the senate. The constitution then provided for the Board of Regents to appoint boards of trustees for each of the institutions (State of South Dakota, 1889 State Constitution, Article XIV, sections 3 and 4). The constitution was amended effective in 1897 to establish a single Board of Regents for higher education and this structure has remained essentially the same (with minor changes) since that time. The 1897 amendments eliminated the provisions for institutional boards. The South Dakota Board of Regents' Policy Manual cites the original purpose of the board as explained by the board chair in 1898:

> The fact that the people of South Dakota, by amending their Constitution have given the management of the State University, the Agricultural College, the three normal schools and the School of Mines to a single board is convincing evidence that the people have decided that there can be no conflict of interest or [rivalry] existing between the institutions, but that they are each a necessary part of the educational equipment of the State in which we are all interested. (South Dakota Board of Regents, p. 1)

The original constitution of Idaho established a State Board of Education that was only responsible for K–12 education. In 1913, however, a constitutional amendment added to the state board's responsibilities oversight of public institutions of higher education. The reasons for this action represent a classic rationale for consolidation:

> By the end of the first decade of the 20th century, the institutions of higher education [in Idaho] were . . . fighting over shares of the tax dollar. Long after the need ceased to exist, the normal schools continued to maintain large preparatory programs and duplicated the offerings of the university. The separate boards of the institutions and their presidents spent considerable time at legislative sessions lobbying for appropriations. (Guerber, 1998, p. 5)

In 1913, Kansas created a centralized three-member Board of Administration to govern the five state schools of higher education, each of which had previously been governed by a separate board. In 1917, the Board of Administration was reconstituted and its authority expanded to include the schools for the deaf and for the blind as well as the penal, correctional, and charitable institutions. As noted in the following periods, Kansas would make further changes in the governing structure but would maintain a single statewide board (Kansas Board of Regents).

During the Progressive Era, states also enacted broad governmental reforms, including highly prescriptive procedures related to control and auditing of public expenditures, human resources, purchasing, capital development, and other matters. These requirements were designed to reduce corruption and the influence of private interests and applied to universities to the extent that these institutions were state agencies with no independent legal standing. Efforts to exempt public universities from procedural controls dating from this era remain at the heart of efforts to increase institutional autonomy today.[3]

## PERIOD 2: CONSOLIDATION ERA (WORLD WAR I THROUGH WORLD WAR II)

The severe economic conditions of the Great Depression coupled with rising concerns about political intrusion into higher education motivated states to take bold action to consolidate governance of their public colleges and universities (e.g., Georgia, Kansas, Oregon, and North Dakota). Efforts to insulate higher education from direct political control of the governor and to curb political intrusion were dominant themes in the period.

For example, the University System of Georgia was created in 1931 by an act of the state legislature eliminating the existing 26 boards of trustees and creating a single board to coordinate and govern the entire system. After highly controversial political intrusion by the governor over the issue of racial integration in the late 1930s and early 1940s, Georgia voters in 1943 enacted a constitutional amendment granting the Board of Regents constitutional status (Fincher, 2003). In response to political meddling by the governor and Board of Administration, in 1925 the Kansas legislature again separated control of the state higher education system from the other state institutions and created the first entity equivalent to the modern-day Board of Regents. In 1939, the legislature recreated the nine-member Board of Regents (Kansas Board of Regents). Oregon created a single Board of Education in 1931 to curtail the regional jockeying and competition occurring across the state's higher education sector. This board was intended to coordinate and govern the campuses and to ensure that they focused on state needs rather than just on institutional interests (Oregon University System, 2011). Finally, in North Dakota, the creation of the State Board of Higher Education in 1938 was a response to the desire to keep undue political influence out of the operations of the state's public colleges and universities. The board was intended to govern the institutions and serve as a buffer from state government (Geiger, 1958; Lane & Kerins, in press).

## PERIOD 3: CAPACITY BUILDING, EXPANSION, AND STANDARDIZATION (WORLD WAR II TO THE 1970s)

In the Capacity Building, Expansion, and Standardization period, states sought to accommodate demand for higher education. Two trends drove this demand: a significant increase in individuals pursuing higher education and calls for consolidation across all forms of state government. Early in this period, large-scale consolidation occurred as a means to aid the state in expanding access and meeting the needs of students within the massification movement. In particular, the offerings at former teachers colleges were expanded and community colleges were created. By the end of this period, consolidation was becoming a standard practice across the nation and nearly all states adopted a statewide coordinating or governing structure.

In 1945, for example, Arizona consolidated the governance of the University of Arizona and the state's teachers colleges in Tempe and Flagstaff under a single Board of Regents, eventually elevating the teachers colleges to universities and expanding their academic offerings. The most significant change, however, came in 1948, when the State University of New York (SUNY) was instituted. SUNY was a far-reaching initiative that established a public university system in a state that had previously been served (and dominated) primarily by independent higher education institutions. The system initially represented a consolidation of 32 unaffiliated public institutions, including 11 teachers colleges. A system of community colleges governed by local boards subsequently developed within SUNY's overall coordinating framework. As was the case in other consolidated systems formed from institutions that had their own governing boards, the SUNY structure retained campus councils with limited advisory powers within the overall governing authority of the SUNY Board of Trustees and chancellor.

From 1960 through the early 1970s, U.S. higher education saw not only an explosion of enrollments but also its greatest movement toward centralization. Kerr (1971, p. xii), reflecting on this movement, observed, "[t]he freestanding campus with its own board, its one and only president, its identifiable alumni, its faculty and student body, all in a single location and with no coordinating council above it, is now the exception whereas in 1945 it was the rule."[4] He continued by proposing that the multi-campus system could be viewed "as one facet of bureaucratic centralism in American society—in its government, its industry, its trade unions, its education at all levels" (Lee & Bowen, 1971, pp. xi–xvii).

By the early 1970s, every state—with the exception of Michigan—had one or more statewide governing boards responsible for most, if not all, the public universities, or they had a statewide coordinating entity (Berdahl, 1971; McGuinness, Epper, & Arrendono, 1994).[5, 6]

From 1960 through 1973, 14 states[7] established new or reconfigured existing consolidated *governing* systems. The City University of

New York, for example, was established in 1961 through consolidation of New York City's public institutions under a single governing board. The California Master Plan legislation of 1960 established two systems, each composed of institutions with similar missions. In Tennessee, the state's four-year colleges and universities were merged into a single system with its community colleges.[8] Other states consolidated universities with diverse missions—flagship research universities, as well as comprehensive colleges and universities that had evolved from normal schools—under a single board and system executive (a system president, chancellor, or commissioner). In all these states, the rationale for consolidation was the need to reduce political conflict; eliminate unnecessary duplication of academic programs and activities; and create a means for more rational planning, resource allocation, and accountability.

Some of the most far-reaching changes in the latter part of this period occurred in North Carolina (1971) and Wisconsin (1973). North Carolina merged the existing multi-campus University of North Carolina System with the other nonaligned state universities under a single Board of Governors. Reflecting the existence of local boards prior to the merger, the North Carolina legislation retained boards of trustees for each campus but with certain powers explicitly delegated by the system Board of Governors. In Wisconsin the push for centralization resulted in merging the former multi-campus state university system with the existing multi-campus University of Wisconsin under a single Board of Regents and with the campus chancellors reporting to a system president.

By the early 1970s, the basic architecture of state higher education coordinating and governing structures that would remain in place for the next 40 years was in place. Almost one-half the states had consolidated the governance of public colleges and universities under one or two statewide boards. The remaining states retained a degree of decentralization in governance but established statewide coordinating boards.[9]


## PERIOD 4: THE RISE OF DECENTRALIZATION (1980s)

The 1980s witnessed the beginning of a fundamental shift away from the almost century-long trend toward centralization. Nationwide, the picture of change was mixed. Some states continued to consolidate while others rejected consolidation, instead choosing to decentralize, deregulate, and increase institutional management flexibility.

Continuing the earlier trend toward consolidation, Texas consolidated the University of South Texas into the Texas A&M system (Texas Higher Education Coordinating Board, 2011). Following an earlier pattern, the emphasis in Texas continued to be on consolidation of smaller institutions into either the University of Texas system or the Texas A&M system in part because of the perceived prestige and political advantage of being associated with the dominant state systems. In other states, centralization continued, but with a different emphasis. Three states, Maryland, Massachusetts, and Pennsylvania, enacted broad governance changes that established or realigned higher education systems, but each of these changes included provisions that granted the systems more autonomy from state regulation. Maryland, for example, consolidated the state college system and the flagship system of the University of Maryland to create the University System of Maryland. Massachusetts established the University of Massachusetts system by consolidating several state colleges with the flagship university system. The new structure also established a statewide board, the Board of Higher Education, that both coordinated and governed the state colleges and community colleges, but institutions also retained local boards whose powers were subordinated to the statewide board. Pennsylvania (1983) transferred the oversight of the state universities, the institutions that evolved from normal schools, from the State Education Department to a new Board of Governors that would oversee these institutions as part of the Pennsylvania State System of Higher Education. The state granted the new system substantially increased autonomy from state regulatory controls closer to that accorded the state-related universities.[10] The new law retained campus-level advisory boards, but overall authority was assigned to the statewide Board of Governors.

In contrast to continuing centralization in a few states, decentralization, management flexibility, and deregulation emerged as central themes in the mid-1980s. Kerr anticipated this change in 1971:

[T]he future is not likely to be simply a mirror of the past. Bureaucratic centralism is under attack in many places from many sources. The new theme is local control, volunteerism, and spontaneity. From right and from left comes the challenge to simplify and to personalize. It is unlikely that the multi-campus systems of higher education in the United States will escape from the impact of these new demands. (Kerr, 1971, p. xiii)

The movement toward deregulation began early in the decade with actions by several states, including Kentucky and Maryland, to increase the management flexibility of their universities (Mingle, 1983). In New York, the Independent Commission on the Future of the State University of New York (1985) found that "SUNY is the most overregulated university in the nation. Given the vast array of laws and practices that govern New York State agencies, a fundamental and basic change in SUNY's structure is required to allow the university to carry out the functions for which it was created" (pp. 30–32). The commission made far-reaching recommendations to disentangle SUNY from state financial and regulatory controls, several of which remain challenges in 2012.

In the mid-1980s, New Jersey began a 20-year process of granting the state colleges and universities, except Rutgers University, increased autonomy. Following the pattern in other states in the 1960s, New Jersey had transferred its former normal schools from the state education department to the jurisdiction of the state higher education coordinating entity, but the state government also retained extensive regulatory controls. Beginning in the 1980s, the state rejected proposals to form a consolidated state college system and instead granted state colleges increased autonomy and formed a state-chartered nongovernmental entity to provide voluntary coordination of the state's nine state colleges and universities. Laws enacted in 1986 and 1994, then subsequent legislation enacted over the next decade, increased the institutions' operational flexibility in key areas of establishing tuition levels, contracting, and human resources.


## PERIOD 5: RESTRUCTURING AMID A CHANGING STATE ROLE (1990s–2003)

The themes of decentralization continued from the previous period. Most importantly, however, period 5 was also the beginning of a fundamental change in the role of the states that would evolve over the next three decades.

## More Aggressive State Role in Higher Education

Specifically, the states would establish a more aggressive position in promoting reforms designed to link higher education to state priorities. Again, Kerr (1991) foresaw these changes, observing that the country was entering a "state period in higher education" following what he described as a "federal period" from 1955 to 1985 (p. 264). He noted governors'—who he believed had become some of the most influential actors in higher education—and other state leaders' recognition of the importance of higher education to interstate competition: "With all the concern about jobs in economic development, the states are becoming even more competitive and advancing their higher education systems, since one of the greatest assets a state can have in the competition with other states and with foreign countries is its system of higher education" (pp. 264–265).

Throughout the nation's history, states have played important roles in establishing and funding higher education institutions, but prior to the 1980s states generally granted public colleges and universities considerable autonomy in setting substantive policy directions on issues such as curricular decisions and research priorities. The most direct state involvement was through the state budget process for operating and capital expenses and, depending on the state, procedural regulations (e.g., human resources, purchasing, and accountability for public expenditures) applicable to all state entities.

The late 1980s and early 1990s marked a decisive break from the past as national organizations such as the Education Commission of the States (1986) and the National Governors Association (1991) called for states to hold colleges and universities accountable for student learning, and states took more aggressive actions to develop institutional capacities in research and development (R&D). This more forceful stance by the states was accompanied by a shift in their role from developing and subsidizing the capacity of their public institutions to more targeted policies (e.g., finance and regulation) designed to link that capacity to explicit state goals. Continuing the theme of the previous period, the new state role placed greater emphasis on deregulation and decentralization balanced by new modes of accountability (MacTaggart, 1998). This new state role evolved over the subsequent 25 years with refinements within the general theme of greater state policy direction for higher education systems (see table 3.1).

Table 3.1. Shifts in State Higher Education Policy

| From | To |
|---|---|
| Master planning for rational development of public institutions and systems; planning for static institutional models | Strategic planning linking higher education to state priorities; planning for dynamic market models |
| Focus on providers, primarily public institutions | Focus on clients: students/learners, employers, and governments |
| Service areas defined by geographic boundaries of the state and monopolistic markets | Service areas defined by enrollment patterns without regard to geographic boundaries |
| Clients served by single providers (e.g., a public university) | Clients served by multiple providers (e.g., students enrolling simultaneously at two or more institutions through online learning and other means) |
| Reliance on traditional modes of delivery through on-campus academic programs and services | Promoting new modes of delivery and competency-based certification of learning (e.g., Western Governors University) |
| Centralized control and regulation through tightly defined institutional missions, financial accountability, and retrospective reporting | Decentralized governance and management using state policy tools to stimulate desired response (e.g., incentives, performance funding, consumer information) to state priorities |
| Subsidy of institutions and formulas based on costs of inputs—on cost reimbursement, not performance | Targeted subsidy and performance funding linked to public priorities (a public agenda) and emphasizing performance, productivity, and innovation to improve student success and completion at lower cost to students and the state |
| Low tuition complemented by need-based student aid | Shift of costs to students through higher tuition and increasing emphasis on non-need or "merit-based" aid |
| Policies and regulation to limit competition and unnecessary duplication | Deregulation and increasing flexibility for institutions to develop new programs provided that these are consistent with institutional missions |
| Quality defined primarily in terms of resources (inputs such as faculty credentials or library resources) as established within tertiary education | Quality defined in terms of outcomes, performance, and competence as defined by multiple clients (e.g., students/learners, employers, government) |
| Policies and services developed and carried out primarily through public agencies and public institutions | Increased use of nongovernmental organizations and mixed public/private providers to meet public/client needs (e.g., developing curricula and learning modules, providing student services, assessing competencies, providing quality assurance) |

Source: McGuinness (2006), modified.

*Reinventing Government and Public Governance*

Proposals for "reinventing government" and trends in public governance (the overall of national and state governments) provided a context for the changes in the state role in higher education. These broader forces led to proposals for radical decentralization, deregulation, greater reliance on market forces, and a shift of funding priorities and accountability measures from inputs to outcomes (Osborne & Gaebler, 1992; Peters, 2001).

Elsewhere in the world, especially in Europe, the arguments were intensifying about the fundamental role of government, moving from central control and significant subsidization of higher education institutions to steering at a distance, reduced funding, and devolution of authority. These deliberations also focused on the adoption of new policy tools that would allow public institutions to become more market driven, but with the intention that they would be more responsive to the public interest (van Vught, 1989; Williams, 1995). These changes emerge as major themes in higher education throughout Europe and the world through the 1990s and beyond (OECD, 2008).

*Questioning the Value of Systems*

These changes in the public governance of and the state role in higher education led some to argue that systems would continue to be a dominant form of governance for public higher education. In addition, some asserted that, while systems needed to increase flexibility and responsiveness to changing conditions, the focus should be on sharing best practices about "what works" in system organization and leadership and bringing about major system change (Gade, 1993; Johnstone, 1992; Kerr & Gade, 1989; McGuinness, 1991 and 1996). Others called for a more fundamental examination of the effectiveness of systems. Callan (1994), for example, described systems as "vestiges of past and possibly obsolete models and concepts. . . . Governing and coordinating structures and processes will either change with their social environment or become redundant" (p. 16).

*Advancing a Public Agenda*

The state role in public higher education evolved further in the mid-1990s as leaders increasingly emphasized development of a "public agenda"—a long-range plan for increasing a state's competitiveness, benchmarked to the best performing states and, in some cases, the best performing countries.

The goals of a public agenda are not about institutions, per se, but are about their state's population and economy, such as the percentage of the state's population with a postsecondary education credential, the success of the population in moving through the education pipeline from preschool to a postsecondary education credential, and the competitiveness of the state's economy in terms of per capita income. These issues are distinctly different from those that traditionally concern system and institutional leaders.

Pursuing a public agenda requires policy decisions that cut across higher education sectors and across levels of education from preschool through lifelong learning. Moreover, these decisions link with state economic development and innovation strategies across other public policy domains. The emphasis of states on developing public agendas has placed particular pressures on systems. Formed primarily to govern and advocate for their constituent institutions, systems have increasingly been called upon to provide broader policy leadership to link the higher education enterprise with long-term state goals. Few systems, however, have had the capacity to provide this broader policy leadership. Recognizing this challenge, the National Center for Public Policy and Higher Education (2005) argued that sustained policy leadership in higher education must include, among other aspects, a broad-based public entity with a clear charge to increase the state's educational attainment, prepare citizens for the workforce, and articulate and monitor state performance objectives for higher education.

In half the states, most if not all public institutions are encompassed within one, two, or three governing systems; and there is no overall entity for coordination of the system as a whole. In these states, there is no clear state-level venue for shaping a public agenda. As noted earlier, public higher education governing systems face challenges in balancing their governing responsibilities (often for only one higher education sector) with the broader obligations to provide statewide policy leadership for a public agenda (McGuinness & Novak, 2011). For example, in a state with both a university system and a community college system, the university is not in a position to shape a public agenda on its own without collaboration of the other system and, above all, without leadership and support from the governor and state legislature.

### Changes in Higher Education Systems during Period

As in the previous decade, actual changes in systems during the 1990s and early 2000s were mixed. Some of the changes reflected the broader trends described previously while others evolved from state-specific issues and political agenda. A few states abolished systems, and others further consolidated them.

Three states, West Virginia, Illinois, and Colorado, dismantled their higher education system structures and reinstituted separate institutional governing boards—decisions that reflected unique state circumstances and politics rather than any broader trends. In 1990, West Virginia split its consolidated system into two systems, one for universities and another for state colleges and community colleges. In 2000, these systems were dismantled, and separate institutional governing boards were created, although all public institutions continued to be coordinated by a statewide agency. Illinois enacted legislation in 1995 that eliminated two systems, the Illinois Board of Governors and the Illinois Board of Regents, and established individual governing boards for each of the public universities previously within the systems. In 2003–2004, Colorado enacted a series of far-reaching reforms reflecting the market-oriented philosophy of a conservative governor and state legislature to decentralize the governance by eliminating the Board of Trustees of the State Colleges in Colorado (the governing board for Adams State College, Mesa State College, Metropolitan State College of Denver, and Western State College) and creating separate governing boards. The reforms also separated Fort Lewis State College from the Colorado State University System and placed it under the authority of a separate governing board (Western Interstate Commission on Higher Education, 2010).

During this period, the case of Florida was unique in that the state initially dismantled a consolidated system and then reconstituted it two years later. In 2001, Florida enacted legislation to abolish the Board of Regents, the statewide governing board for the State University System of Florida, and established separate governing boards for each of the nine state universities. In 1998 Florida enacted a constitutional amendment to create a single governance structure for the state's public schools, community colleges, and state universities to be implemented by 2003. The state legislature enacted implementing legislation in 2001 that eliminated the Board of Regents for the Florida University System, separate governing boards for each of the state universities, and assigned overall policy leadership for the system to a newly established position of secretary of education for the whole P–20 system. Concerned that these changes would lead to costly duplication and competition among the state universities, former governor and then-current U.S. senator Robert Graham organized a successful campaign to reestablish a statewide governing board for the university system. In 2003, Florida voters adopted a constitutional amendment to reestablish a statewide consolidated system under a new governing board, the Florida Board of Governors. Within the new system, universities retained separate governing boards, but the authority of these boards became subject to the new statewide board (Venesia & Finney, 2006).

In a slightly different form of decentralization, New Jersey deregulated its state colleges through the New Jersey Restructuring Act of 1994, which granted the institutions more autonomy; abolished the State Board of Higher Education and Department of Higher Education; and established a new coordinating body, the Commission on Higher Education and Presidents Council (McGuinness, 2006). While these changes did not involve dismantling of a consolidated system, they reflected a new emphasis on decentralization and deregulation, and a greater reliance on market forces in state higher education policy.

While these states were dismantling systems and decentralizing authority, other states were increasing consolidation. A number of these decisions were taken to resolve long-standing debates about the role and missions of systems of two-year institutions, community colleges, and technical colleges. To address these concerns, states moved in two directions. Several states consolidated two-year institutions with university systems while other states deliberately separated two-year institutions from universities with the intent of promoting greater mission differentiation. First, Arkansas, Minnesota, and Montana consolidated two-year institutions within the governance structures of existing universities. Arkansas (1996 and 2001) linked previously free-standing community colleges and technical institutions to the state's major universities, while Minnesota in 1995 ended decades of debate by consolidating all state universities (other than the University of Minnesota), state technical colleges, and community colleges under a single entity, the Minnesota State College and University System. Through the authority of the constitutional Board of Regents, in 1994 Montana created two multi-campus universities each with a single governing board structure by consolidating all public institutions, including two-year campuses, under the state's two major universities, Montana State University and the University of Montana.

Second, other states (Kentucky and Louisiana) took deliberate steps to separate the governance of two-year institutions from that of universities, arguing that separation of governance was essential to maintain mission differentiation. The Kentucky Postsecondary Education Reform Act of 1997 divided community colleges from the University of Kentucky and consolidated them with the state's technical institutions under a new statewide governing board, the Kentucky Community and Technical College System. In 1998, Louisiana removed its technical colleges from the oversight of the elementary and secondary education board and consolidated them and the community colleges under the jurisdiction of a new statewide governing board, the Louisiana Community and Technical College System. In 2000, West Virginia passed legislation, which began a several-year transition of community colleges previously appended to four-year colleges and universities to a new statewide system, the Community and Technical College System of West Virginia, established in 2003.

## PERIOD 6: RESPONSES TO RECESSION AND SLOW ECONOMIC RECOVERY (2003 THROUGH THE PRESENT)

As the preceding discussion illustrates, periods of governance change tend to coincide with periods of severe economic pressure. The slow recovery from the 1999–2001 Recession followed by the Great Recession (2008–2010) led states to take dramatic actions intended to improve the cost-effectiveness of their public higher education systems. Again, the pattern across the country was mixed, with a few states taking dramatic steps to centralize governance but with the dominant pattern continuing to emphasize deregulation and decentralization.

Two states (Louisiana, Connecticut) debated further consolidation of systems and institutions. The rationale for these changes mirrored the classic arguments for establishing consolidated systems in other periods of economic crisis:

- Placing the governor in a more direct role in shaping higher education policy
- Establishing a centralized means to enforce major restructuring to achieve cost reductions
- Achieving economies-of-scale in administrative and support services
- Eliminating what were perceived as unnecessary layers of bureaucracy and boards
- Curbing unnecessary duplication and competition among public institutions

Louisiana debated but rejected a proposal from the governor to eliminate the state's four system boards (the Boards of Supervisors for Louisiana State University, the Louisiana Community and Technical College System, the Southern University System, and the University of Louisiana System) and consolidate all public institutions under a single board. As an alternative, Louisiana strengthened the powers of the statewide coordinating board, the Louisiana Board of Regents (Governance Commission, 2012). Governance debates continue, including proposals to eliminate the Southern University System, to realign institutions among systems, and to restructure the Louisiana State University System (AGB, 2012).

The most far-reaching change took place in Connecticut, which adopted the governor's proposal to eliminate the statewide coordinating board (the Board of Governors) and consolidate two systems (the Connecticut State University System and the Connecticut Community and Technical System) and the State Board for Academic Awards under a single Board of Regents and president who is appointed by the governor (State of Connecticut, 2011). The University of Connecticut was not included in the new consolidated system, although the new Board of Regents has responsibility for strategic planning across the whole system, including the University of Connecticut.

As the nation emerged from the Great Recession and began the slow process of economic recovery, the basic profile of consolidated systems across the country remained essentially unchanged from a quarter-century ago, but the tensions that could lead to dismantling or significant weakening of these systems were building. Sharp reductions in state funding of higher education accelerated the fundamental changes in the state role summarized earlier. State priorities shifted again. While continuing to stress the themes of a "public agenda," states pressed for improvements in productivity, cost-containment, and innovation designed to improve student success and degree completion at lower cost to the state and to students.

## CONCLUSION

The forces leading to the establishment of modification of systems have changed over the past century depending on broader economic and social trends and state-specific circumstances. Consolidation frequently coincided with periods of severe economic stress. While a few states have established new consolidated systems in the past 20 years, the dominant trend has been toward decentralization and deregulation between the state and systems and within systems. Overall, systems remain among the more stable elements of the nation's public higher education system. In this respect, systems can serve as a "platform" for leading change and linking the component institutions to public priorities. At the same time, the "closed" bureaucratic structure of systems and their dominant internal governing responsibilities can be significant barriers to the capacity of systems to respond to the demands of the 21st century.

## NOTES

1. This chapter uses the term *system* as defined by the National Association of System Heads (NASH). NASH has defined a public

higher education system "as a group of two or more colleges or universities, each having substantial autonomy and headed by a chief executive or operating officer, all under a single governing board which is served by a system chief executive officer who is not also the chief executive officer of any of the system's institutions" (NASH, 2011). Such a system is to be distinguished from a "flagship" campus with branch campuses. It also differs from a group of campuses or systems, each with its own governing board that is coordinated by some state body. Since NASH is an organization of system heads, the organization's definition does not include multi-campus universities such as the University of Minnesota, where the president of the main university heads the system with no intervening system executive between the university and the governing board.

2. Technically, the University of California (UC) could also have been classified as a consolidated system as the Los Angeles campus developed from a former normal school, and the Santa Barbara campus was transferred from the California State University System to the UC system. However, Lee and Bowen (1971) defined UC as a flagship system because the Berkeley campus served as the primary hub around which the rest of the system was initially organized.

3. The legal status of systems differs greatly across the country. Systems in states such as Maine were formed as public corporations with substantial autonomy from state procedural controls. In contrast, in states such as Oregon, institutions retained their status as state agencies, with some management responsibility consolidated under a state board that had limited, if any, independence from state procedural controls. The Board of Trustees of the University of Maine and the Oregon State Board of Higher Education are both statewide governing boards. However, the Maine board is the board for a public corporation whereas the Oregon board is a state entity with statutorily defined governing, management, and administrative powers.

4. This passage is from the foreword to Lee and Bowen's (1971) study of multi-campus systems. Kerr included the foreword as a "vignette" in his 1991 publication, *Great Transformations* (Kerr, 1991), because he felt that the observations were still relevant twenty years later.

5. Three small states had essentially no overall coordinating entity. Delaware had three institutions: the University of Delaware, Delaware State University, and Delaware Technical College. Vermont had two boards: the Board of Trustees of the University of Vermont, a privately chartered institution supported by state funds, and the Board of Trustees for the Vermont State Colleges. Wyoming had the Board of Trustees of the University of Wyoming, the single public four-year institution in the state. The Community College Commission coordinated the state's seven locally governed community colleges.

6. It is important to distinguish between statewide *coordinating* boards and *governing* boards. Coordinating boards are state entities commonly responsible for functions such as statewide planning, budgeting and resource allocation, program approval and other regulatory functions, and administration of state-level projects. However, coordinating boards do not have authority to govern institutions. In contrast, statewide and system "governing" boards commonly have the authority to appoint system and institutional presidents and chancellors, develop and implement policies related to human resources, and engage in other functions carried out by college and university boards of trustees.

7. California (1960), Florida (1965, succeeding Board of Control established in 1905), Illinois (1965 and 1967, reconfiguring existing systems), Maine (1968), Montana (1972), Nevada (1969), New Hampshire (1963), North Carolina (1971), Rhode Island (1970), Tennessee (1972), Texas (1975, the Texas State University System), Utah (1969), West Virginia (1970), Wisconsin (1971, implemented in 1973).

8. The University of Tennessee operates as a separate public higher education system.

9. Two federal laws had an important impact on the establishment of state planning agencies. The Higher Education Facilities Act of 1963 required all states to establish state facilities planning commissioners that were broadly representative of the public and institutions of higher education. The Education Amendments of 1972 extended the earlier requirement by mandating that in order to be eligible for federal funding for planning and certain categorical programs states had to establish so-called 1202 Commissions that were broadly representative of the general public

and postsecondary institutions. In most cases, states designated existing coordinating boards. However, if these boards did not exist, the states established new entities—most often with only limited planning and advisory powers.

10. The Commonwealth of Pennsylvania has several different types of universities that receive state support. The Pennsylvania State System of Higher Education is publically owned and governed by the Commonwealth. The Pennsylvania State University, Lincoln University, Temple University, and the University of Pittsburgh are legally chartered by the Commonwealth as private corporations but receive public funding as "state-related" institutions. The Pennsylvania State University evolved toward its current role from its original charter as the Farmers' High School of Pennsylvania. The other institutions are private institutions that the Commonwealth subsequently designated as "state-related" institutions eligible for state funding: Lincoln University (1972), Temple University (1965), and the University of Pittsburgh (1966). More information about the structure of higher education in Pennsylvania can be found at: http://www.portal.state.pa.us/portal/server.pt/community/institution_types/8713.

## REFERENCES

Association of Governing Boards of State Universities and Colleges (AGB). (2012). Leadership characteristics sought in the next president of the Louisiana State University System and recommendations on a restructured LSU System office. Retrieved from Louisiana State University System website: http://www.lsusystem.edu/overview/docs/AGB-report.pdf.

Berdahl, R. O. (1971). *Statewide coordination of higher education.* Washington, DC: American Council on Education.

Callan, P. M. (1994). The gauntlet for multi-campus systems. *Trusteeship, 2*(3), 16–19.

Couturier, L. K. (2006). Checks and balances at work: The restructuring of Virginia's higher education system (National Center Report No. 06-3). Retrieved from http://www.highereducation.org/reports/checks_balances/.

Dahl, R. A. (2005). *Who governs? Democracy and power in an American city*, 2nd ed. New Haven, CT: Yale University Press.

Education Commission of the States. (1986). *Transforming the state role in undergraduate education: Time for a different view.* Denver, CO: Author.

Fincher, C. (2003). *Historical development of the University System of Georgia, 1932–2002*, 2nd ed. Athens, GA: Institute of Higher Education, University of Georgia.

Gade, M. L. (1993). *Four multi-campus systems: Some policies and practices that work.* Washington, DC: Association of Governing Boards of Universities and Colleges.

Geiger, L.G. *University of the Northern Plains: A history of the University of North Dakota 1883–1958.* Grand Forks: University of North Dakota Press, 1958.

Governance Commission (2012). Response to House Concurrent Resolution 184 Regular Session of Louisiana Legislature. Retrieved from State of Louisiana Board of Regents website: http://www.regents.doa.louisiana.gov/assets/docs/Administration/Governance/GovernanceCommissionReportFINAL.pdf.

Guerber, S. (1998). A brief history of education in Idaho. Retrieved from Idaho State Department of Education website: http://www.sde.idaho.gov/site/schoolsbudget/docs/Guerber%20presentation%20to%20SBOE,%20May%201998.pdf.

Independent Commission on the Future of the State University. (1985). The challenge and the choice: Report of the Independent Commission on the Future of the State University. Retrieved from State University of New York website: http://www.suny.edu/SUNYNews/pdf/ChallengeChoice.pdf.

Johnstone, D. B. (1992). Central administration of public multi-campus college and university systems: Core functions and cost pressures, with reference to the central administration of the State University of New York. Albany: State University of New York. Retrieved from the ERIC Database. (ED348902).

Johnstone, D. B. (2005). Role, scope, mission, and purposes of multi-campus systems. Retrieved from Special Task Force on UW Restructuring and Operational Flexibilities website: http://legis.wisconsin.gov/lfb/UW_Task_Force/Documents/2012_02_08_Role_Scope_Mission%20and%20Purposes%20of%20Multi-campus%20Systems_D%20Bruce%20Johnstone.pdf.

Kansas Board of Regents. (n.d.). A brief history of the Kansas Board of Regents system. Retrieved from http://www.kansasregents. org/history.

Kerr, C. (1971). Foreword. In E. C. Lee & F. M. Bowen, *The multi-campus university: A study of academic governance* (pp. xi–xix). New York, NY: McGraw-Hill.

Kerr, C. (1991). *The great transformation in higher education, 1960–1980*. Albany: State University of New York Press.

Kerr, C., & Gade, M. L. (1989). *The guardians: Boards of trustees of American colleges and universities*. Washington, DC: Association of Governing Boards of Universities and Colleges.

Lane, J. E., & Kerins, F. J. (in press). Middle Border region: Higher education in Idaho, Montana, North Dakota, South Dakota and Wyoming. In L. Goodchild, P. Limerick, & D. Jonson (Eds.), *Higher education in the American West: Past, present, and future*. Houndmills, Basingstoke, UK: Palgrave Macmillan.

Lee, E. C., & Bowen, F. M. (1971). *The multi-campus university: A study of academic governance*. New York, NY: McGraw-Hill.

MacTaggart, T. J. (1998). *Seeking excellence through independence: Liberating colleges and universities from excessive regulation*. San Francisco, CA: Jossey-Bass.

McClure, E. (1999). The structure of higher education in Montana: Meandering the murky line. Retrieved from Montana legislature website: http://leg.mt.gov/content/Publications/fiscal/Education/Eddye-McClure-Report.pdf.

McGuinness, A. C., Jr. (1991). Perspectives on the current status of and emerging policy issues for public multi-campus higher education systems (AGB Occasional Paper No. 3). Washington, DC: Association of Governing Boards of Universities and Colleges.

McGuinness, A. C., Jr. (1995). *Restructuring state roles in higher education: A case study of the 1994 New Jersey Higher Education Restructuring Act*. Denver, CO: Education Commission of the States.

McGuinness, A. C., Jr. (1996). A model for successful restructuring. In T. J. MacTaggart & Associates (Eds.), *Restructuring higher education: What works and what doesn't in reorganizing governing systems* (pp. 203–229). San Francisco, CA: Jossey-Bass.

McGuinness, A. C., Jr. (2006). *A conceptual and analytical framework for review of national regulatory policies for tertiary education*. Paris: Organisation for Economic Co-operation and Development.

McGuinness, A. C., Jr. (2010). The states and higher education. In P. G. Altbach, P. J. Gumport, & R. O. Berdahl (Eds.), *American higher education in the twenty-first century: Social, political, and economic challenges* (pp. 139–169). Baltimore, MD: Johns Hopkins University Press.

McGuinness, A. C., Jr., Epper, R. M., & Arrendono, S. (1994). *State postsecondary education structures handbook*. Denver, CO: Education Commission of the States.

McGuinness, A. C., Jr., & Novak, R. (2011). The statewide public agenda and higher education: Making it work. *Trusteeship, 19*(2), 25–29.

Mingle, J. O. (1983). *Management flexibility and state regulation in higher education*. Atlanta, GA: Southern Regional Education Board.

National Association of System Heads (NASH). (2011). About NASH. Retrieved from http://www.nashonline.org/about-nash.

National Center for Public Policy and Higher Education. (2005). State capacity for higher education policy. National Crosstalk. Retrieved from http://www.highereducation.org/crosstalk/ct0305/news0305-insert.pdf.

National Governors Association. (1991). *Time for results: The governors' 1991 report on education*. Washington, DC: Author.

Oregon University System. (2011). 80-year chronology of the Oregon University System. Salem, 2011. Retrieved from http://www.ous.edu/sites/default/files/about/chanoff/80yearboardchronology2012.pdf.

Organisation for Economic Co-operation and Development (OECD). (2008). Thematic review of tertiary education. Retrieved from http://www.oecd.org/education/highereducationandadultlearning/thematicreviewoftertiaryeducation.

Osborne, D., & Gaebler, T. (1992). *Reinventing government: How the entrepreneurial spirit is transforming the public sector*. New York, NY: Plume.

Peters, B. G. (2001). *The future of governing*, 2nd ed. Lawrence: University of Press of Kansas.

State of Connecticut. (2011). An Act Implementing the Revenue Items In the Budget and Making Budget Adjustments, Deficiency

Appropriations, Certain Revisions to Bills of the Current Session And Miscellaneous Changes to the General Statutes. House Bill No. 6652. Public Act No. 11-61. Retrieved from http://www.cga.ct.gov/2011/ACT/PA/2011PA-00061-R00HB-06652-PA.htm

South Dakota Board of Regents. (2012). South Dakota's unified system of higher education: The constitutional trust and purposes for a new century. In South Dakota Board of Regents Policy Manual. Retrieved from http://www.sdbor.edu/policy/1-Governance/documents/1-0.pdf.

State of South Dakota. (1889). Report of Committee on State Institutions, South Dakota Constitutional Convention held at Sioux Falls, July, 1989, vol. 2, p. 171. Retrieved from http://www.archive.org/stream/constitutionalde02soutiala/constitutionalde-02soutiala_djvu.txt.

Texas Higher Education Coordinating Board. (2011). *History of Texas public university systems*. Austin: Author.

University of Iowa Libraries. (2012). Records of the Iowa State Board of Education and Board of Regents. Retrieved from http://www.lib.uiowa.edu/spec-coll/archives/guides/rg04/rg04.02.htm.

van Vught, F. (Ed.). (1989). *Governmental strategies and innovation in higher education*. London: Jessica Kingsley Publishers.

Venesia, A., & Finney, J. E. (2006). The governance divide: The case study of Florida. Retrieved from National Center for Public Policy and Higher Education website: http://www.highereducation.org/reports/governance_divide/FL/FL_case_study.pdf.

Western Interstate Commission on Higher Education. (2010). *An evaluation of Colorado's College Opportunity Fund and related policies*. Boulder, CO: Author.

Williams, G. L. (1995). The "marketization" of higher education: Reforms and potential reforms in higher education finance. In D. D. Dill & B. Sporn (Eds.), *Emerging patterns of social demand and university reform: Through a glass darkly* (pp. 170–193). Tarrytown, NY: Elsevier Science.

# Part II

## CHALLENGES TO SYSTEM INNOVATION

### UNPACKING THE TENSIONS

# 4

## Higher Educational Autonomy and the Apportionment of Authority among State Governments, Public Multi-Campus Systems, and Member Colleges and Universities

### D. BRUCE JOHNSTONE

ABSTRACT

Public colleges and universities operate within a complex field of competing interests and authorities. Individual institutions and their campus heads attempt to maximize their state tax revenues, their prestige, and their freedom from external authority, whether from a system head, a system governing board, or the government. Faculty deans want much the same freedoms but seek their autonomy from their institutional administrations as well as external authorities. Moreover, university departments and individual faculty members seek autonomy from all of the aforementioned. Meanwhile, state governments—including governors and legislatures—seek efficient use of tax revenues, an appropriate assurance of equitable student participation (subject to widely varying interpretations and policies, including admission standards and tuition fees), as well as a fair allocation of state revenues and institutional missions by legislative district. Public college and university systems, with system governing boards and system CEOs, vary in structure but have been constructed in most states to negotiate between governments and institutions, on behalf of the institutions to the state for revenue and maximum autonomy, and on behalf of the larger public interest—almost as a proxy for the state—to the member institutions. This chapter begins with a discussion of the changing notions of autonomy and then discusses issues surrounding the apportionment of authority.

## AUTONOMY AND AUTHORITY IN PUBLIC HIGHER EDUCATION

Autonomy in the context of public higher education is a devolution of authority from the state to the institution itself—or, as we shall discus in this chapter, to a system of institutions acting on behalf of the state (or on behalf of the greater public good). This autonomy can be, but is not always, further devolved to the separate institutions or campuses comprising the system. At its most elemental, then, autonomy in public higher education is a condition of freedom from state authority. Authority in public higher education may, however, embrace a host of very different decisions within the operations of a public college or university, only some (or many, or most) of which the state may choose to devolve to the institution or the system—or, in turn, the system may choose to devolve to the institution. These responsibilities may involve, for example, the authority to determine institutional mission (e.g., a comprehensive research university, a teaching college, or a specialized institution); what to teach; whom to hire; who is to head the college, university, or system; and what fees to charge.

The devolution of state authority over public higher education is complex and never complete or absolute. For example, rather than vesting all authority over public higher education in a government ministry or a state bureaucracy, as in most other countries, the sharing of public authority in the United States among governors, state legislatures, and public governing boards, while removing certain elements of authority from the direct control of state governors and legislatures, still preserves substantial ultimate authority in the hands of whomever selects the members of the public governing board (e.g., the governor alone, or the governor with consent of a body of the legislature, or the voters of the state). Also, as long as public colleges and universities, whether systems or individual campuses, are dependent on state operating budgets for a critical core of their unrestricted operating revenues, whatever independence or autonomy may have been gained from the state government may be compromised by the very considerable power of the state purse and the conditions that may be attached to receipt of state tax revenues.

Just as the state may devolve only certain authorities to the institution or system—that is, grant more or less autonomy—so also a multi-campus system may devolve only certain elements of authority to its member institutions and retain others. To the individual college or university, then, the extent and nature of its perceived autonomy may lie more in what the system governing board and management have delegated to the campus than what the state initially (and perhaps long ago) gave over to the multi-campus system. Finally, and further complicating the concept of autonomy in public higher education, is the necessary sharing of whatever authority the state has given over, or devolved, to the governing board and chief executive officer of a multi-campus system and then to the chief executive officers of the member colleges and universities. This authority is further shared with the institutional (and sometimes the system-wide) faculty, generally but not exclusively in the respective faculty senates. This latter sharing is partly codified in system and campus bylaws, partly in powerful traditions of shared governance within the academy (especially in four-year colleges and universities), and partly in whatever ways state governments are able to reach in to shape governance and decision making at the system and institutional levels (e.g., as in the placement of students and faculty on system governing boards or the requirement of common system-wide undergraduate course numbers and curricular content).

## HIGHER EDUCATIONAL AUTONOMY AND THE WESTERN UNIVERSITY TRADITION

Amid all this situational complexity, university autonomy, whatever its meaning and extent, has come to be viewed as something fundamental to higher education. Autonomy gained currency as essential to universities with the advent of the modern, classical, Western university, which was dedicated to the search for truth and built upon the Humboldtian principles of the freedom of the faculty to teach, to study, and to publish, and the freedom of the student to learn. Beginning in the 19th century, the emerging Western universities were centers of social, political, and religious inquiry and criticism. Although reliant on the state for capital and operating revenues, universities were also—or at least were assumed by frequently conservative and often authoritarian European governments—to be bastions of dissent and potential threats to the established social and political orders. Thus, universities in 19th-century Europe established principles of academic freedom and institutional autonomy, which were gradually embraced by European states in university framework laws or even constitutions. Autonomy meant freedom from state interference: the freedom to hire and promote faculty and staff; the freedom of the faculty to select (and limit the authority of) its leader, the rector; and the freedom to select its students, set the curriculum, and establish the requirements and standards for degrees. The state paid the salaries (increasingly through forms of protected civil service), built the physical plant, funded the laboratories, and controlled the degrees to be awarded. The notion of autonomy—to the degree that it was granted—essentially meant enlarging the freedom of the faculty from state governmental control and the right, instead, to *self-government*, which meant government in the hands not of rectors or management but of the senior faculty. This concept of self-government only carried in part into the organization of U.S. higher education (Duryea, 2000).

## PUBLIC HIGHER EDUCATION IN AMERICA AND THE EMERGENCE OF THE MULTI-CAMPUS SYSTEM

By the *powers reserved* clause of the U.S. Constitution, education, including higher education, was an authority reserved to the states rather than to the national government. In creating their first public universities, most states turned to the already established private college and university model of the lay governing board (taken from Dutch, Scottish, and Irish sources) to serve as an agent of the state (Duryea, 1973). Along with public governing boards came campus heads (called either presidents or chancellors) who were chosen not by the faculty, as were European university rectors, but by public university governing boards, which were composed of prominent individuals, generally appointed for terms and without remuneration by state governors (in a few instances by popular election). Thus, as America imported the idea of the research university from the European continent in the latter half of the 19th and early 20th centuries, the notion of university autonomy, which in a European context had to do with the insulation of the university—meaning the *faculty*—from the government, now had a third locus of contesting authority, which was the public governing board and its chief executive officer, serving as agents of the state and the public interest but simultaneously as a buffer against the direct authority of the established government. Finally, within the past 50 years (albeit in varying shapes and sizes), most public institutions in the United States have come to be governed not simply as single institutions but as systems of institutions, with the rich variations described in this volume.

Public governing boards, whether of singular institutions or multi-campus systems, thus play a special and at times inherently conflicting role in what Perkins (1973) called "a bridge—representing the university's interest to society as well as society's interest to the university" (p. 238). As an agent of the state—whether appointed or elected—the governing board represents the interests of the public, including the efficient use of tax revenues, the need for the university to attend to the needs of commerce and the larger economy, and the role of colleges and universities in promoting social and political goals such as equity and diversity (sometimes in opposition to the faculty's paramount interests in scholarly prestige, selectivity, and academic meritocracy). At the same time, the governing board needs to advocate on behalf of the institution or system to the state government, especially for resources, with the political leverage that the board is presumed to have via its gubernatorial appointment and legislative approval or its direct election, as well as to shield the university from the political or popular slings and arrows that are often sent in the direction of the academy.

Since the advent of the multi-campus public system, most public colleges and universities have had to negotiate with (that is, seek a measure of autonomy from) an appointed or elected system governing board and system CEO—sometimes in addition to a local or institutional board, which is most often advisory and not truly governing, but which can still constitute another locus of competing pressure on both the faculty and the management of the college or university. In many states, there are also statewide planning boards that are generally advisory and not truly governing but that constitute yet another potentially significant source of advocacy for the larger public interest in the areas of resource allocation and academic program approval. Meanwhile, the multi-campus system governing board and system head have the responsibility of withholding autonomy from the campuses when such autonomy may not be in the public interest. System leaders may have to limit institutional ambitions, for example, if a comprehensive university college desires to transform itself into a research university, or a research university wishes to add professional schools that may not be needed, or selective public colleges and universities want to take advantage of their favorable market positions to charge very high tuition and fees. Such campus wishes may be opposed by the public system governing board not in response to a directive from the state government but rather on behalf of what the governing board (often on the advice of its appointed system head) perceives to be in the larger public interest. At the same time, the public governing board will attempt to negotiate additional freedom from state controls on behalf of itself as a system, as well as of the member colleges and universities, where it perceives such autonomy will serve the interests of both the institutions and the public. Thus, the focus of this chapter is on the nature of higher educational autonomy in the context of public multi-campus systems. Specifically:

1. How is higher educational authority to be apportioned—or institutional autonomy limited—among state governments, individual public colleges and universities, and public multi-campus systems?
2. What are the natural tensions between public multi-campus systems and their member colleges and universities?
3. What are some alternatives to public college and university system governing boards and system management (that is, system presidents or chancellors and system administrations) in balancing the campus need and desire for autonomy with the public's need for efficiency, accessibility, and accountability?

## THE APPORTIONMENT OF AUTHORITY AMONG
## STATE GOVERNMENTS, PUBLIC MULTI-CAMPUS SYSTEMS,
## AND MEMBER COLLEGES AND UNIVERSITIES

Higher educational autonomy still (loosely) means freedom from external restraint, but whereas in a much earlier European context it largely meant freedom of individual members of the faculty from state controls or reprisals, we now must ask whether the autonomy we seek to preserve or enhance is the freedom:

- *For* what or whom—as among system board and system head, the institutional head, or members of the faculty, either individually or collectively;
- *From* what or whom—as among the state, either politicians (i.e., governors or legislators) or state bureaucrats and officials (e.g., of departments of education or state budget offices), or system governing boards and system administrators acting as proxies for the state;
- *To do or decide what*—as among such critical *academic* decisions as the determination or alteration of institutional mission; the establishment of faculties, departments, and academic programs; or setting the standards for admission or the awarding of degrees—or *managerial* decisions, such as the terms and conditions of faculty and staff employment, the allocation or reallocation of budget revenues, the acquisition or disposal of property, the setting of tuition fees, and other decisions critical to college or university operations.

Thus, the governing board and management of a college or university system may seek autonomy—that is, freedom from state bureaucratic budgetary controls—to reallocate budgeted revenues among the several campuses, pleasing some and dismaying others. The chief executive officer of an individual college or university within a system may seek autonomy to raise its tuition to a level that it believes it requires but that the governor, legislature, and system governing board may believe to be contrary to the larger political and social goal of widened higher educational participation and accessibility. The faculty of arts and sciences of one system institution may, for example, wish for the autonomy to establish new degree programs without having to obtain the approval of the state higher educational planning board or the system governing board—potentially disregarding demonstrated public need or the impact on other colleges or universities, public or private. Alternatively, the faculty of the department of biology of a member research university may seek to require all transferring students to take its introductory biology course (or pass a special examination) to proceed to upper-level biology courses—in the face of state legislative or system-level rules seeking more seamless transfer opportunities and forbidding such requirements. The chief executive officer of a member college or university may seek autonomy—perhaps from the system governing board or from the state office of employee relations—to establish a new academic track or otherwise to change the terms and conditions of employment of the academic staff. Perhaps the head of a campus, with the full support of a local advisory board, may seek permission from the state and the system to establish a public-private partnership with a local private hospital and development company to build a biomedical research complex. All of these scenarios, and so many other examples, suggest the evolving complexity of the quest for autonomy by some element of public higher education from the real or perceived restrictions of another level of authority.

## TENSIONS BETWEEN SYSTEMS AND MEMBER INSTITUTIONS

As multi-campus system governing boards and system administrators act on behalf of state government and as agents of the statewide public interest, tensions between systems and member institutions—generally seeking maximum autonomy—are inevitable. These tensions will differ depending, for example, on the types and degrees of authority that have been delegated to the system (as opposed to being retained by other agencies of the state), the influence accorded in a particular state to nongoverning higher educational planning boards, the scope or reach of the multi-campus system (that is, whether the system is a single comprehensive system encompassing all or most public colleges and universities or is divided by sectors or regions), and the real or putative degree of difference in the prominence or esteem accorded to so-called *flagship* campuses. Eight common tensions are described here.

## 1. Determination and Alteration of Institutional Missions

Many four-year comprehensive colleges have become doctoral-granting universities, and many more are thought to aspire to this status. More recently, some two-year community colleges have begun to offer bachelor's degrees. This *academic drift* in the direction of increasing orientation to research is worldwide and is thought to be fueled by the desire of faculty and academic leaders to attain the prestige, the time away from teaching obligations, and the higher salaries generally associated with research universities (Massey & Zemsky, 1994; Morphew & Huisman, 2002). This drift may be supported by (or sometimes even originate with) local politicians, who want the most prestigious institutions in their region. Such institutional upgrading may also be sought by politically prominent citizens, institutional advisory boards, and local media.

However, not all faculty of predominantly teaching colleges are able to assume the scholarly profiles of research university faculty, nor would such an alteration, even if possible, necessarily be affordable or otherwise in the public interest. The advantages of such a decision—that is, whether to allow a four-year college to transmogrify into a research university—being left to the system governing board as opposed to state government are twofold. First, the governing board, although an agent for the state, is presumably less influenced by the need for votes or other extraneous interests than are politicians. Second, the governing board and system administration, with the full knowledge of the capacities of all the member institutions, and with a larger grasp of the costs and benefits of such an institutional mission transformation, is likely in the best position knowledgably to consider such a request or at the very least to be accorded a prominent role in the ultimate governmental decision to accede to or deny the request of a comprehensive college to transform into a research university.

## 2. The Approval of Campus Requests to
## Add or Dissolve Academic Programs

It is in the nature of faculty and academic administrators to wish to add programs (and occasionally to dissolve them) to keep up with their perception of changing student demand as well as with changes in academic fields and the professions. The faculty and leaders of an institution are in the best position to know when such a change should be made, but there are other interests that the system board and administration must accommodate. For example, a proposed new program may cut seriously into the enrollments of another member campus—or even into the enrollments of colleges or universities that are not within the system but that are in the larger public interests of the state. There may not be the sufficient resources to establish an academically worthy program—or the resources proposed to be reallocated may weaken other programs. Finally—and probably the most difficult for a system board to make when attempting to serve all the member campuses and accommodate the legitimate needs of one of them to grow and keep up with its peers—the board may decide that the proposed new program is duplicative and too wasteful of state resources. (The system board and administration may also perceive that if the system does not act, the governor and legislature may begin to attack all programs they believe to be duplicative.)

## 3. Undergraduate Admission Numbers

The admission of students is a decision properly left to individual campuses. However, there are both institutional and system interests in the numbers of students admitted by any particular campus—or at least in the extent to which a member campus is encouraged or allowed to deviate to any significant extent from a target, or expected, number of new admissions. Member campuses are motivated to meet—and in no instance to fall below—the total enrollment expectations that underlie their respective state operating appropriations. Whether this appropriation is rigidly enrollment-based, there is always an expectation of student numbers (at least of undergraduate numbers and particularly of in-state undergraduates) below which campuses do not want to fall lest either the state or the system reduces their instructional appropriations. Given the uncertainties of underlying yields and student return rates, then, the prudent undergraduate enrollment policy for a campus is to make certain that the target is not missed by aiming always for a slight overenrollment. In a large system (such as the California State University System or the State University of New York), the result of each member campus's attempt to overenroll even by a very small margin means that the system as a whole will inevitably overenroll by a large margin. The state may be pleased by such a demonstration of instructional productivity, but the message to the state may also be either that the system is getting more instructional dollars than it needs or that the target enrollments for the revenues received need to be adjusted upward—both consequences being unfortunate for the system. Such deliberate and essentially unauthorized increases in enrollments also may erode admission standards and strain faculty, staff, and facilities. Additionally, the financial temptation to concentrate such overenrollments on out-of-state and international students because of the higher tuition fees, which the campus may defend on the claim of social and cultural diversity, may alienate politicians, especially when political tensions are rising anyway and when the rising admission standards for in-state students are creating problems for politicians whose constituents cannot get their sons and daughters enrolled in *their* colleges and universities. A system may then attempt to discourage, or at least limit, such campus overenrollments.

## 4. A Change in the Standards for Admission

A related tension may arise in public systems with stable or even declining overall enrollments when one institution (perhaps one of the more selective institutions) attempts to maintain (or even expand) its enrollment and its share of state revenues by slightly lowering its admission standards. This practice allows the institution to dip into the pool that may be said to have *belonged*, perhaps quite appropriately, to one of the less selective institutions. This conflict does not mean that selective institutions should not aspire to grow, or that the relative shares of target enrollments and public revenues need be fixed for the member campuses of a system. The system needs, however, to be certain that a campus aspiring to grow in undergraduate enrollment can do so without lowering its standards of admission and without *poaching* the applicant pools of less selective campuses that might be a better fit for the students being poached.

## 5. The Setting of Tuition Fees

Average public college and university undergraduate tuition, while varying by state, system, and frequently by sector within systems (generally highest in the research universities and lowest in the community colleges), has been increasing dramatically albeit fitfully for decades. That is, higher education has witnessed periods of frozen tuitions followed by sudden dramatic increases. In most states, tuitions have increased over time at rates considerably in excess of consumer prices generally and even in excess of median family incomes.[1] The causes are many and complex. At the heart of the increases lie increasing per-student costs, driven relentlessly upward partly by ambition and partly by higher education's resistance to the substitution of capital and technology for labor, further magnified in many states by surging enrollments. Meanwhile, states, facing equally mounting cost pressures from Medicare and other health care costs, elementary and secondary education, corrections, and other public needs, unable to deficit finance state operations[2] and politically constrained by resistance to increasing taxes, have turned to increasing tuition fees as a way to reduce the fiscal burden of their public colleges and universities. Increases in public sector tuitions have been eased by the provision of means-tested financial assistance (albeit increasingly in the form of loans). At the beginning of this upward trend in public sector tuition, the increases were frequently supported by economists and policy analysts who pointed out that public colleges and universities with very low tuition—especially the very selective ones that were attended in disproportionate numbers by sons and daughters of the more affluent, whose families could well afford and would gladly pay higher tuition fees—constituted an unnecessary and regressive governmental subsidy.

At the same time, politicians continue to be fearful of student and voter backlash to increases in public sector tuition fees. This anxiety may stem from a genuine concern for a possible diminution of access and participation. It may also reflect sensitivity to a widespread public reaction to the extremely inflated price tags of elite private residential colleges and universities. Alternatively, it may reflect a mounting concern over governmental spending generally, exacerbated by the cuts that states have been forced to make throughout their public sectors and heightened by the suspicion that public colleges and universities would not need the revenue if they were just more efficient. This view may be held by those of all political persuasions, but it is especially held by those who view most of the public sector, *especially public universities*, as wasteful and who would hasten its further downsizing or privatization. In most states, these views have set up a conflict between governors and legislators—who continue to cut higher education budgets but who also continue to resist regular tuition increases that would keep up with increasing higher educational cost pressures—and campus heads, especially at the more selective institutions, where the cost pressures may be greatest and where the students and families could probably most afford a tuition increase. These campus heads, as opposed to governors and legislators, tend to prefer regular increases in tuitions to keep up with their rising costs.

System governing boards and system heads may thus be caught in the middle. Governing boards may feel pressure from appointing governors but may also see the larger public interest of a so-called *rational tuition* policy,[3] which would support regular albeit modest tuition increases that meet both legitimate campus revenue needs as well as the need to control costs for students and families, in preference to periods of overtly politicized tuition freezes followed by very large and inevitably controversial tuition increases. At the same time, governing boards and system heads may have to resist pressures from the heads of more selective campuses to implement a more market-based tuition policy that would see tuitions rise the most at the most selective institutions, which are likely to view their peer institutions as other elite private colleges and universities rather than other public institutions, even within the system.

## 6. The Disposition of Tuition Dollars

Public systems of higher education differ (often because of underlying state regulations) in the allocation of tuition dollars to the member campuses—whether all tuition dollars collected go directly to a campus account, to be drawn out at its discretion, or whether a predetermined tuition dollar total for each campus has been anticipated within the campus's budget appropriation, such that the state needs to collect at least the amount of dollars already dispensed to replenish its general fund. In the latter case—that is, where the tuition revenue has, in a sense, already been *advanced*—campuses frequently complain that *their* tuition dollars simply go to the state and are never seen by the campus (or by its faculty or its students). Although in a public accounting sense such a complaint is not strictly accurate, it plays well politically to students and faculty and to local advisory boards, especially when the state is, in fact, replacing state tax dollars with tuition dollars and then depositing the tuition that it had advanced to the campuses in the state's general revenue fund. Furthermore, depositing all tuition in the state's general revenue fund does prevent, or at least delay, the additional dollars earned from overenrollments going to the campuses that rightly believe they have earned them—and that may need them to pay for the additional adjunct staff that they have had to hire in order to accommodate the overenrollment.

On the other hand, a system may wish to be able to balance the campuses that have overenrolled, perhaps inadvertently, with those that have underenrolled, also perhaps unintentionally, due simply to the uncertainties and inevitable fluctuations in admission yields and return rates. A campus that consistently underenrolls may need a lower enrollment target and a diminished appropriation—just as a campus that consistently overenrolls due to a high yield and return rate, both of which are to be desired and rewarded, may need a higher target and appropriation. In any given year, however, a system may wish to balance at least some of the tuition revenue shortfalls of the underenrolling campuses with some of the extra (and presumably unanticipated) tuition revenue from the overenrolling campuses. Furthermore, the ability of a system to retain some of the unanticipated and therefore unappropriated tuition revenue gives the governing board and system administration a tool with which to discourage persisting and excessive overenrollments, especially of the *poaching* variety.

## 7. Senior College Acceptance of Community College Associate's Degree Graduates

Not all community college associate's degree graduates aspire to pursue a bachelor's degree at a public senior college. However, particularly in a comprehensive public system that includes both two- and four-year colleges (but even in a system of only four-year college and universities), most state governments and most public systems expect four-year colleges and universities to accommodate, if at all possible, the associate's degree graduates of the state's community colleges—and to do so with as seamless an academic transition as possible. In some states, this process may require senior colleges to hold back purposefully on first-time freshmen matriculates to have sufficient capacity to accept community college transfers in the undergraduate upper divisions. However, in all systems, the need to accommodate successful community college graduates as transfers necessarily conflicts with the principle in most systems of leaving admissions decisions to individual campuses. Clearly, conditions of financial austerity combined with mounting demographically driven enrollment demands worsens the potential friction between a state and a system that wants to accommodate community college transfers and the member senior colleges that may have neither the capacity (especially in very high-demand academic majors) or the inclination to accept students who, in spite of their associate's degrees, may not be perceived by some faculty members to meet the academic standards that a particular college or university department requires.

## 8. Senior College Acceptance of Community College Associate Degree Credits

Some senior colleges in a system will attempt to overcome the reluctance of undergraduate departments to accept community college transfers by accepting the transfer *student* (see item 7) but not necessarily all the community college transfer *credits* for the purpose of counting toward timely graduation (i.e., in approximately two additional years, or 60 to 70 additional credits). Some states and state systems have attempted to address this difficulty by adopting common course titles and numbers in both the community and the four-year colleges and simply mandating the acceptance by the senior college of the course credits wherever the course was taken provided the grade was satisfactory. Other systems spend resources, time, and political capital by urging and assisting two- and four-year college departments to formulate articulation agreements that specify precisely what community college credits will be accepted for purposes of graduation as well as toward completion of the four-year college departmental major.

## LIMITS TO AUTONOMY

The system-campus tensions enumerated here (and there can be many others) suggest limits to the autonomy of individual public colleges and universities—limits that are frequently imposed by the system governing board and system officials acting in their capacities as agents for the larger statewide public interest. In the absence of such limits, public colleges and universities—that is, single institutions via their presidents or chancellors and their faculty senates—would presumably be free to define their own missions. That is, they could purport to be (or, if possible, to change into) a research university, a teaching college, or a specialized institution, limited only by the capabilities of their faculty, the interests of their students, and the resources at their disposal, like any private nonprofit institution. They would be free to add or dispense with programs according to the market and affordability, limited only by institutional and program accreditation and of course by their own sense of academic integrity—but again, just like any private nonprofit college or university. Similarly, the fully autonomous public college or university would presumably set its tuition as the president or chancellor and the institutional governing board decided was best for the institution.

However, the *public* in public college or university carries an obligation to a public good that is sometimes greater than the institution itself and in some cases greater even than the public system. The apportionment of authority in public higher education is among (a) *state governments* via laws, regulations, and executive authority, including agencies such as state departments of education; (b) *individual institutions*, via campus presidents or chancellors, campus faculty senates, and sometimes local campus boards; and (c) *public systems*, via system governing boards, system administrations, and system faculty bodies. The proper apportionment of these authorities—and thus the proper limits to public higher educational autonomy—is a legitimate matter of continuing public policy debate. I, with a background of campus president, system chancellor, and university faculty member, would suggest the following apportionment.

*To state governments*, effectively limiting both system and individual campus autonomy, generally belong:

- The determination or alteration of basic institutional mission (e.g., as from a bachelor's /master's degree comprehensive college to a research university);
- The ability of an institution or a system to add or delete advanced graduate faculties, such as schools of medicine, dentistry, public health, or law (and perhaps, but more controversially, other academic degree programs such as a PhD in bioengineering or a master's of business administration);
- The overall operating budget appropriation and some requisite level or levels of enrollment or other measures of output for the tax revenues that are awarded;
- Stipulations of and limits upon state liability for debts, torts, pensions, and other state financial obligations; and
- Ultimate control over tuition policies (but with the setting of the actual tuition fees desirably delegated to system boards).

*To the individual college or university campus*—that is, allowing full authority (institutional autonomy) over:

- The selection of campus vice presidents, deans, directors, and other campus administrators;
- The appointment and promotion of academic and professional staff;
- The assignment of faculty to courses and to other duties (consistent with established policies and collective bargaining contracts);
- The admission of students at all levels and to all faculties, and the establishment of standards for degrees;
- The determination of all curricula (for approved programs) as well as the methods of instruction;
- The reallocation of revenues among the various departments and programs;
- The execution of purchase orders and contracts; and
- The ability to seek, retain, and spend philanthropic revenue, grants, and contracts (frequently through campus-related foundations).

*To the system.* Finally, there are elements of college and university operations that are best removed from state government and that—at least according to some, including myself—are best devolved to an authority representing a public interest that is larger than the individual college or university and that is also removed from the immediate reach of a governor or a state legislature. In other words, they are best delegated to a public multi-campus system governing board. System limits to campus autonomy will be contested, but a case can be made for multi-campus system authority over, for example:

- *The appointment of campus presidents or chancellors (based always on campus recommendations).* This ultimate appointing authority is not to select the campus head but rather to assure an appropriate selection process—one that incorporates the views of elected faculty representatives, is open to external candidates, and is not sharply divided between a local board and the faculty.
- *The approval of campus requests to propose to state government the alteration of basic campus missions.* The ambitions of some faculty and leaders of large public bachelor's/master's comprehensive colleges to become research universities may be virtually endemic—fueled by campus heads, some faculty, and frequently by powerful local civic and political leaders. Sometimes, such a transformation is appropriate. At other times, it may transform a first-tier comprehensive college into a third-tier research university and impose additional costs on the state taxpayers—to little or no additional public benefit. Although this decision is ultimately up to state governments, it is well to have the public system governing board and system administration deeply involved and in a position to either advocate for, or discourage, such academic drift.
- *The allocation of public revenues among the disparate campuses of the system.* All states have at least one public research university (California has 11), plus many more comprehensive and specialized colleges and an even greater number of two-year institutions. Each institution can and will make a case for being seriously underfunded. It is likely that some are more underfunded than others, although the

*proper* division of increasingly scarce state tax revenues as among comprehensive colleges, community colleges, large research universities with medical centers and hospitals, small universities without medical centers, and other specialized institutions is almost impossible to determine, even with sophisticated allocation formulas. What is almost certain, however, is that the allocation of state tax revenues among the state's public institutions is best *not* left to the legislature, with powerful politicians favoring *their* college, nor to a state budget office with little understanding of the differences in missions, costs, and revenue needs among the campuses and the sectors. Again, this is what a multi-campus system, properly functioning, is best able to do.

- *The setting of tuition fees.* Campus administrations and local boards can be overly concerned with the need for tuition revenue to the exclusion of concern for access and the mounting undergraduate debt loads. State governments, on the other hand, may vacillate between an eagerness to continue lowering the tax burden of public higher education—that is, cutting the budget and further shifting the cost burden onto parents and students—and the populist rejection of any tuition increase whatsoever, even to the point of causing major financial distress for public institutions. In theory, at least, a system governing board and system CEO should be able to bridge this chasm between the financial needs of the campuses and the financial needs of students and families, all the while appreciating the fiscal dilemmas facing the governor and legislature.
- *The establishment of campus- and mission-appropriate policies and procedures for academic appointments, promotions, and tenure.* While actual appointments and promotions are best left to individual campuses, the policies and procedures should be similar across campuses—at least within sectors. Compensation should also be at least similar, and if the faculty and staff of a system are unionized, then the system governing board and administration should be in the forefront of the contract negotiations. If collective bargaining contracts by law are the province of the state government, then the system (plus campus representatives)

should participate in the negotiation of such contracts and play a significant role in contract implementation and griev- ance procedures.

- *Policies governing the admission of community college transfers and the acceptance of community college transfer credits.* Like the admission of students generally, the admis- sion of undergraduate student transfers should be left as much as possible with the individual campuses. At the same time, as mentioned in the preceding section, the acceptance of transfers and the awarding of transfer credits is an area of potential tension, especially between community colleg- es and the more selective senior colleges and universities. Whether formally and officially, as in the famous California Master Plan, or informally, most states support community colleges, whether in a comprehensive college and university system or in an exclusively community college system, in part for the purpose of siphoning off a substantial number of high school graduates in order to provide postsecondary educational opportunities that are less costly to the student, less costly to the state, closer to home, more accessible to the less academically prepared, and less subject to the influence of those university faculty who may not understand, nor fully support, the complex missions of public community colleges. Thus public system governing boards and system administrations may play the critical role in negotiating the legitimate but disparate interests of community colleges, the senior colleges, and students seeking to transfer.

## ALTERNATIVES TO PUBLIC COLLEGE AND UNIVERSITY SYSTEMS

Public college and university systems are subject to periodic criti- cism. Some criticism originates within the aforementioned tensions between system governing boards and system administrations, and the member campuses—especially those that consider themselves the flagship campuses. Criticism of the system may come from campus heads, or from deans and members of the faculties of one or more of the graduate or professional schools. It may be encouraged, or even originate with, members of a local campus advisory board or with local politicians. Such criticisms may be that the system:

- is insufficiently appreciative of the special nature and needs of the research universities—which have more in common with other public flagships and even with elite private universities than with some or even most of the other member campuses of the system;
- imposes unnecessary and time-consuming constraints on new academic programs;
- blocks the establishment of the higher tuition fees that could provide much-needed revenue—and would not unduly deny access;
- uses its excess tuition revenue to correct for deficiencies from other member campuses; and
- imposes a governing authority that is too distant and that has agendas other than the advancement of a particular campus.

A different source of criticism—but a source that complements the criticisms from certain member campuses—is that the system is simply another layer of government that adds to the costs of public higher education and that adds little or no public value. Such a criticism often comes from those who view much of government as unnecessary and costly to the taxpayer. They may believe that system administrations add procedures that are time consuming—both to themselves and to member campus faculty and staff—but that add little value to any ultimate product (in this case, to the learning of the students or the knowledge created through research) and that mainly justify the system and procedures that have been erected—and the positions and salaries of the administrators who have erected them.

Most sympathetic observers of public higher education, whether critics or defenders of systems, however, would concur that some authority—beyond the president or faculty of a single university, and extending even beyond a local, or single campus, advisory, or governing board—needs *at the very least* to allocate campus missions and public tax resources and to hold the campus accountable for their use. The allocation, or apportionment among member campuses, of missions and state tax revenues are among the most important things that public college and university systems do (in addition to the approval of programs, the promotion of access, the encouragement of cost-effective sharing of library and technology resources, and other functions) and need to be done by some authoritative entity. At the same time, there are possible alternatives to multi-campus systems as these have evolved and are described throughout this volume. Four such alternatives are:

1. *Neither system nor campus governing boards*: With neither system nor campus governing boards, institutional missions and academic programs would be under the direct authority of state government: perhaps through a state department of education or a state department of higher education and training, with additional authority as well reclaimed by the state budget office, the state comptroller, the attorney general, and other state executive offices. As in national systems of higher education in many other countries, committees of the legislature (or parliament) would have heightened authority, enhancing the fortunes of those colleges and universities with politically powerful patrons. State revenues would be allocated by the state fiscal office, again privileging those institutions in political favor. Institutional presidents or chancellors would negotiate maximum autonomy for their institutions along with maximum revenues (and as little accountability as politically possible). Faculty and staff would presumably negotiate contracts directly with governors and legislatures, like all other state employees, and would seek the most favorable compensation and job protection (for example, limiting the authority of management to alter teaching loads, class sizes, or to utilize nontenure significant appointments).

2. *Governing boards for each campus*: Separate campus governing boards would presumably be filled, as are most system boards, with gubernatorial appointments, possibly modified by legislatively mandated board members representing, for example, faculty, staff, students, and appointees of the legislature. Several states have separate governing boards for land-grant or other flagship universities; Michigan governs each of its public campuses this way (i.e., without a multi-campus system board or administration). The separate governing boards would add to the first option listed here (i.e., neither system nor campus governing boards) a presumably educationally enlightened authority representing the public interest for each state college and university. The advantage would be governing boards

each of which could unequivocally seek what the board and the chair believed to be in the best interest of their institution. A potential disadvantage is that institutions and their presidents or chancellors who now have only a system board to contend with—and a board that is theoretically buffered and enlightened by a system head—would each have real gubernatorially appointed governing boards and chairs with their own political agendas and only a single campus to focus them on. Another possible disadvantage of separate governing boards and no system board is that the all-important distribution of campus missions and state revenues among the several public colleges and universities would, as in item number 1, be in the hands of either (or both) the governor's office or the education and financial committees of the legislature (and the political clout with these politicians that the board chair of the moment happened to have).

3. *Shared governance between a system board and individual campus boards.* In this example (proposed by the University of California, Berkeley), some of the authority currently held by the system board would be shifted to strengthened campus boards, which would then become, albeit with limited authority, true *governing*, rather than mere *advisory*, boards. The system board might continue its authority, for example, over member campus missions and community-senior college relations, as well as over the allocation of state tax revenues among the member campuses. The separate campus governing boards, however, might have authority over the appointment of campus heads and other senior administrators, campus-specific appointment and promotion policies, the setting of tuitions and other fees, relations with campus foundations, and other such elements of authority. The advantage would be more autonomy for the campuses with their own boards but with continuing overarching authority of a system board. Possible disadvantages would be the potential for politicized campus boards, as cited in the example of the separate governing boards, plus the potential for confusion and occasional conflicts between the system and the separate campus boards, as well as a heightened potential for conflict between campus and system heads.

4. *Enhanced authority to statewide higher educational planning boards.* Many states with multi-campus system boards also have statewide higher educational planning boards that have cognizance over all higher education, public and private, but that are primarily

or exclusively advisory rather than governing. In the absence of a multi-campus college and university governing board (or boards), a planning board—strengthened by legislation to a governing board—might assume the role of the educationally enlightened but authoritative board representing the state's public interest. However, state higher educational planning boards generally have cognizance—even if more advisory than authoritative—over all postsecondary education and all institutions, both public and private. It is not clear whether such an arrangement should be viewed as a proposed elimination of the multi-campus governing board or boards and the transfer of their governing authority to the statewide planning board—or as the elimination of the statewide planning board and the expansion of the cognizance of the multi-campus governing board or boards to embrace all of public and private higher education. More functional might be a combination of numbers 3 and 4: that is, the devolution of some of the critical authority currently associated with multi-campus governing boards to enhanced individual campus boards and then the addition of some of the most critical functions associated with statewide planning boards to a revised mission of multi-campus boards. (Such an arrangement, however, would lose or at least compromise the presumed allegiance of multi-campus system boards to public higher education.)

Any of these alternatives to the multi-campus system (and there are probably others) is theoretically possible. In the not-unbiased opinion of this author, however, none achieves the multi-campus system's ability to combine public higher educational advocacy with appreciation of the uniqueness of each public campus and the representation of a public interest that is larger than any particular institution. But the most critical conclusion of such an exploration of alternatives to multi-campus systems, at least to this author, is a reaffirmation of the fact that some authoritative, knowledgeable buffer entity or entities—whether single campus, multi-campus, or both, bridging the complementary but also the diverging interests of individual institutions and the larger public interest and appropriately supported by enlightened higher educational leaders—has become indispensable to U.S. higher education in the 21st century.

NOTES

1. See College Board (2012) for trends in college costs.
2. In this case, *deficit finance* means that the state government spends more money to support state finances than it receives in revenue.
3. *Rational tuition* is a term that has been increasingly used by those seeking to allow tuition to increase regularly and predictably (usually maintaining a constant percentage of underlying instructional costs) rather than being set in a political theater as a political compromise between those opposing any increase (on principle) and those seeking increases for the sake of the university's revenue streams.

REFERENCES

College Board. (2012). *Trends in college pricing*. New York: Author. Retrieved from http://trends.collegeboard.org/sites/default/files/college-pricing-2012-full-report_0.pdf.

Duryea, E. D. (1973). Evolution of university organization. In J. A. Perkins (Ed.), *The university as an organization* (pp. 15–37). New York, NY: McGraw-Hill.

Duryea, E. D. (2000). *The academic corporation: A history of college and university governing boards*. New York: Falmer Press.

Massey, W. F., & Zemsky, R. (1994). Faculty discretionary time: Departments and the "academic ratchet." *The Journal of Higher Education*, 65(1), 1–22.

Morphew, C. C., & Huisman, J. (2002). Using institutional theory to reframe research on academic drift. *Higher Education in Europe*, 27(4), 491–506.

Perkins, J. A. (1973). Conflicting responsibilities of governing boards. In J. A. Perkins (Ed.), *The university as an organization* (pp. 203–214). New York, NY: McGraw-Hill.

# 5

## THE CHANGING ROLE OF HIGHER EDUCATION SYSTEMS IN FINANCE

JANE V. WELLMAN

ABSTRACT

Systems have always had a prominent role in the acquisition and allocation of state resources, through the role they play in the development and defense of the state budget for the institutions that are part of them. In the current environment, a number of forces have combined to change the historic system role in finance, including the reduction of public funds for higher education, growth in tuition dependency, a pattern within systems of a substitution of front-end fiscal controls toward greater campus autonomy in the use of resources, and a shift to performance or outcomes-based budgeting. As finances change, the system role is also changing. Primary attention is moving from acquisition and allocation of state funds to greater attention on resource management, finding ways to leverage efficiency and effectiveness, and identifying the best balance between public needs and institutional capacity.

State systems are relatively new organizational constructs in higher education, having evolved in the United States since the Second World War and in some states as recently as the 1980s. Designed to carry out largely administrative functions and not to operate academic programs, they were developed by state governments to manage the orderly growth of institutions through a coordinated approach to strategic planning, resource acquisition, and program planning.[1] In addition to a prominent role in developing, negotiating, and allocating the state budget for their institutions, systems were also designed to promote efficiency and effectiveness in the use of state funds, both through the planning function and by disciplining campus missions through program review. In contrast, the system role in academic policy has historically been more deferential to campus decision making and to shared governance with faculty.

This chapter speaks to the role of system offices in the financing of their member institutions that comprise them, and the ways in which that role is changing in the current environment. The focus is on governing board systems, defined as multi-campus systems with a single governing board and a chief executive who is not also the chief executive or academic head of a campus in the system. The distinctions between governing board systems and other types of multi-campus confederations or consortia are somewhat blurry, so these comments may well generalize to other types of state-level systems including community college boards and state coordinating boards.

## THE DIFFERENT FACETS OF THE SYSTEM FINANCING ROLE

Systems have historically played myriad roles in the financing of their institutions, from state or system-wide planning and budgeting to the determination of student tuition and fee policies, the management of collective bargaining and employee benefits, and capital outlay programs. As is true of most aspects of systems, there is a continuum within their roles, with some systems playing a central role in setting funding levels for their institutions and others acting more as pass-through agencies for distributing allocations made by the legislature. Responses to a 2011 survey on the role and function of system offices (National Center for Higher Education Management Systems [NCHEMS], 2012), listed in table 5.1, shed some light on the range of fiscal roles played by systems, with answers ranked by the percentage of systems claiming to have a "major role" in these areas.[2]

As the survey results show, the system role in finances is most prominent, likely as it affects planning, development, and defense of the state operating budgets; the allocation of state funds to campuses;

Table 5.1. System Central Office Fiscal Functions, Ranked by Percentage of Systems Reporting Function to Be a "Major Role"

| *System Role* | |
|---|---|
| Prepares a system-level strategic plan | 93% |
| Maintains the audit function for campuses and for the system | 85% |
| Prepares an operating budget with a strategy to fund the strategic plan | 81% |
| Prepares a facilities plan for the system including broad parameters about where new enrollments will be accommodated | 74% |
| Determines campus mission and role within parameters (if any) set by the state | 70% |
| Develops and negotiates annual operating budget | 70% |
| Allocates appropriated funds to campuses | 70% |
| Oversees the administration of the budget including review of change proposals | 66% |
| Centrally manages tuition funds including interest | 52% |
| Purchases goods and services | 48% |
| Responsible for capital financing including loan programs and innovation financing | 48% |
| Develops and manages bond funds | 48% |
| Operates the institutional treasury and invests funds | 44% |
| Conducts collective bargaining | 37% |
| Manages the retirement system separately from the state | 25% |
| Manages health and benefit programs | 22% |
| Establishes indirect cost recovery rates | 15% |
| Manages and monitors research grants, and ensures compliance with contract and grant requirements | 11% |
| Analyzes resource use including efficiency/effectiveness analyses and benchmarking | 7% |

*Source*: NCHEMS (2012), based on a survey of 54 system offices, with 27 systems (50%) responding.

and the management of the central audit function. The following are some key findings from the survey about the role of system offices in institutional finances:

- In 70% of the reporting systems, the state allocation goes from the state to the system and is subsequently disbursed from the system to the campuses. In the other 30% of systems, state funds are allocated directly to the campuses, without going through the system office. These figures may overstate the system role in directing how funds are used, however. Even in some of those states where allocations are made to systems, the system may have limited authority over allocations, allocating funds to campuses based on predetermined formulae, budget language, or other controls over spending set by the state.
- While 70% of the systems reported having state allocations funneled through the system office, only 50% indicated that they retained any role in the collection or disbursement of tuition. For the other 50%, tuition revenues are held at the campus level. Similar to the previous point, those systems that do handle tuition revenue may have limited discretion to allocate such funding other than to the institution on whose behalf it was collected.
- Two-thirds of systems are involved, in some form, in the administration of institutional spending and in review of institutional budget changes over the course of the year.
- Most systems (85%) engage in a central audit function for their constituent campuses. Such activity appears to be focused on fiscal reporting, not extending into a strong *analytical* role in looking at how resources are used. Only 7% report system-level work focused on designing performance benchmarks or analyzing the efficiency and effectiveness of institutional resource allocation. Several systems also perform other central administrative functions on behalf of their institutions. Such functions can include collective bargaining, the management of employee benefits, the management of bond funds, central purchasing, and responsibility for capital finance including loan programs and innovation financing. Consolidating such functions at the system level may provide a cost savings through economy of scale and enhance the system's ability to coordinate institutional activities. In the case of collective bargaining, the system role

can be a very powerful lever into the management of employee relations. In unionized states, the central bargaining role forces greater system-level involvement in faculty and staff affairs than would be the case without it.

Some of the variations in system offices' financing roles are related to the large differences between states in their basic approaches to the financing of public institutions. Some states have historically provided very generous subsidies for their public institutions, and as a result these colleges and universities have been able to keep tuition low. Other institutions have higher in-state tuitions, as a result of lower subsidy levels. There are regional patterns in state finances, as well, reflecting state political histories and the relative presence, or lack thereof, of private institutions that could be alternatives to public institutions.

The system role in finances outside of activities supported by state funds or tuitions tends to be weak or nonexistent. For example, management of research and public service contracts and grants and oversight of auxiliary enterprises including teaching hospitals are typically handled at the campus level. As activities supported by these revenue sources comprise a growing share of institutional budgets, particularly at research universities, the system—and state—role in controlling the flow of resources is diminishing. An exception is the State University of New York, which operates a separate system-wide research foundation that both serves as the fiscal agent for external research grants and helps to coordinate and support research across the system.

## THE CHANGING FISCAL CONTEXT
## FACING PUBLIC SYSTEMS

The fiscal situation throughout higher education—public, nonprofit private, and proprietary institutions alike—is changing quite rapidly and is characterized by increasing enrollments, rising tuitions, and declining public subsidies. These trends are causing huge changes to approaches to the acquisition and management of funds, as well as to the traditional roles played between states, systems, and campuses.

*Enrollment Growth and Goals for Increased Attainment*

Finances need to be put into context in relation to enrollment trends and national goals for increased degree and certificate attainment. Nationwide postsecondary enrollments have grown by 70% since 1980, with almost half that growth occurring between 2000 and 2010. (See table 5.2.) At the same time, postsecondary attainment—defined as the proportion of the population with some type of post–high school degree or credential—has increased at roughly a half a percentage point a year. If we are to meet national goals for increased attainment, growth will need to reach 2 to 4% *per year*. While private institutions and nontraditional forms of delivery will play an important role in achieving these goals, the majority of the work will be done at public institutions, most of which are part of state systems. The educational challenge is daunting, and the funding challenge equally so.

Table 5.2. Nationwide Enrollment Growth in U.S. Education, 1980–2010

| Enrollment Growth in U.S. Education | 1980 | 1990 | 2000 | 2010 | 40-year % change | 2000–2010 % change |
|---|---|---|---|---|---|---|
| Public Elementary/ Secondary | 40,877 | 41,217 | 47,204 | 49,386 | 20% | 5% |
| Private Elementary/ Secondary | 5,331 | 5,648 | 6,169 | 5,984 | 12% | -3% |
| Public Postsecondary Undergraduate | 8,442 | 9,710 | 10,539 | 13,428 | 59 % | 27% |
| Private Postsecondary Undergraduate | 2,033 | 2,250 | 2,616 | 4,116 | 102% | 57% |
| Graduate and professional, public and private | 1,621 | 1,859 | 2,156 | 3,006 | 85% | 39% |
| All postsecondary, public and private, undergraduate and graduate | 12,096 | 13,819 | 15,311 | 20,550 | 70% | 34% |

*Source:* Snyder and Dillow (2011).

## Declining State Funds and Growing Tuition Dependency

The single biggest fiscal challenge facing public higher education is the pattern of declining state revenues and growing tuition dependency. In the past 20 years, nationwide state and local appropriations for public institutions have declined, as a share of state spending, as a share of institutional spending, and in relation to enrollment increases. (See table 5.3.) The figures in table 5.3 are nationwide averages

Table 5.3. 2000–2010 Change in Revenue Sources for Public Higher Education, Per Capita, in 2010 CPI Adjusted Constant Dollars

| Source of Revenue/Year | Public Research Universities | | Public Master's Universities | | Community Colleges | |
|---|---|---|---|---|---|---|
| | 2000 | 2010 | 2000 | 2010 | 2000 | 2010 |
| Net Tuition | $5,489 | $8,611 | $4,114 | $6,360 | $2,324 | $3,269 |
| 10-Year % Change | | +57% | | +55% | | +40% |
| State/local appropriations | 10,682 | 8,132 | 7,725 | 5,859 | 8,029 | 6,388 |
| 10 -Year % Change | | - 24% | | -24% | | -20% |
| State Funds + Tuition Per Capita | 16,1711 | 16,743 | 11,839 | 12,219 | 10,353 | 9,657 |
| 10-Year % Change | | +3% | | +3% | | -7% |
| Federal Contract and Grants | 5,248 | 8,389 | 1,586 | 2,158 | 1,695 | 2,537 |
| Auxiliary Enterprises | 9,193 | 11,445 | 3,276 | 3,725 | 1,252 | 1,310 |
| Private Gifts, Endowments | 2,369 | 2,338 | 464 | 362 | 222 | 158 |
| Total Operating Revenues | 32,962 | 38,755 | 17,155 | 18,413 | 12,440 | 12160 |
| State + Tuition Share of Total | 49% | 43% | 69% | 66% | 83% | 79% |
| State-Only Share | 32% | 21% | 45% | 32% | 65% | 53% |

*Source*: Delta Cost Project (2012). All figures are nationwide averages, adjusted for FTE enrollment and in 2010 CPI-U constant dollars. From the Delta matched set database.

Figure 5.1. State Expenditures by Major Functional Area, FY1987–FY2011

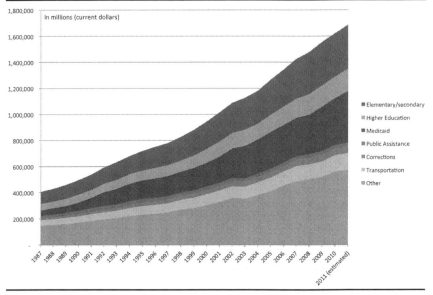

*Source*: National Association of State Budget Officers, *State Expenditure Reports*, FY1987–FY2010.

for the institutions in each sector. While the precise figures differ by state and institution,[3] the pattern of reduced state subsidies, growing enrollments, and rising student tuitions is now common across all 50 states. Just since 2000, state revenues per Full-Time-Equivalent (FTE) student have declined by an average of 24% at public four-year institutions and 20% at community colleges. State funds now average just 21% of total revenues at research institutions—a smaller source of revenue than either tuition or federal contracts and grants. The decline in the proportion of state funds clearly relates back to the importance of the system role in the financing of these institutions. For research universities in particular, the system role is now less important fiscally than it was just ten years ago.

State budget officials note that overall funding for higher education has increased fairly consistently over the last twenty years. With the exception of the recent past following the Great Recession, they are right in that state and local tax appropriations for higher

Figure 5.2. Distribution of State Expenditures, FY1987, FY1991, FY2001, and
FY2011

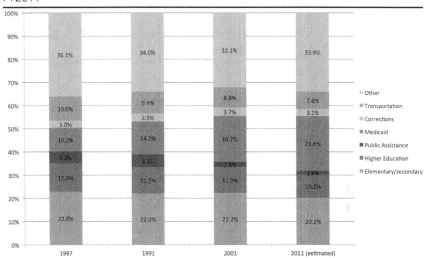

*Note*: "Other" includes state contributions to pensions and health insurance, children's
health insurance program (CHIP), institutional and community care for mental health, public health programs, economic development, state police, parks and recreation, housing,
and general aid to local governments.

*Source*: National Association of Budget Officers, State Expenditure Reports, FY2010 and
FY1996, Table 3.

education *have increased* almost every year. The funding increases
have not, however, been sufficient to sustain spending needs in light
of growing enrollments and increased costs for employee benefits
such as health care.

Higher education is not alone as an area experiencing state revenue declines. As figure 5.2 illustrates, declines have occurred in every
area of state spending except Medicaid. Since other areas have not
been able to subsidize state funding reductions with tuition increases,
budget cuts and reductions in service, while also common in higher
education, are actually deeper elsewhere. For example, state aid to
local governments, parks, social support services, environmental protection, and K–12 education have all been subjected to deep budget
cuts in the years since the start of the Great Recession in 2008. Even

so, state funding for higher education has been cut more than twice as much on a per capita basis than has state support for functions. Support for higher education has dropped by an estimated 20% per capita nationwide; spending reductions for Medicaid and correctional programs have averaged around 7% per capita.[4] Lawmakers know that, if need be, institutions can raise tuition to replace lost state revenues.

At public four-year institutions, revenue from tuition has increased by over 50% per student in the last 10 years, and in most states it now constitutes a larger funding source than do state contributions. After accounting for increases in tuition and adjusting for enrollments, state funding, at public four-year institutions grew by just 3% between 2000 and 2010, less than a half a percent per year above inflation. At community colleges, the patterns are different in that funding cuts and tuition increases are smaller, but enrollment growth has been much greater. Nationwide, combined state and local per capita revenues for public community colleges have declined by 7% since 2000. In the same period, however, federal revenues for vocational education have increased considerably, and are now a major source of revenue for that sector (see table 5.3).

### Unpredictability of Funding

The problem of declining state revenues is exacerbated by the irregularity of funding, with large shifts in revenues from year to year (see figure 5.3). State appropriations for higher education have followed a zigzag pattern over time, increasing more quickly than funds for other areas in good times and declining faster following recessions. The unevenness of funding has presented particular problems for systems and the institutions that comprise them, because it has thwarted efforts to approach finance strategically and develop multiyear strategies to pay for increased degree attainment. It has also contributed to parallel zigzags in student tuition and fee revenues—which spike in years of budget cuts and do not increase and may even decrease in good budget years. Tuition policies that provide for regular, moderate increases in tuition would help students and families plan and pay for college. But efforts to rationalize those policies, and to stabilize

Figure 5.3. Annual Percent Change in Higher Education Appropriations, FY1960–FY2012

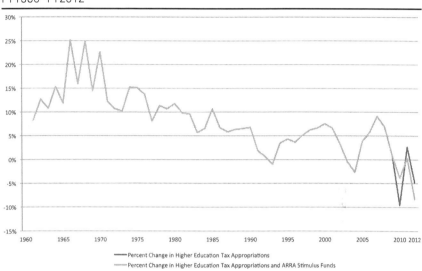

*Source*: Annual Grapevine reports, FY 1960–FY 2012 http://grapevine.illinoisstate.edu/index.shtml

tuition and fee practices, are difficult to enforce because of the unevenness of state funds. Also, unlike private nonprofit institutions, which can build operating reserves to cushion against revenue losses, public institutions largely remain in a year-to-year budget balancing situation, without substantial control over major parts of their financing.

Projections suggest that state revenues will not recover soon to take pressure off of tuition increases or cost-cutting. The United States Government Accountability Office projects that state general fund revenues will grow at an average of 3% per year over the next decade—a welcome level of growth compared to the 2010–2012 period, when state revenues actually declined overall for two consecutive years (Government Accountability Office, 2012). Spending on Medicaid, however, is projected to grow an average of 8% per year for the next decade, suggesting that the basic structural pressures that have caused state funding reductions for higher education will continue.

*Growing Federal Role for Tuition Assistance and Operating Support*

Historically the federal role in higher education finance has been to pay for functions rather than for institutions via contract and grant funding for research, student financial aid grant programs, and subsidies for federal loans. It provides relatively little direct aid to institutions, and systems have correspondingly not directed much attention to the federal government for the development of their institutions' educational missions. Federal funds are crucial for research and service, but these activities have been a campus, and not a system, function. As student tuition revenues have grown, the federal role in student grant aid has become an indirect but important source of subsidies.

Good estimates do not exist for the proportion of tuition dollars that the federal government subsidizes, though nationwide roughly 20% of tuition revenue is currently supported with federal *grant* dollars. The federal share of tuition subsidy is highest (approximately 43%) for community colleges, where the population of Pell grant recipients is largest. The federal share is lowest (approximately 7%) at private four-year institutions.[5] The federal government also plays an increasingly important role in funding vocational and technical education at community colleges. Federal funding in this area almost doubled between 2000 and 2010 and now equals almost a third of state funding.

The total federal investment in institutions of higher education exceeds the value of grants and contracts because of student loan programs' growing cost to the federal government. If current trends of increasing federal subsidies and declining state funding to higher education continue, in 10 years the federal share of funding to public institutions will be larger than the remaining subsidies from state funds. At the same time, the states will be paying more into Medicaid. These obligations carry huge implications for the future policy role of the federal government vis-à-vis states, systems, and institutions.

## RESPONSES TO CHANGING FINANCES

If the United States is to fulfill its goal to increase postsecondary attainment, it will have to find new ways to pay for it. New revenue streams, and different ways to price programs, will be part of the solution. Greater attention to efficiency and effectiveness—and to leveraging the potential of systems to set expectations for performance, including increases in productivity—will contribute as well. Consequently, systems are evolving to adapt to the new climate through changes in regulatory relationships with the state and within the institutions, renewing their focus on issues of efficiency and productivity to find the most appropriate intersection of public needs with institutional capacity. Systems are also playing a stronger role in the evaluation of resource use and in measuring cost effectiveness among their institutions.

## Deregulation from State Controls

In the past few years, a number of systems (e.g., SUNY, Oregon, and Wisconsin) have successfully used their changed fiscal circumstances to argue for greater regulatory freedoms from their state governments in a variety of ways, including how tuition revenues are captured and used, how permissions are granted to reallocate funds across budget categories, and to encourage multi-year investment approaches to funds. Tuition revenues, previously collected and held by the state in New York, are now retained at the campus level. In Oregon, following a change in state law in 2011, tuition revenues may now be used to make up for losses in general funds. Until the law changed, tuition reserves could not be used even as institutions were closing classes and restricting enrollments. Wisconsin institutions now may reallocate funds across budget categories without seeking prior state approval to do so, which provides incentives to institutions to achieve efficiencies that will make money available for academic priorities.

States and systems are also seeking ways to build multi-year investment approaches to improve strategic capacity to meet postsecondary attainment goals. For example, an experiment with a new investment approach to institutional finances is underway in Oregon, led by a new State Education Investment Board whose responsibilities span elementary, secondary, and postsecondary education. The first focus of the board has been to define a performance compact with each sector, which in turn will become the basis for funding agreements with the state. Performance compacts are negotiated agreements between the board and the institutions, which set forth broad expectations for performance in key areas such as new enrollments, the share of enrollments that will be from in-state versus out-of-state students, expectations for increased degree production, and other goals. Oregon is also changing governance structures for higher education. In addition to the statewide investment board, there is a (new) Oregon Higher Education Coordinating Commission. The commission operates in conjunction with the governing board of the Oregon University System, campus-level boards for some public four-year institutions, as well as statewide and local boards for the community colleges. It remains to be seen how this new governance structure will work.

### Strains on "Public" and System Identity

The deregulation of systems is just one manifestation of how changed finances have affected governing relationships in public higher education. Across the country, a number of institutions—typically the flagship institutions or medical centers—have sought to redefine their relationships with their system, either to withdraw from it entirely or to have greater regulatory freedoms within it. One of their first priorities is to seek greater autonomy over tuition and fee levels and collections. To date, secessions have not been successful, as system offices (joined by many of the institutions within them) have argued that their collective interest is best met by staying together in dealing with state policy makers.

Rhetoric aside, the public identity of these institutions remains very strong, and even the wealthiest among them still needs the state appropriations that are a substantial proportion of their general fund base. However, the sense that these institutions might be better off if left to their own devices in a deregulated market has rekindled interest in campus-level governing boards, including ones with the ability to hire and fire institutional presidents. Under these circumstances, the system office financial role could continue to diminish, and its function could become more analogous to the policy and advisory role carried out by coordinating boards in the past. As that transition occurs, the ability of the system—and the state—to use funding policies to steer institutions toward common purposes will be further diluted.

*Shift to performance- or outcomes-based budgeting.* The system role in allocating resources to campuses is also evolving from program-based systems (PBS) to formula-funding models, funding compacts, and now increasingly to performance- or outcomes-based efforts. All these models are predominantly incremental, with the base budget calculated according to prior year appropriations and adjustments that account for fixed costs, inflation, workload (enrollment), and other priorities. In performance-based systems, adjustments to the budget are based on evidence of improvements in performance, such as student retention or degree production, either instead of or in addition to enrollment-based funding.

There was a flurry of interest in performance-based budgeting in higher education in the late 1990s and early 2000s, but these efforts were dependent on new money to fund performance and were largely abandoned in light of the declines in state funds. A new generation of performance-based models is now being promoted across the country by organizations such as the National Governors Association and several foundations (e.g., Bill and Melinda Gates Foundation and Lumina Foundation) that are active in higher education finance. The new models are typically more focused on increasing incentives for institutions to retain and graduate students and less on student access or enrollments. Efforts to implement some form of performance- or outcomes-based budgeting are now in place or are being put in place in the majority of public systems. Some of these approaches are data- and formula-heavy (e.g., Ohio, Tennessee, and Texas) and are based on historic patterns that differentiate spending by discipline and level of instruction, while also building incentive funds to recognize increases in degree progression and attainment. Others (such as in California, Missouri, and Nebraska), look more like budget compacts, with allocations made in lump sums, accompanied by incentives for increases in performance and sanctions for failure to reach goals. A number of systems (e.g., the Pennsylvania State Higher Education System and the University of California system) have additionally created incentive- or performance-based systems that go beyond their state's efforts, seeding system-level investment pools into campus innovations or to reward performance on system goals.

The situation is quite fluid, as a number of large state systems are piloting new efforts at some type of performance-budgeting that have yet to be fully implemented. One of the problems has been that new funds to pay for incentives were in short supply in the years following the 2008 recession. With employee benefit expenses rising faster than any other area, virtually all new money has gone to pay for those costs, and funding either for enrollments or outcomes has not been available. Other concerns have been that shifting entirely to outcomes-based funding will create disincentives for institutions to increase enrollments and that quality will be threatened in the event that standards are loosened as institutions push more students through to achieve degrees.

It remains to be seen whether performance- or outcomes-based budgeting leads to enhanced attainment. Some gains in degree completion have occurred, but these increases have happened in places without performance budgeting as well as in some that do have it. Research also shows that performance-based approaches have resulted in greater consensus between states, systems, and institutions about mutual goals and expectations for results (Desrochers & Delta Cost Project, 2012; Dougherty & Reddy, 2011). They have also improved institutional attention to student flow and to data that shows where students are both entering and leaving their institutions.

The findings of a 2011 survey of college and university business officers, however, revealed that only about 20% were experimenting with performance-based funding (see tables 5.4 and 5.5). Seventy-five percent of the respondents characterized their strategies as incremental. The survey also asked CFOs about their perceptions of the effectiveness of their budget model. Without asking them precisely what they meant by "effective," a bare majority of the CFOs reported their systems to be effective in the sole category of "managing resources during good times." When asked about how the models helped in using data, developing new business plans, setting priorities, and managing resources during difficult times, less than 30% of CFOs reported that their budget models were effective.

*Consolidation of Administrative and Support Functions.* Diminishing state funding has also motivated a number of systems to step up efforts to use the system to push down costs in administrative and support activities, to achieve greater efficiencies, and to free up funds to be reinvested in academic programs. While these practices are probably occurring to some extent in all systems, the scope of the efforts within the University System of Georgia, University of Maine System, University of North Carolina system, and the University of

Table 5.4. Budget Models by Colleges and Universities, FY2007–2008 and 2010–2011

| | All Institutions | Public | Nonprofit | For-Profit | Public Doctoral | Public MA | CC | PNP Doctoral | PNP Master's | PNP Bass |
|---|---|---|---|---|---|---|---|---|---|---|
| *What budget model was used by your campus three years ago (FY 2007–2008)?* | | | | | | | | | | |
| Formula | 27.1 | 37 | 16.8 | 22.2 | 44.7 | 28.6 | 39.3 | 16 | 14.8 | 16.9 |
| Incremental | 68.6 | 68.9 | 68.5 | 66.7 | 87.2 | 78.6 | 60.4 | 60 | 76.5 | 65.7 |
| Performance-Based | 12.2 | 12.8 | 11.6 | 11.1 | 14.9 | 14.3 | 12.1 | 16 | 6.2 | 14 |
| RCM | 10.2 | 7.5 | 13 | 11.1 | 6.4 | 5.4 | 6.4 | 40 | 9.9 | 11.2 |
| Zero-Base | 2.8 | 16.4 | 24.7 | 44.4 | 2.1 | 7.1 | 24.3 | 8 | 21 | 28.1 |
| *What budget model has your institution used in the current fiscal year (FY 2010–2011)?* | | | | | | | | | | |
| Formula | 26.1 | 34.8 | 17.1 | 22.2 | 44.7 | 25 | 35.8 | 16 | 14.8 | 17.4 |
| Incremental | 60.2 | 59.3 | 62.3 | 22.2 | 78.7 | 73.2 | 47.4 | 56 | 71.6 | 58.4 |
| Performance-Based | 29.6 | 21 | 18.2 | 22.2 | 292.5 | 19.6 | 20.8 | 24 | 14.8 | 19.1 |
| RCM | 14.2 | 11.8 | 17.1 | | 21.3 | 8.9 | 8.7 | 48 | 12.3 | 15.2 |
| Zero-Base | 30 | 25.6 | 33.2 | 77.8 | 0 | 16.1 | 37.6 | 20 | 25.9 | 37.6 |

*Source:* Green, Jaschik, & Lederman (2011).

Table 5.5. Perceived Effectiveness of Budget Models

| | Overall | Managing Resources during Good Times | Managing Resources during Difficult Times | Setting or Reassessing Priorities | Developing Business Plans for New Programs | Deliver Business Plans for Online Education |
|---|---|---|---|---|---|---|
| How would you rate the effectiveness of the budget model used at your institution? | | | | | | |
| All Institutions | 39.7 | 49.9 | 56.7 | 27.6 | 20.9 | 15.8 |
| Public Institutions | 36.7 | 51.1 | 33.8 | 28.5 | 21.0 | 17.8 |
| Doctoral Institutions | 23.4 | 38.3 | 23.4 | 23.4 | 19.1 | 17.0 |
| Masters Institutions | 32.1 | 55.4 | 28.6 | 21.4 | 21.4 | 19.6 |
| Community Colleges | 44.5 | 55.5 | 40.5 | 32.4 | 22.0 | 19.1 |

Source: Green, Jaschik, & Lederman (2011).

California system are particularly noteworthy. Helped in many in-stances by independent consultants, these systems have conducted performance, organizational, and funding reviews that have un-earthed evidence of many layers of superfluous functions in infor-mation technology, grants management, personnel, accounting, and procurement.[6] These analyses are leading to reorganizations to con-solidate functions and eliminate redundancies. In the University of California's Working Smarter initiative, for example, campuses and the system are working to improve performance and reduce costs in administrative areas to meet system-level goals for spending reduc-tions or revenue increases of $500 million in five years. Efforts to date have already identified cost savings of over $200 million across the system, along with $90 million in increased revenues.[7]

An emerging pattern among systems is for centralized functions to be carried out through a lead campus. That is, services are per-formed by one or more of the institutions with the best capacity to do the work, not necessarily within the system office. (Examples of this practice can be found within the University of North Carolina and the University of California systems.) Therefore, the centraliza-tion of services and the consolidation of functions are not resulting in expansions in the central system office in terms of either staff or authority. Rather, a greater sharing of activities is occurring across multiple institutions. This pattern of systems is also emerging as a new model in private nonprofit and proprietary education, where variations of systems are being used to increase efficiency and ensure quality control. For example, Yale now leads a "shared services" consortium among private institutions, drawing on the expertise of a former budget officer in Ohio who pioneered shared services in higher education under the Ohio Board of Regents. In addition, several emerging powerhouses in for-profit education effectively operate as systems, including the Education Management Corporation, Bridgepoint University, and the University of Phoenix. The corporate entity is responsible for administrative, financial, and support functions including consolidated admissions, student aid, fund management, and strategic academic planning, while the campuses are responsible for program delivery and educational quality control.

*Increasing System Attention to Cost Growth in Employee Benefits.* The rising costs of employee benefits are one of the biggest spending challenges facing public systems. Nationwide, average benefit costs rose by more than 5% per year between 2000 and 2010—the biggest single area of spending increases anywhere in public higher education. In an era in which state funds are flat, and new money comes increasingly from tuition increases, continued cost growth in benefits will mean that tuition increases will all go to pay for cost increases in benefits. Changes in accounting standards are creating more pressure on these systems, as future obligations for payments (for retirement and for retiree health benefits) now must be shown as current debt. This practice will require institutions to spend more on debt service, which in turn will increase the costs of borrowing, as bond ratings will inevitably decline.

Several systems have started to tackle the benefits problem. For example, the University of Nebraska sought to eliminate its post-employment retirement liability, and the University of Maine System has engaged in a "bend the trends effort" (University of Maine System, 2011). Nebraska was able to eliminate completely its other post-employment benefits (OPEB) liability, which, if unaddressed, would have required 3% per year increases in state funds to the system for that cost alone. Maine reduced the rate of growth in benefits costs by half.

*System Attention to Educational Productivity.* System interest in efficiency and effectiveness is not confined to administrative and service costs; systems are also working with their campuses to address educational productivity. They are also seeking to identify ways to decrease educational production costs and excess time and tuition that drive up costs for students. In addition to work at the campus level, a number of systems have established new policies on credit accumulation, student articulation and transfer, increasing college work in high schools, and expanding credit by examination and distance-based learning. A few examples follow.

*Credit accumulation.* A number of systems have reexamined policies on credit requirements, to seek ways to reduce redundant or repeated credits and to limit state funding (and increase tuition charges) if students remain in school beyond what is required for their degrees. A number of systems have announced new policies limiting BA credit requirements to no more than 120 (except where specialized accreditation requires more credits). They have also developed initiatives to work with campuses to identify ways to improve counseling and scheduling so that students are not put in the position of running up credits while waiting to get into required classes. A systematic survey of these types of initiatives has not been conducted, so it's hard to know the range of types of activities. But something seems to be working: IPEDS data collected by the Delta Cost Project show credits against degree attainment declined an average of 10 credits per degree among public institutions in the 2002–2009 period alone (Delta Cost Project, 2011).

*Improved articulation and transfer.* Attention to the transfer function, and to pathways that ensure that students can move across institutions without suffering a loss of credits, has long been a system-level concern in most states. The cost crisis has rekindled attention to transfer and articulation, to further smooth the pathways by guaranteeing community college students a "slot" in a senior institution upon successful completion of a transfer core curriculum. Systems are also renewing efforts to save both state and student costs by encouraging enrollment in public community colleges and less expensive regional universities. There are a number of examples of this work; one of the most comprehensive has been announced by the

University System of Georgia as part of its initiative to increase college attainment.[8]

*Elimination or consolidation of high cost/underperforming academic programs.* Systems are also doing more to use their program review authority to evaluate costs and outputs of current programs. As one example, the Pennsylvania State System of Higher Education (PASSHE) has used its program review authority to trigger more intensive reviews of degree programs that are both underenrolled and have failed to produce sufficient graduates over a period of time. Programs that are found to be meeting unique system or regional needs are left alone, but those that fail to increase performance are either restructured or eliminated.

*Improving fiscal accountability indicators.* Finally, several systems are reworking their internal and external accountability systems, to improve their focus on outcomes for public priorities and to bring new attention to fiscal accountability as well as academic performance. System reporting about finances has traditionally had an accounting focus, via the production of annual financial statements showing total revenues and expenditures and year-end fund balances. The new generation of fiscal performance indicators is more likely to examine patterns in unit costs and outcomes. The University System of Maryland, one of the first to initiate a broad system-level "efficiency and effectiveness" policy, also has been a pioneer in a system dashboard of performance indicators organized around their fiscal and program goals. The University of Texas System has also been a leader in developing sophisticated fiscal performance indicators, through a web-based tool that documents trends in unit costs and allows users to generate comparison data on a number of benchmarks including costs of degree production along with traditional categories of revenues and expenditures.[9] Both the Maryland and Texas systems include issues about faculty workload practices in their broader agendas for efficiency and accountability.

None of these areas of system attention are entirely new because of systems' historic focus on efficiency and effectiveness. As the NCHEMS (2012) survey shows, however, in 2012 just 7% of systems claimed to be playing a major role in looking at how resources were used or in developing indicators of fiscal performance.

In addition to a greater emphasis on public accountability and transparency, this new generation of system-level work in institutional finance focuses much more on the intersection of academic performance and fiscal policy than has historically been the case. New types of data and different skill sets will be needed to carry out these functions.

## CONCLUSIONS

More than any other factor, finances have shaped the historic relationships between states, systems, and institutions. As finances change, the system role is also changing. Primary attention is moving from acquisition and allocation of state funds to greater attention on resource management, finding ways to leverage efficiency and effectiveness, and identifying the best balance between public needs and institutional capacity. These changes do not mean that systems are spending less time on state finance than they used to. In fact, most of them are probably spending more time and political capital in this complicated area. Understandings about financial roles and responsibilities for systems, campuses, states, and the federal government are evolving very rapidly. The need for system-level attention to finance is arguably greater than ever, to leverage capacity, enforce mission differentiation, advocate on behalf of institutions to public officials, and attend to student flow and success, using a wide spectrum of educational delivery models. The challenge ahead is both how to pay for higher education and how to find the right balance of regulatory and market models to do so.

## NOTES

1. The evolution of state systems and discussions of the differences between systems and coordinating boards may be found in Glenny (1985); McGuinness (1997); and Richardson, Bracco, Callan, and Finney (1998).
2. The survey also addressed other system office functions, including student and academic affairs, communication, and economic

development. The complete survey is available in the Improving System Governance section of the National Association of System Heads website: http://www.nashonline.org/strategic-initiatives.
3. Details about differences in state funding of public institutions may be found in the State Higher Education Finance survey of state finances for public institutions (http://www.sheeo.org), as well as in the state-level data reported by the Delta Cost Project (http://www.tcs-online.org).
4. Estimates of state funding reductions per capita were developed by the author in an analysis of state funding for higher education prepared for the National Association of State Budget Officers (2011).
5. The federal share is based on the amount of Pell grant aid applied to tuition as reported in the Integrated Postsecondary Education Data System (IPEDS). Since the number of students who receive Pell grants is limited, it is not the same for all students. The figures reported here are averages based on federal IPEDS data.
6. Bain & Company's review of the University of North Carolina at Chapel Hill, which has become the prototype for other such reviews around the country, is available at http://universityrelations.unc.edu/budget/#Bain.
7. See http://workingsmarter.universityofcalifornia.edu/ for details.
8. For more information about the University System of Georgia initiative, see http://www.usg.edu/news/release/public_colleges_finalize_plans_to_help_more_georgians_earn_degrees.
9. Available at http://www.txhighereddata.org/Interactive/Accountability/.

## REFERENCES

Delta Cost Project. (2011). *Trends in college spending 1999–2009.* Retrieved from http://www.deltacostproject.org/resources/pdf/Trends2011_Final_090711.pdf.

Delta Cost Project. (2012). *Revenues: Where does the money come from? A Delta Update, 2000–2010.* Retrieved from http://www.deltacostproject.org/.

Desrochers, D., & Delta Cost Project. (2012). *Performance/*

*outcomes-based budgeting: What are the experiments? What is the evidence of effectiveness?* (NASH Issue Brief, April 2012). Retrieved from National Association of System Heads website: http://db.tt/nRAaz196.

Dougherty, K., & Reddy, V. (2011). *The impacts of state performance funding systems on higher education institutions* (CCRC Working Paper No. 37). Retrieved from Community College Research Center, Teachers College, Columbia University website: http://ccrc.tc.columbia.edu/Publication.asp?uid=1004.

Glenny, L. A. (1985). *State coordination of higher education: The modern concept.* Denver, CO: State Higher Education Executive Officers.

Government Accountability Office. (2012). *State and local governments' fiscal outlook.* April. Retrieved from the GAO website at: http://www.gao.gov.

Green, K. C., Jaschick, S., & Lederman, D. (2011). *The 2011 Inside Higher Ed survey of college & university business officers.* Retrieved from http://www.insidehighered.com/download?file=insidehigheredcfosurveyfinal7-5-11.pdf.

McGuinness, A. (1997). *State postsecondary education structures sourcebook.* Retrieved from Education Commission of the States website: http://diginole.lib.fsu.edu/cgi/viewcontent.cgi?article=1004&context=ecs.

National Association of State Budget Officers (2011). *2010 state expenditure report.* Retrieved from the National Association of State Budget Officers website: http://www.nasbo.org/publications-data/state-expenditure-report.

National Center for Higher Education Management Systems (NCHEMS). (2012). *A survey of multi-campus public system offices.* Retrieved from National Association of System Heads website: http://www.nashonline.org/strategic-initiatives.

Richardson, R. C., Jr., Bracco, K. R., Callan, P. M., & Finney, J. E. (1998). *Designing state higher education systems for a new century.* Washington, DC: Oryx.

Snyder, T. D., & Dillow, S. A. (2011). *Digest of education statistics 2011.* Retrieved from National Center for Educational Statistics website: http://nces.ed.gov/pubs2012/2012001.pdf.

State Budget Crisis Task Force. (2012). *Report of the State Budget Crisis Task Force*. Retrieved from http://www.statebudgetcrisis. org/wpcms/wp-content/images/Report-of-the-State-Budget-Crisis-Task-Force-Full.pdf.

University of Maine System. (2011). Report from the Employee Plan Task Force. Retrieved from University of Main System website: http://www.maine.edu/pdf/FinalEHPTFReportoftheTaskForce-toChancellorwithExhibits.pdf.

# 6

## REORGANIZING HIGHER EDUCATION SYSTEMS

*By Drift or Design?*

KATHARINE C. LYALL

ABSTRACT

U.S. higher education systems are facing significant financial, political, and market challenges. Some systems appear to be adrift, responding without direction to environmental winds, while others seem to be charting a new course for their students, faculty, and institutions. Instead of continuing to operate as state agencies, higher education system offices have a unique opportunity to develop new governance, financial, and management models that fit the market-oriented environment of the 21st century. To complete this task, they will need to redefine their responsibilities in ways that will assist their institutions in facing the very real challenges ahead. New ideas worthy of consideration have appeared in several states and from our competitors abroad. Higher education systems will change, whether by drift or design. This chapter examines new roles for systems to pursue and describes possible new structures that could be adopted to meet changing environmental demands.

> It used to be the role of governments to provide for the purpose of universities; it is now the role of universities to provide for the purpose of governments.
>
> —Sir Howard Newby, CEO, Higher Education
> Funding Council of England

M ost public higher education systems in the United States emerged as part of the unprecedented growth of colleges and universities during the 1960s. As demand for affordable higher education expanded to meet post–World War II economic needs, burgeoning college-aged populations, and soaring personal ambitions, new institutions and campuses were founded, existing institutions doubled or tripled in enrollment, and many state legislators worked to ensure that their constituents had access to a local campus at modest tuition levels (Berdahl, 1971; Millett, 1984). The spectacular growth in access to U.S. higher education is reflected in the fact that immediately after World War II, only about 5% of the U.S. working-age population (25 years or older) had completed at least four years of college, while in 2011 about 30% had at least four years of college-level education (U.S. Census Bureau, 2012). The rapid expansion of higher education left many state governments looking for efficient ways to meet the increased administrative and financial demands. The growth in institutions corresponded to more vigorous competition for operating budget subsidies to staff, equip, and administer an increasing number of academic programs, majors, and certificates. Governors and state legislators often found themselves struggling in their efforts to meet the expectations of parents, students, faculty, and institutions for the financial support that could maintain the promise of access and affordability. To enhance the coordination of their higher education systems, most U.S. states organized their public colleges and universities into some kind of statewide higher education system (or multiple systems). These systems vary in the scope and range of their responsibilities, from statewide *coordination* of academic programs at one end of the spectrum to *governing* institutional policies and activities at the other (Johnstone, 1999). Moreover, in many cases ordinary state revenues could not provide for all the needs of higher education, and state governments issued bonds and used other borrowing mechanisms to raise the funds needed to support enormous new investments in physical facilities including residence halls, laboratories, classrooms, and athletic facilities. While this financial maneuvering solved certain short-term problems, it created debt-service liabilities stretching decades into the future.

Gradually, political leaders realized that states would be unable to sustain this growth in financial obligations, even in the best of economic times. However, competitive political pressures made it nearly impossible for political processes to restrain it. Thus, government leaders began charging higher education system leaders with the responsibility of limiting the proliferation of campuses and programs, eliminating uneconomical programs, managing consolidated capital and operating budget requests that set priorities among institutions, and stemming lobbying by individual institutions for budget items outside a statewide context. These roles eventually led system offices in many states to be viewed internally as the government's hatchet man and externally as the primary public representation of the state's higher education sector.

After a half-century of successful operation, the financial, organizational, and political assumptions on which these systems were constructed are changing. Governance structures put in place 40 to 50 years ago no longer ensure that states' needs are fulfilled or effectively add value to their component institutions. In many states, the higher education system has been a weak advocate for maintaining state support, serving more as a conduit that passes cuts in state appropriations to institutions. Old regulatory mandates to monitor institutional-mission creep and minimize program duplication are less valued in an environment that looks to market competition or managed competition to ensure quality and responsiveness to students, donors, state governors, legislators, and alumni. As a result of these massive changes, some systems appear to be purposefully designing new structures and defining new strategic goals, while others appear to be adrift, searching for a new role and reacting to political winds and institutional pressures.[1]

It is in the midst of these changes that the leaders of higher education systems need to consider what role systems will play in the future. Moreover, they must discern how systems should be configured to meet the needs of the states they were designed to serve and to add value to the work of the institutions of which they are comprised. This chapter examines new roles for systems as well as possible new administrative, financial, and governance structures that could add value to both states and their component institutions.

## CHANGING FINANCIAL WINDS

Some of the most significant winds of change are coming from state fiscal environments. Competing demands for state funds, including obligations to K–12 education, Medicaid, and state pensions, have steadily crowded out higher education as a state financial priority (Carnevale, Smith, & Melton, 2012). Accelerated by the Great Recession, which sharply reduced revenues in most states, and the ready substitute of tuition for state subsidies, states' support for their public colleges and universities has eroded significantly at a time when global economic pressures demand more college-educated populations (Lane & Johnstone, 2012). In fact, despite the highest rate of growth in enrollments in public institutions since 1970, state and local support of higher education has failed to keep pace, with per student subsidies falling to the lowest level in 25 years (State Higher Education Executive Officers [SHEEO], 2012). This trend will likely persist because even when state revenues recover, they will be needed for infrastructure maintenance, to replenish public pension funds, and to meet other long-deferred public obligations (SHEEO, 2012).

As a state's share of the institutional budget decreases, the relationship between the state and campus changes. New sources of revenue carry new constituencies whose agendas begin to overshadow more traditional expectations of "the public interest." In this scramble for sustainability, it is easy for the public interest to be pushed aside or reduced to an afterthought. State higher education systems have important roles to play in keeping public goals for higher education alive, defining which of these goals can be pursued in the new fiscal contexts, and identifying which goals must be given back to state government or rolled out to private entities. Here, perhaps, is another example of Sir Newby's maxim: While governments used to define "the public interest" of their citizens and the respective roles of public and private sectors, defining the public interest is now left largely to universities and partisan politics. In the current environment, universities may have an advantage if they grasp the opportunity to redefine their missions in sustainable, realistic terms.

Finally, and most basic of all, the underlying view of the beneficiaries of higher education has shifted, as have views on the appropriate size and role of government. Despite a number of studies (e.g., Lane & Johnstone, 2012; Wolfe & Haveman, 2003) that showed that the benefits of higher education are roughly equally split between individuals and society, current policies continue to shift costs from public to private sources. Until we reach some kind of consensus about the appropriate role of government and the division of responsibilities between federal and state levels, higher education would do well to define its role and seek a sustainable financial future on its own terms. Systems should provide a structure for this conversation within the academy. Political representatives should be invited to join in; but the system should retain the leadership role.

## NEW ROLES FOR HIGHER EDUCATION SYSTEMS

Systems' roles have been evolving to meet their states' new economic needs for a more educated workforce, greater innovation, and the exploitation of new ideas. Even as state support for higher education has declined, public universities have increased enrollments, attracted more federal and private funding for research, and developed foundations or other vehicles for commercializing new ideas discovered on campus. In exchange, higher education institutions have demanded more flexibility to operate independently from rigid state government procedures that hamper their ability to compete effectively in national and global environments (Kelderman, 2011). However, systems also need to consider how they can enhance their contributions to fulfilling state needs and helping institutions accomplish their missions. The following are potential areas of strength that higher education systems may consider pursuing.

### Defining, Facilitating, and Meeting Statewide Needs

One classic role of systems is to coordinate the efforts of all institutions to meet statewide needs. To that end, systems orchestrate the assets of their component campuses to ensure that specific manpower needs are identified and component institutions meet these needs. No single institution can or should be expected to provide all skills or respond to the demands of all businesses and public entities. Without mechanisms for identifying and prioritizing statewide manpower needs and for negotiating appropriate cost-sharing with employers, resources cannot be targeted efficiently and academic programs cannot be effectively managed. It is increasingly the duty of systems to respond to demands for new programs, accreditations, and professional training by insisting that such expansions be conditional upon adequate sources of revenue.

*"Insure" Institutions against the Risks of Innovation*

All institutions need to adapt to the new environment, but not all
have the resources necessary to engage in risk-taking, particularly
when failure may be highly likely. The risk of innovation can be almost fatal if enrollments decline or unanticipated costs arise, especially for smaller institutions. Systems can facilitate institution-level
innovation by guaranteeing a limit to possible losses when new programs, new technology, and new methods of instruction are tried.
For example, a system can create an "insurance" fund that covers
some or all the cost of a failed innovation attempt (a system may
want to ask its institutions to assume some financial responsibility,
similar to a deductible, so that they are vested in the success of the
endeavor). The extent of such insurance, the length of time it runs,
and how it is financed would need to be discussed and adopted as a
system-wide policy. Without such insurance, however, it is unrealistic
to expect innovation to proceed rapidly or across institutions of different sizes.

*Protect Academic Freedom and Ethical Performance*

Traditional core academic values—academic freedom of thought and
expression, ethical behavior in conduct and reporting of research,
humane treatment and fostering of students—are placed under great
stress when colleges and universities are thrust into a market-based
environment. Recently, higher education leaders have had to grapple
with such issues as the determination of the proper line between corporate sponsorship of research and suppression of research findings,
the acceptability of scholarships tied to students' subsequent employment with a particular firm, and the response to a state legislature's
ban of free inquiry into stem cells or other scientific work. Systems
must champion core academic values and defend the academy from
improper intrusion or demands from supporters and detractors alike.

Individual institutions need the security of an environment with
clear and firm values, the assurance that they will not be played
against other institutions in the system to concede core values, and
the knowledge that they will be supported when disciplinary measures or honest confession of error are necessary. Beyond systems,

institutions have no other source of such support; neither governments nor courts nor the public will take this responsibility. Higher education is fallible, but it is still identified in national polls as among the top three public institutions in which Americans have a "great deal of confidence" (Harris, 2010). Systems should take this very seriously, with their boards regularly articulating and affirming it.

## Monitor and Assess State, National, and Global Competition

Public and institutional policy making in a more competitive environment should be grounded in realistic views of both the challenges and the opportunities that such competition presents to states and their colleges and universities. The growing demand for higher education has led to the entry of new players into the state, national, and international environments. For example, there has been a rapid increase in the number of private (for-profit and nonprofit) higher education providers (Kinser et al., 2010). In some cases, public universities are now opening campuses in other states to attract new enrollments (Lane, Kinser, & Knox, 2012). Internationally, many countries have made sizeable investments in their education infrastructure, looking both to enhance the competitiveness of their workforce and to attract students from other countries (Lane, 2012).

To compete in these changing markets and make up for shrinking government subsidies, systems and their institutions may no longer be able to fulfill certain public missions or may have to adapt these missions to the new environment. It may be, for example, that reform of state government procedures could liberate universities to make more effective use of existing resources. Alternatively, reorganizing governance arrangements within a system, giving campuses their own boards, or delegating certain responsibilities directly to campuses may be the next step in evolution of sustainable higher education.

Systems have an important role to play in staffing, researching, and translating the competition into understandable challenges for their states and institutions. For example, annual reports from the Organisation for Economic Co-operation and Development (OECD) (2012) indicate that the United States is slipping in the ranks of the world's 34 developed economies in its share of population with college degrees. The United States lacks sufficient STEM graduates, it is

said, and is not preparing enough nurses and health care professionals for an increasingly elderly population (Carnevale & Rose, 2012).
The assertions go on, and it should be the role of systems to examine them carefully; research and publish the facts for their state and
component institutions; and equip faculty members, administrators,
trustees, and elected officials to recognize realistic opportunities to
address these concerns.

## Find and Foster Campus Leaders

Arguably, the most important responsibility of systems is succession
planning for campus leadership. System officials need to be continually focused on finding and fostering campus leaders, particularly individuals who can thrive in the new market-oriented environment.
Leaders need to foster innovation and change while preserving conti-
nuity of core academic values and cultures. These tasks often demand
skills and personalities different from those required of past leaders;
they also call for redesign of the relationships between leaders at the
campus and system levels. Confusion reigns when the pace of and
expectations for change differ between system and campus leaders.

In many way, attempts by several flagships (e.g., University of
Oregon, University of Wisconsin-Madison, and University of California-Berkeley) to separate from their respective systems after the
Great Recession began to evidence the growing tensions between institution leaders who are attempting to respond to market challenges
and opportunities but who feel constrained by what is often perceived
as outdated governance and financial models. These cases illustrate a
larger frustration that systems no longer help campus leaders obtain
funds, buffer them from government intrusion and demands, or compete with other universities for faculty members and research monies.
They feel caught in regional orientations and structures while trying
to compete in national and global venues. Systems, seemingly caught
flatfooted by these wider visions for their campus, have responded
by challenging or even removing innovative presidents to protect traditional system power rather than using these ideas to fashion new
missions for both system and campus.

For systems to survive and thrive in the 21st century, they need to
redefine and reaffirm the roles of campus heads, being more explicit

(and perhaps humbler) about what the system can do to support its campuses, what campus heads are expected to accomplish in fund-raising and academic competitiveness, and how receptive the system may be to new ideas that may alter governance and power relations within it. Job descriptions for campus heads need to reflect a realistic portfolio of expectations for the environment that they are offered. In a larger sense, just as institutions are concerned with how to develop the next generation of the professoriate, systems need to attend to fostering the next generation of campus leaders.

## Create Incentives/Disincentives for Sustainability

Sustaining a higher education system in the new market environment requires institutions to work in a setting of incentives and disincentives, rather than an environment of mandates and regulations, to achieve specified goals efficiently. A tenet of human nature, as well as a market environment, is that rewards and penalties often work best to generate a desired performance. Higher education leaders regularly observe this phenomenon when seeking to achieve a campus-wide or system-wide innovation. Universities traditionally run with modest individual rewards and powerful institutional rewards. Compared to business, for example, there are few bonuses for individual performance; but there may be significant rewards to a department or program for exceptional achievements in research, teaching, or fundraising. Furthermore, traditional state public-sector operating procedures often embody *dis*incentives for exactly the behavior sought. For example, when an institution saves operating funds through energy efficiencies, the state budget office may reclaim the monies for an unrelated expense, such as building prisons. Alternatively, an institution may seek salary recognition for an extraordinary research or teaching accomplishment only to learn that it can only be offered if the prospective recipient has in hand a competitive employment offer from another institution. Moreover, development officers may solicit a substantial donation of computer technology and discover that such equipment must be put out for competitive bids.

There is an important opportunity for systems to identify, lobby for, and convert higher education operating policies in ways that adopt incentives and disincentives in place of mandates and regulations. (I do not argue here for elimination of public health and safety requirements, or similar regulations, but for freeing up daily business operations to incentivize performance.) Similarly, systems could join higher education purchasing consortia that multiply savings through group contracts. To make these incentives work, however, savings must remain available for reallocation within the higher education system to strengthen quality and access. It is illogical to expect institutions and systems to operate in a market environment but deny them the rewards for performance the market would bestow. Universities are not private businesses, but they can and should run their business functions in an efficient manner; state policies that prohibit this should be waived or eliminated.

## REDESIGNING HIGHER EDUCATION SYSTEMS FOR THE 21ST CENTURY

While systems should consider new goals, they should also evaluate the organizational structures that guide their activities. In the evolution of higher education systems, whether by drift or design, the primary factor driving change is the movement away from a highly subsidized budget model to one that is driven by market forces. For most of their existence, the heart of effective higher education systems has been control of the budget and budget process. Without a central budget process, it has been nearly impossible to establish statewide funding priorities, incentivize inter-institutional collaboration, or speak with one voice about the needs and opportunities of higher education. Moreover, the credibility of system administration among component institutions and the wider public is often derived from their management of the budget process. As the proportion of institutional budgets coming from state funding diminishes, the power derived from this central budget function declines as institutions raise larger and larger portions of their operating resources from nonstate sources.

These shifting financial realities have led many systems to diversify how they deal with the variety of their constituent institutions. In decades past it was possible to manage multiple institution types using the same set of criteria and policies. However, in a more market-driven economy, some institutions, often the so-called flagships, are better equipped to succeed in obtaining new funding lines, which in turn leads them to want to separate from their system. In contrast, many smaller institutions often do not have the resources to operate independently and continue to benefit from being part of the system. Moreover, the separation of any one institution from the collective threatens the ability of the system to perform its coordinative functions. The chief challenge in redesigning higher education systems for a market environment is finding a realistic and constructive way of working with the flagship university that fosters its unique capacities for innovation and self-financing while keeping smaller institutions engaged in a common educational effort. Here are some approaches that have been tried or are already in use.

### Supplement System Boards with Local (Institutional/Campus) Governing Boards

To allow constituent institutions greater flexibility, some systems have adopted a two-tiered governing model. In this model, a system-level board coordinates and governs the entire system, but certain powers are devolved to boards of individual institutions. Typically, system-level boards retain responsibility for developing and managing a unified budget; appointing campus heads; and approving establishment of new schools, colleges, or campuses. Institutional boards may have responsibility for recruiting and appointing faculty and staff members, approving new academic majors, institutional fundraising, and personnel policies. Such a combination of boards is in place, for example, at the University of Utah, the University of North Carolina, and the University of Maine. Most recently, it has been proposed to create separate boards for some or all 10 members of the University of California system, which would devolve certain functions to campus boards while preserving overall system authority with the central Board of Regents (Brigeneau et al., 2012; see also chapter 7).

Experience shows that institutions benefit from the presence of local boards because of their members' closer knowledge of and identification with the institutions, greater fundraising appeal to alumni and other advocates, and personal support and advice for the campus head (Association of Governing Boards, 2010; Worth, 2008). It may be easier for flagships and specialized smaller campuses to recruit members to institutional boards of trustees because of their shared experience and interest in the specific areas of focus and expertise on these campuses. That is, the boards of flagships and specialized campuses may attract individuals who may not be interested in (or be interesting to) a composite, system-wide board. The prominence, focus, and experience characteristic of the membership of a flagship's or specialized campus's board are often quite different from the characteristics needed of board members charged with overseeing an entire system to foster all institutions, large and small.

At the same time, a disadvantage of local boards is the potential for confusion or outright conflict with the system board if each board's mission and scope of responsibility are not clearly articulated and honored. Where local boards are not authorized, we can expect to see "quasi-boards"—advisory committees, alumni councils, and other entities—take over an increasingly important role in situations in which systems cannot or are reluctant to lead, such as fundraising, lobbying, and public relations. In addition, it is likely that flagship (and possibly other) institutions will undertake more initiatives through legally separate satellite enterprises—university research parks, independent research institutes, and other subsidiaries—which are protected from state intervention and can appoint their own governing boards focused on advancing their mission rather than primarily on managing the political and public images of the institution.

### Stabilize the Financial Base

In an era of financial instability, is very difficult for systems and their component institutions to pursue aggressive transformation in support of their long-term sustainability. As long as a significant amount of institution funding is tied to the political cycle, this instability is not likely, at least in most states, to dissipate. The insecurity that results from such financial unpredictability causes everyone to hold their breath and make only incremental changes in the delivery of higher education.

One approach to this dilemma has been to convert current levels of state funding to an endowment or trust, the income from which would flow to the university. Universities would match the state portion of the endowment with private contributions, and the entire endowment would be professionally managed using rolling average payout ratios. Thus, state expenditures for higher education would be frozen at current levels, institutions would no longer make requests for (or compete for) future state funding, there would be some stability for the university's basic instructional budget. Moreover, the university would be partially buffered from consequences of state fiscal management or mismanagement. Universities would know the estimated "floor" to their long-term income but would also have incentives to maximize private donations and to restrain growth in programs and enrollments to economically sustainable levels.

For example, in 2010 the University of Oregon's president, Richard Lariviere, proposed that the state issue up to $1 billion in bonds, the proceeds of which would be placed in the university's endowment, to be augmented by private fundraising. The state would use its annual appropriation to higher education, about $65 million, to finance the bonds each year for 30 years. At the end of 30 years, the state's contributions to higher education would, in theory, come to an end, and the university would use the proceeds from the endowment to operate the institution.[2]

This model is not without risk, but it does have some advantages. In addition to stabilizing a university's future public revenue stream, it would save considerable time and expense associated with lobbying for a public subsidy every year, and it would eliminate competition for state budget resources with other public campuses. More predictable revenue for the instructional mission could also make tuition increases more predictable, enabling families to plan better for college expenses. The risks to an institution include the possibilities that the endowment might fail to achieve the rate of return needed to equal current support, the university might fail to raise the required matching funds, or rampant inflation might erode the real purchasing power of the income.

Another approach might be to consider *income-contingent financing* under which public universities (or states) would be authorized to borrow at a low rate of interest an amount of money sufficient to finance all new undergraduates tuition-free. Students would still have to finance their own living expenses (just as they would if they did not attend college). Graduates would then be obligated to repay, as part of their subsequent income tax filings, the tuition subsidy for a set number of years, after which any balance would be forgiven.

An example of this model was recently suggested by students at the University of California-Riverside. The plan, dubbed "Fix UC," proposed that students would repay their college costs at 5% of their income for 20 years (Abramson, 2012). This approach would shift public subsidies from funding *institutions* to funding *students*. That is, students would receive grants from the states that they could use to pay for their tuition and fees, which would likely increase substantially as institution's would no longer receive appropriations from the state. It is a long-term strategy and would need to be administered by a higher education system or other entity protected from government manipulation.

The U.S. government now permits student borrowers with high debt levels relative to their incomes to convert their federal loans to income-based repayments, making payments over a longer period. Making the program "opt out," rather than requiring graduates to apply and qualify, could substantially reduce repayment burdens for millions of new graduates (Supiano, 2012).

While institutions have historically turned to their state governments for assistance with raising funds, many universities and systems now have better credit ratings—and thus lower borrowing rates—than the states of which they are a part. In such cases, it would make sense for a higher education system to borrow directly against its future tuition revenues or state appropriations. In the case of the endowment model, states would have to ensure that the annual appropriation payments would not change for at least the term of the bonding period. For the repayment model to be successful, institutions would likely need assistance from the state or federal government to collect repayments, specifically through the income tax system, and remit them back to the higher education system. Both models would create a self-financing system that might be more stable than relying on the political fortunes of state budgets.

*Reconfigure Governing Board Membership*

A higher education system's founding legislation usually specifies the composition of its governing board and is rarely amended, although some boards have been modified to add seats for students and alumni. The membership of today's public higher education governing boards, however, often does not reflect new institutional revenue sources. Most, if not all, members are typically appointed by the governor (or, in a few states, by popular election) although state support for these systems often accounts for less than a third of their budgets. Indeed, at 12 of the nation's top public research universities, less than 25% of their budgets comes from public sources.[3] In most systems, student support via tuition now equals or exceeds state contributions, with this trend promising to continue. It should not be surprising that the growing shareholder constituents—students and private donors—are demanding more participation in governance to determine the future of the enterprise.

As the kinds of investors supporting public university systems change, states should consider whether the current composition of their governing boards optimally positions them to compete in the national and global marketplaces. Especially for major research institutions, having trustees with successful leadership experience in businesses and nonprofit organizations of similar scale and competitive reach is increasingly critical; local and regional citizen trustees are valuable, but experience in and exposure to the larger global environment are also essential. University systems whose boards are limited by statute or practice to in-state residents or have operating policies that limit the recruitment of trustees with wider experience should consider how such restrictions might be altered to achieve more useful governing boards.

## Plan and Negotiate a Common Technology Base

Both administrative and instructional applications of communications technology are evolving rapidly, but technology systems are often aggressively marketed to higher education institutions with exaggerated promises of flexibility and compatibility. Like cutting-edge businesses, universities use computing systems extensively to deliver basic services as well as for operating applications. Computing capacity and facilities are often key factors in attracting and retaining top students and faculty members. However, in this area, educational and business models diverge significantly. Most corporations that use technology widely plan for and make budget provisions for updating their computing systems every three to five years; universities often have inadequate maintenance provisions and little or no reserves for regular system updates and replacements. Public institutions frequently must depend on volatile state budget appropriations to determine if and when systems can be replaced.

In addition, the significant costs associated with technology purchases and upgrades needed to support large public universities can make them targets of political intervention. In some cases, universities are required to use computing systems acquired primarily to fit the needs of other state agencies rather than those that facilitate instruction and research. Inside the university, faculty and staff will have differing views on which system(s) are best, and interdepartmental as well as inter-institutional debates can paralyze efficient decision making.

Since technology is now clearly established as a prerequisite for positive higher education performance, it is essential for systems to lead in the identification of technology options, provision of plans and funds for regular upgrades and replacements, and negotiation of purchases using educational discounts. In particular, higher education consortia can significantly control technology costs. Savings that result from quantity purchases should be returned to the higher education budget rather than gobbled up by state deficits. Centralizing the planning and funding of technology infrastructure requires system staff to work effectively with campus computing staffs to meet the varying needs of each institution. As this function has often developed as a decentralized campus responsibility, a clear mandate from the system governing board or other statewide entity may be necessary to reorient decision making and redistribute responsibilities between systems and their component institutions.

A related system responsibility involves coordinating and encouraging the appropriate use of online instruction to extend access and improve graduation rates, particularly by reaching rural and dropout populations not able to come to campus. While the faculty must provide the content and delivery of such instruction, systems can encourage this practice by providing incentives (and limited insurance) for individual and departmental innovation, by facilitating throughout the system the transfer of credits earned online, and by policing the quality and application of such credits to degree completion. The lines between institutional credits are eroding quickly, and avoiding policies through which campuses compete for each other's students requires some system-wide policies and policing. A shared funding formula might also improve the situation, as all institutions in the system would benefit from additional credits earned anywhere in the state.

## WHAT ARE WE TO MAKE OF ALL THIS?

The political, economic, and social environment in which public higher education must operate is in unusual ferment. The purposes, expectations, and missions of universities are being transformed by large trends whose origins are often outside the institutions themselves. Public higher education systems are increasingly considered to be part of the problem, as they are viewed primarily as state agencies designed to manage funding reductions and regulate institutional activities. Too often institutions do not see any value added to being part of a system, and with declining state resources, systems are challenged to fulfill their coordinating role between institutions and state governments. To progress in the purposeful redesign of systems to meet the demands of the 21st century, their leaders need to recognize that they now operate in a market-based (or market-oriented), rather than a public agency, world. That is, resources are inherently limited, demands are multifaceted, and competition from inside and outside the United States is expanding. It is essential for systems and their component institutions to make wise choices, focus their missions, and identify ways to remain sustainable.

There are many ways in which systems can encourage and pursue incremental changes in university operations, such as moving to three-year undergraduate programs, incentivizing and capturing energy savings, enrolling more nonresident (full-paying) students, and making more use of online instruction. It is time, however, to consider real structural change as well. Structural changes entail reallocation of power and authority, reassignment of responsibility and accountability, and greater risk-taking. Systems need to be the source of new ideas for sustaining their own, very important business of public education. The performance of systems, as well as the performance of campuses, will determine whether the statewide system structure remains or disintegrates under persistent fiscal pressures.

Systems must identify the tradeoffs that they face and explain them clearly to the public. They should encourage each of their component institutions to innovate and fulfill its portion of the public good; defend institutions in the face of unwarranted political or ideological attack; and celebrate the academy's mission and its successes, even in the face of cynics who may believe that the "public interest" is a quaint idea whose time has expired.

How these tasks are accomplished, whether by drift or design, will determine much of what U.S. public universities can contribute to the growth of the country in the coming decades. The global environment is alive with competitors who have already redesigned their higher education policies. We must hurry to stay in the game.

## NOTES

This work extends ideas previously discussed in Lyall (2011).

1. The emergence in several states of proposals to separate their flagship institutions from system oversight and coordination are reflective of the growing desire among institutional leaders and some elected officials to allow those institutions with the ability to compete in the broader educational market to do so. The knee-jerk rejection of these proposals by systems to date is not a constructive response.

2. State legislation (Senate Bill 242) adopting this idea would have effectively ended the university's status as a state agency and created a state Higher Education Commission to coordinate all seven public universities and 17 community colleges. Individual universities would be free to establish their own governing boards. The Oregon Senate voted unanimously for the bill in March 2011, but the Oregon University System put forward an alternative proposal that would include all seven universities, and President Lariviere agreed with the governor to delay the request of the so-called flagships or the flagship for one year. However, at the time of this writing the proposal does not seem to be moving forward.

3. The 12 public research universities receiving less than 25% of their financial support from their states in 2008 were the University of Michigan, the University of Virginia, Pennsylvania State University, Ohio State University, the University of Iowa, the University of Illinois, the University of Wisconsin-Madison, Indiana

University-Bloomington, Michigan State University, Purdue University, the University of Texas, and the University of North Carolina-Chapel Hill. The calculations were made by the University of Wisconsin System Office of Budget in 2011 using Integrated Postsecondary Education Databases (IPEDS) data.

## REFERENCES

Abramson, L. (2012, February 7). UC students propose alternative to tuition increases. National Public Radio. Retrieved from http://www.npr.org/2012/02/07/146479925/uc-students-propose-alternative-to-tuition-increases.

Association of Governing Boards. (2010). *Policies, practices, and composition of governing boards of public colleges, universities, and systems.* Washington, DC: AGB Press.

Berdahl, R. O. (1971). *Statewide coordination of higher education.* Washington, DC: American Council on Education.

Brigeneau, R., Breslauer, G., King, J., Wilton, J., & Yeary, F. (2012). Modernizing governance at the University of California: A proposal that the Regents create and delegate some responsibilities to campus boards. Research and Occasional Paper Series: CSHE.4.12. University at California, Berkeley.

Carnevale, A. P., & Rose, S. J. (2012). The convergence of postsecondary education and the labor market. In J. E. Lane and D. B. Johnstone (Eds.), *Universities and colleges as economic drivers: Measuring higher education's role in economic development* (pp. 163–190). Albany: State University of New York Press.

Carnevale, A. P., Smith, N., & Melton, M. (2012). *STEM* . Washington, DC: Georgetown University Center for Education and the Workforce. Retrieved from http://www.mcla.edu/About_MCLA/uploads/textWidget/4175.00013/documents/stem-complete.pdf.

Harris Polls. (2010). Annual reports for 2001–2010. Retrieved from www.pollingreport.com/institut.htm.

Johnstone, D. B. (1999). Role, scope, mission, and purposes of higher education systems: Management and leadership challenges of multicampus systems. In G. Gaither (Ed.), *The multicampus system: Perspectives on practice and prospects* (pp. 3–20). Sterling, VA: Stylus.

Kelderman, E. (2011, March 31). N.Y. budget takes another bite out of SUNY and omits most regulatory freedoms. *The Chronicle of Higher Education*. Retrieved from http://chronicle.com/article/NY-Budget-Takes_Another-Bite/126968.

Kinser, K., Levy, D. C., Silas, J. C., Bernasconi, A., Slantcheva-Durst, S., Otieno, W., Lane, J., Praphamontripong, P., Zumeta, W., & LaSota, R. (2010). *The global growth of private higher education*. San Francisco, CA: Jossey-Bass.

Lane, J. E. (2012). Higher education and economic competitiveness. In J. E. Lane & D. B. Johnstone (Eds.), *Colleges and universities as economic drivers: Measuring higher education's contributions to economic development* (pp. 1–30). Albany: State University of New York Press.

Lane, J. E., & Johnstone, D. B. (Eds.). (2012). *Colleges and universities as economic drivers: Measuring higher education's contributions to economic development*. Albany: State University of New York Press.

Lane, J. E., Kinser, K., & Knox, D. (2012). Regulating cross-border higher education: A case study of the United States. *Higher Education Policy*. doi: 10.1057/hep.2012.23.

Lyall, K. (2011). *Seeking sustainable public universities: The legacy of the Great Recession*. (Research and Occasional Paper No. CSHE.10.11). Berkeley: Center for Studies in Higher Education, University of California. Retrieved from http://cshe.berkeley.edu/publications/publications.php?id=384.

Millett, J. D. (1984). *Conflict of higher education: State government coordination versus institutional independence*. San Francisco, CA: Jossey-Bass.

Organisation for Economic Co-operation and Development (OECD). (2012). *Education at a Glance 2012: OECD Indicators*. Paris: Author.

Oregon Senate Bill 242. (2011). 76th Oregon Legislative Assembly, regular session. Relating to education; creating new provisions.

State Higher Education Executive Officers (SHEEO). (2012). State higher education finance report FY2011. Retrieved from http://www.sheeo.org/projects/shef-%E2%80%94-state-higher-education-finance.

Supiano, B. (2012, July 6). Income-based repayment of student loans: If only borrowers knew. *The Chronicle of Higher Education*.

Retrieved from http://chronicle.com/article/Income-Based-Repay ment-of/132703/.

U.S. Census Bureau. (2012). Years of school completed by people 25 years and over, by age and sex: Selected years 1940 to 2011. [Table A2]. Retrieved from the U.S. Census Bureau website at http://www.census.gov/hhes/socdemo/education/data/cps/histori-cal/index.html.

Wolfe, B., & Haveman, R. (2003). Social and nonmarket benefits from education in an advanced economy. In Y. K. Kodrzycki (Ed.), *Education in the 21st century: Meeting the challenges of a changing world*. Retrieved from http://www.bostonfed.org/economic/conf/conf47/.

Worth, M. J. (2008). *Sounding boards: Advisory councils in higher education*. Washington, DC: Association of Governing Boards Press.

# 7

## BOARD GOVERNANCE OF PUBLIC UNIVERSITY SYSTEMS

*Balancing Institutional Independence and System Coordination*

## C. JUDSON KING

ABSTRACT

Modes of board-level governance for public universities and especially public university systems should be reexamined in view of major forces that are emerging to create enormous challenges and opportunities for public higher education. In order to sustain the public mission and rise to these challenges and opportunities, there is a growing need to enhance funding from a variety of sources, many of them private, and to map them onto new initiatives, partnerships, and directions of change. Boards of public universities need to develop new dimensions, including several of the characteristics that private-university board members have honed over many years. Promising alternatives to consider, alone or in combination, are public boards with mixed public-private membership, delegation of some responsibilities of university-system boards to subsidiary boards for individual campuses, more serious consideration of outsourcing components of public higher education to private universities, and possibly in some cases even conversion of public universities or components of them to private status.

Higher education is undergoing vast changes, having to confront a variety of economic, political, technological, and social challenges. Many of these changes were not contemplated decades ago when the higher education systems in the United States were first created. Despite the changing environment, the governance of these systems has remained fairly stagnant (see chapter 3 for a history of systems). This lack of change has resulted in governance structures designed to meet the challenges of the past, not the present.

The administration and governance of higher education systems were created as means to bridge the gap between the state government and the public colleges and universities. The assumption was that state government was the most important stakeholder as it was the primary source of funding and, in essence, created the institutions to serve a public good. However, state funding now covers a minority of the total cost of educating students. In order to sustain their quality and breadth of operations, many universities have increasingly modeled the financial behavior of private universities (e.g., massive fundraising) and pursued other market-based fiscal strategies (e.g., private-public partnerships, raising tuition). Yet, it is usually the case that governance systems of public university systems do not facilitate the pursuit of these alternative forms of resource acquisition to the extent that is needed.

The main objective of this chapter is to examine the changes that would be desirable in board-level governance of university systems in light of changing circumstances of public higher education. The chapter begins with an overview of the many challenges now confronting public higher education and explores new sources of revenue. It then examines the existing governance structure of higher education systems, including the core tenets of public governance. The chapter then describes possible alternatives to the existing system governance structures and sets forth a set of criteria by which those alternatives can be evaluated. The conclusion assesses functions that could be devolved to campus-level boards to help them deal with the challenges discussed at the beginning of the chapter.

## A TIME OF CHANGE

Public universities in the United States are in a time of intense financial stress as well as significant opportunities relating primarily to advances in technology. These circumstances require difficult but necessary change. There are as well several major forces affecting higher education. Patterns of immigration, historical disadvantage, and diversification create the need for institutions to do a still better job of providing higher education to all peoples, so as to provide a vital route for upward mobility and to enable the best and the brightest from all areas of society to accomplish what they are inherently capable of doing. Since their inception, that has been the primary mission of public university systems. The most visible and immediate changes come from (1) diminishing support from state governments, which in the United States are the bodies to which most public universities belong; and (2) the emergence of online learning and the global education marketplace.

First, the reasons why public support for higher education has shrunk in the United States are complex and differ somewhat from state to state, but a common theme is severe pressure on state budgets from other sources, such as health care and public pension obligations that must now be met. These pressures, coupled with reluctance to increase taxation for revenue, result in stark state funding scenarios for public universities. Underlying these phenomena is a largely unspoken debate as to whether higher education is a public good (i.e., something that has far-reaching benefits and should therefore be financed by government) or a private good (i.e., something that has benefits only for those pursuing their education and should thus be financed by the individual). The Morrill Land-Grant Act of 1862 and subsequent legislation directly recognized higher education as a public good, opening higher education to the best and the brightest among the entire populace.

As a result of these financial stringencies, state funds have dropped steadily as a fraction of the revenues of public universities. When I came to the University of California, Berkeley, half a century ago, the portion of support from state funds was well over 50%. When I was provost for the university in the late 1990s and early 2000s, that figure was around 22%. Today it is 11% (University of California, 2012).[1] This story is in no way unique to California; Virginia and Michigan have the dubious distinction of having led the way in reduced state funding years before.

Some of the recent decline in the ability of states to fund public higher education is a consequence of the Great Recession of 2008–2009 (Zumeta & Kinne, 2011). It is therefore logical to ask whether the state financial situation for public universities may reverse over time. Some gain is possible, but it is not likely that any gains can offset the longer-term fundamental forces affecting state budgets for higher education. States and public higher education have to adapt to a permanent situation in which the revenue for public universities is a much smaller fraction of total state revenue and needs. However, the need for the public mission in higher education remains as vital as ever. Increased funds from other sources must be found to support the public mission, and to the extent that this increase is insufficient, the quality and/or quantity of public higher education will decrease accordingly.

Second, there are many ventures into global and/or online higher education, such as branch campuses overseas, joint and double degree programs, and the development of online courses and degree programs. Most opportunities in globalization partnerships and online instruction are at the campus level, although there are certainly possibilities for university systems as well. Massive open online courses (MOOCs) have arisen as an important new phenomenon. These activities bear risk, and it is too early in their development for good judgments or generalizations to be made as to which are more successful and sustainable—academically and financially. What is needed is experimentation and experience with various forms of partnership, global instruction, and uses of online instruction, along with how they will serve and create markets. These strategies need to be coupled with sound and knowledgeable judgment, including business expertise and foresight.

Strong feelings and tensions surround these opportunities and risks. The profile is high, and the financial uncertainties are substantial, but so are the potential financial and academic gains. There are clearly associated issues of board-level governance that are complex and require both varied expertise and deep understanding of universities, as was illustrated vividly during the governance crisis at the University of Virginia in June 2012, where the driving force was concerns by board members that the university was not moving quickly or imaginatively enough in the arena of online instruction.

## ALTERNATIVE SOURCES OF FUNDING

Different public universities are in different situations and of necessity will cope in different ways. Generally speaking, though, gaining

greater operating efficiency must be a substantial part of accommo-
dating financial strain. For a number of quite fundamental reasons,
however, universities have more difficulty doing selective pruning
than across-the-board cuts. Several major universities have mounted
large programs to seek and gain more selective and effective ways of
making budgetary cuts in administrative areas, one of them being
the Operational Excellence project at the University of California-
Berkeley campus.

In addition, public universities face a need to develop additional
sources of revenue. The methods used can and should be case specific, but there are several general approaches, including (1) tuition
and fees; (2) private fundraising and endowment development; (3)
economies of scale achieved through educational partnerships; and
(4) research and entrepreneurial activities.

Raising tuition amounts to shifting costs from the state to the
individual, or most often to the individual's family. The extent to
which tuition can be raised for various groups of students (e.g., in-
state, out-of-state, undergraduate, graduate, etc.) is ultimately a market situation for the individual campus, although public policy and
political considerations often set the actual limits lower than what
the market might be able to bear, especially for in-state undergraduate students. To preserve the public mission, a substantial portion
of the revenue raised through tuition increases should be put back
into need-based financial aid. In Australia, New Zealand, and the
United Kingdom, massive government income-contingent loan programs have been created to cover sharp tuition increases and/or what
would otherwise be tuition, thereby shifting the cost from the family
of the student to the future earning power of the student (Browne, et
al., 2010; Harman, 2009). This approach has increased enrollments
of students from low-income families (Harman, 2009).

New tuition revenue can also come from the recruitment of students from outside of the state. Public university campuses can draw
students from other states and other countries, even at the higher
tuition rates charged to nonresident students. Statements from some
major public universities have implied that enrolling about two out-
of-state students covers costs for one in-state student. Of course,
campuses must find a balance in expanding access for nonresident
students while still fulfilling their public mission of serving the citizens of the state.

Another potential source of funding is private fundraising. Starting in the early 1980s many major public universities began to engage in large programs of private development or fundraising. The aims have been to cover some current expenditures and to build endowments in the manner akin to many private universities. Within university systems, fundraising is nearly always done campus by campus rather than at the system level. Private giving is nearly always for specified purposes that are campus specific.

Resource generation can also come from cost savings. One example of this can be the cost reductions achieved from education partnerships. Regional partnerships among educational institutions of different types can be cost effective by enabling each institution to provide to the partnership what it does best. There may also be partnerships among institutions of like nature so as to gain efficiencies of scale and/or complementarity of faculty expertise. International partnerships can make use of the capabilities of information technology, provide multinational experiences for students, and provide opportunities for education-hungry countries, while also generating revenue for the providers. Opportunities in this category tend to be campus specific within university systems.

Finally, public colleges and universities have begun to look at their innovation and research endeavors and other entrepreneurial activities as means for creating new streams of revenue. Research ventures and partnerships can be substantial sources of income, not necessarily directly in view of federal limits on administrative overhead but certainly indirectly by drawing private support, positioning the institution for future research ventures, recruitment of outstanding faculty, and deriving licensing income in the case of successful inventions. Research ventures are specific to the faculty members involved and hence are usually specific to campuses within university systems.

In addition, many campuses, and particularly individual units within them, are increasingly looking at various money-making ventures as ways of preserving their budget situations. Many of these activities serve needs of continuing education in some form, and many are online ventures, but there are also many other varieties of entrepreneurism. Executive education, long established in the world of business, is spreading to other academic fields. Within university systems, these efforts too are specific to campuses.

Not all these strategies will work for all campuses, and the extent to which any campus may engage in these activities will vary based on campus interest, system regulations, and state oversight. In places such as North Dakota, the state legislature has already enhanced institutional flexibility to pursue a variety of entrepreneurial and public-private partnerships as means for enhancing external revenue streams (Lane, 2008). However, in states like New York, the state still retains control over the setting of tuition and has significant restrictions on public-private partnerships (Ottman, 2010). In addition, the type of institution will dictate the most appropriate approaches. Research universities may be more inclined to develop the economic potential of their research enterprise, while community colleges and regional comprehensive institutions may pursue regional educational partnerships.

## EXISTING GOVERNANCE STRUCTURES
## FOR UNIVERSITY SYSTEMS

With the previous information providing a necessary backdrop, we can start with a brief review of current governance systems for universities in the United States. For public university systems, governance resides typically in a board of regents or trustees (Education Commission of the States, 2012), members of which are usually appointed by the governor of the state, subject to confirmation by a state legislative body. Appointments to such public boards are commonly made through a variety of criteria that do not prominently include in-depth knowledge of the university system at hand or even of higher education. For example, the criteria for Regents of the University of California state that regents "shall be able persons broadly reflective of the economic, cultural, and social diversity of the state, including ethnic minorities and women" (Regents of the University of California, 1976). Appointments may also have elements of political payback. More often than not, members of such boards are not themselves graduates or longtime supporters of the institution. Public boards meet in public settings, with media attention, public-comment periods, an inherently political environment, and often much public coverage and interest.

The situation for public university and system boards stands in substantial contrast with that for the boards of most private

universities, whose members tend more to be dedicated alumni and/
or long-term supporters and who are often chosen to provide a balance of relevant expertise. Many are close friends of the institution
who have been financially generous and who serve as effective am-
bassadors to other donors or prospective partners. These boards meet
in private, rather than public, sessions. Private university boards also
differ considerably in size. For example, the governing boards of
Harvard and Yale have 11 and 19 members, respectively, whereas
Carnegie Mellon, Cornell, and MIT have 62, 64, and 74, members,
respectively.[2] Such large boards may have an executive committee.
The main reason for the larger boards is a belief that more direct
and formalized governance relationships help gain greater and more
dedicated involvement, support, and ambassadorial activity from the
individuals involved.

## Maintaining the Public Mission

A paramount need within public higher education is to maintain
the vital public missions of our state universities, including access
for the most capable and deserving students without regard to family resources, while enabling funding of that mission to come from
a variety of sources, many of them private, beyond the diminished
state component. This need must be reflected in governance as well
as practice.

Logically, the various major constituents of a university should be
among those participating in governance. Constituents will become
more involved with, understanding of, and supportive of the university if they are part of governance in meaningful ways. Given the
complex array of functions, constituents, revenue sources, needs, and
opportunities for public universities, it is increasingly important that
boards in public university systems have a deep understanding of the
individual campuses within that system. In addition, various types
of expertise are needed on boards, including, *inter alia*, academic, finance, investment, personnel, business, social, facilities management,
and public affairs. As students pay for a greater percentage of the
cost of their education, they merit meaningful roles in governance,
particularly if their costs of education take the form of a personal
loan. Boards of public universities and systems also need to be more

flexible and nimble. As has been abundantly evident in recent international and online ventures, as well as in competitions such as that for a new research university campus in New York City,[3] the current agility of private universities is much greater than that of the public institutions. The reasons for this situation lie to a substantial extent in board-level governance.

Viewed in another way, the board governance of public universities needs to gain several of the elements found in board governance of private universities, without forsaking the public trust, the public mission, or access. These needs include varied and pertinent expertise among board members, deeper knowledge of the specific campuses, flexibility and agility, and an inherently helpful approach without undue political influence. In a recent book subtitled *A Rescue Plan for America's Public Universities*, Garland (2009) has noted the same sorts of needs. These needs do not contradict the well-established concept that executive action lies with the president or chancellor. Boards set up in appropriate ways can be supportive and helpful without increasing their own independent initiative or executive roles. On the executive side, the appropriate role of the board is selection, recruitment, and review of the president or chancellor.

## ALTERNATIVES TO EXISTING SYSTEM GOVERNANCE STRUCTURES

Many of the existing governance structures were put in place during a different era when the state government was the primary funder and stakeholder. As dependence on state revenue diminishes, campuses are forced to derive new sources of revenue. However, the existing governance structures are not optimal for enabling campuses to pursue these alternatives. As such, it is worth exploring possible alternatives to the existing governance structures.

### 1. Modifying or Augmenting the Composition of the System Board; Mixed Public-Private Appointment Processes

Public university and university-system boards operate in the public arena, subject to public meeting and disclosure laws and typically with a process and criteria for appointments that are embedded into law and give appointment powers to the governor of the state with confirmation by the legislature. It is worth noting, however, that in some states—Delaware, Vermont, South Carolina, and Pennsylvania—there are public universities with boards that have mixed public/private compositions. These board structures result from the particular histories of these institutions.[4] The successor "private" members are appointed by the board itself or by the subset of the board composed of "private" members, rather than by a state government process. An extreme case of this sort of mixed public/private structure occurs for Cornell University, which has a board of 64 members, heavily tilted toward private, successor members[5] but including public members in recognition of the incorporation of Statutory Colleges and a Statutory School (see alternative 6) that are part of the State University of New York existing within Cornell, making it a private land-grant university. If a fully public board were to be converted to a board of mixed composition, it would presumably be done by retaining open-meeting laws and policies and requiring financial disclosure by all members, so as not to reduce the public trust by "hiding" governance.

## 2. Creation of Individual Campus Boards under the Main System Board[6]

The concept here is to create boards for individual campuses that would take on some governance roles that would be delegated by the main system board. This approach should provide greater knowledge of the campus by the campus board, along with the ability for the campus board to be more agile in meeting needs and opportunities and also in addressing issues that are more campus specific. Governance becomes closer to the front line and thereby more visible and understandable to the campus community. The states of North Carolina, Florida, and Utah have board structures of this sort, with the boards at both levels being fully public. The state of Ohio also has a Board of Regents at the state level and public boards at campus levels, but the state Board of Regents is only advisory. The higher boards for North Carolina and Florida are university system boards, while that in Utah is a state board. Garland (2009) specifically recommends the creation of campus boards by the Board of Regents of the University of California. The two-tier structure probably does create a burden of greater board interaction responsibilities for a campus but hopefully largely in ways that are positive for the campus. There can of course also be worries about added and/or excessive intrusiveness from a campus board into campus matters. Numerous issues pertain as to the way in which members of campus boards would be appointed, what would and would not be delegated, and other matters. These are considered in more detail in a subsequent section. The two-layer board structure can also be combined with the "mixed" board concept (see alternative 1), with the "mixed" board membership probably being more palatable politically for the campus-specific boards than for the main system-level board.

### 3. Creation of "Private" Boards with Strong Advisory Roles but No Direct Governance Roles

Advisory boards to public universities are usually not subject to open meeting laws, financial disclosure, and other requirements that pertain to public boards. University leaders who seek involvement of persons who they believe would be reluctant to serve in a public setting have occasionally created or contemplated boards that have no actual decision authority and thereby would not be subject to public meeting laws. A further step sometimes contemplated is to say that the advice from a non-public advisory board is intended to be taken very seriously by the main, public board (e.g., that the main board is expected to accept the advice of the advisory board most or nearly all of the time). This concept leads to a gray area between advice and decision that would probably not stand public scrutiny and possibly not legal scrutiny either. Aside from the question of the wisdom and ethics of avoiding public disclosure, experience has shown that the absence of actual decision-making authority means that advisory boards draw less involvement and support from members.

### 4. Delegating Administrative Responsibility within the Existing Governance Structure

It may be possible to accomplish the desired changes through administrative delegation rather than modification of the governing board structure. This would be delegation from the system board to the system president or chancellor, and/or delegation from the system head to the campus administrations. Administrative delegation can engender more administrative latitude and agility as well as decisions closer to the front line, but the desired changes with regard to board-level roles and actions cannot be accomplished in this way.

## 5. Conversion of Public University Systems or Component Universities or Campuses to Private Status

This change would remove the university(ies) from public oversight and would probably be a very difficult matter politically and legally. In addition to concerns about loss or alteration of the public mission, it would generate complex legal and political issues, such as the worth and obligations associated with the conversion of the retirement system if it is within a state system and how to financially handle the portion of the physical plant that had been built with state funds. A second factor is that the major private universities rely financially to a very substantial extent upon the yield of an already-built endowment. Public universities tend to have far lower endowments, all the lower on a per-student basis. For example, reported 2011 endowments for Stanford, Cornell, and Columbia are $16.5, $5.1, and $7.8 billion, respectively, while the endowments of Berkeley, UCLA, and the entire University of Illinois system are $1.1, $1.5, and $1.6 billion, respectively ("List of colleges and universities," 2012). Except for extremely large and singular gifts, a university cannot build a large endowment in a short number of years.

## 6. Creation of Public Portions of Private Universities

The state of New York has long had Statutory Colleges and Schools, which are publicly funded portions of private universities. They can also be viewed as subject-specific public colleges and schools placed under the aegis of a private university. Cornell has four Statutory Colleges (Agriculture and Life Sciences, Human Ecology, Industrial and Labor Relations, and Veterinary Medicine) and one Statutory School (Hotel Management). Alfred University has one Statutory

College (Ceramics). These units receive their funding through the state budget of the State University of New York (SUNY) system. This is an interesting and potentially very useful approach, and it certainly does succeed in putting public higher education under governance that has substantial elements of a private board. However, it seems unlikely to be useful on a wholesale basis, except in a situation such as the collapse of a public university with this approach then being used to save some of the parts while retaining the public mission for them. There is also a potential combination of alternatives 5 and 6, whereby an entire, or nearly entire, private or privatized university is commissioned by agreement with the state to fulfill a specified public mission. This approach would presumably require a public board.

## 7. Dissolution of the System

Another way of going from a single system board to individual campus or university boards is, of course, dissolution of the state public system into separate universities, each with their own governance. The trend over the years has been to create public systems rather than taking them apart (see chapter 3). There are good reasons why that has been the case, notably to reduce the number of competing hungry mouths that are dealing separately and competitively with the state government and also to gain the benefits of planning across the entire system as well as efficiencies of scale.

## CRITERIA FOR EVALUATING THE APPROACHES

Each of these approaches has both positive and negative aspects. The value of any one approach will be largely dependent upon the intended goals of the governance change and the priorities of those involved. To aid those considering such changes, I have set forth several broader criteria that can be used to assess the relative desirability and workability of the various approaches.

*Ensuring access without regard to ability to pay.* One of the primary missions of public colleges and universities is to provide access to higher education to the citizens of the state. A core consideration of making any governance change should be to ensure that that access is maintained as widely as possible and remains a priority of the campuses.

*Keeping the public trust.* The trust of the public in a public university or university system will best be maintained to the extent that there is complete openness and oversight by a public board, such as through adherence to open meeting and disclosure laws for all boards in a system with multi-tiered boards.

*Effectiveness of governance.* Effectiveness is essentially the capability of a board to produce the desired results. So, any evaluation of effectiveness must include a discussion of what the new governance structure is intended to achieve. There is little or no value to simply implementing a new system if it is not going to facilitate the needed and desired changes.

*Achievability.* Every state context is going to differ markedly in terms of its political landscape, historical developments, and cultural beliefs. These all will have a direct impact on the feasibility of implementing any one of these alternatives. Deciding which alternative to pursue should also take into account how difficult or easy it will be to achieve the desired change.

## DEVELOPMENT OF CAMPUS BOARDS WITHIN SYSTEMS

The intention of campus boards created by, and with responsibilities delegated by, system boards is to enable campuses to respond better to their environments and pursue new resources in line with their missions while maintaining coordination and interactions with the state government at the system level.

Two of the primary issues that would need to be addressed are the membership of campus boards and the ways in which these members are appointed. Some or all members could be appointed by the main system board, giving one layer of insulation from the political process. Alternatively, all members for the initial campus board could be appointed in that way, with some or all continuing and successor appointments then made by the campus board itself.

An interesting question is whether members of the main system board should also be on one or more campus boards. Reasons for doing this would be to provide a liaison between the boards and to give the system-board members greater familiarity with at least one campus. Reasons against this approach could include the larger workload for the individual board members and the fact that dual-board membership would provide a route to the main board that does not go through the chancellor or president of the system. This choice will probably be dictated by the individual campus and system circumstances.

Beyond membership, a primary area of debate will be what areas of authority will be given to campus boards, as opposed to being retained by the system board. The University of North Carolina has already developed campus boards, with a system-board structure.[7] The system board has set forth in its bylaws those areas in which it delegates authority to the campus board, ranging from academic affairs to budgeting to property and buildings. It is also made clear that all activities of the campus board must be in alignment with system policies and that a key role of the campus board is the enforcement of such policies.

The following are some of the main areas of authority and the issues to consider in dividing authority between the system and campus boards.

- *Budgets and audits.* The state budget for a system should be a single budget, submitted by the main board (see discussion of alternative 7). Components of that budget could be recommended by the campus boards, to be taken into account as the chancellor or president of the system prepares the budget that is recommended to the main board. The rest of the campus budgets, beyond the state portion, should be the purview of the campus boards, because of the closer relationship to the sources of those non-state funds. Given that overall fiduciary responsibility usually lies with the main system board, primary audit responsibility should logically lie there, with delegation of some campus-specific responsibilities to the campuses.
- *Setting of tuition.* Tuition is, of course, a very sensitive issue politically. In many states tuition is set by the state government rather than at the system or university level. In those situations, the question of delegating control of tuition from a system board to campus boards is moot. In

states, such as California, where the control of tuition lies with the University of California Board of Regents and the Trustees of the California State University, delegation of tuition setting by the main board to campus boards would be an issue for consideration. It would be a sensitive matter to delegate further the setting of tuition for undergraduates who are residents of the state, but it may be more feasible to delegate setting of tuition for graduate and professional students and/or nonresidents.

- *Enrollment and capacities.* In states where there is a stated or implied commitment for a public university system to accommodate a certain enrollment across the system, that responsibility lies with the system board and system head and cannot logically be delegated other than by assigning enrollment targets to each campus. Such commitments are typically for enrollment of in-state undergraduate students. It could be reasonable to delegate enrollments of non-resident, graduate, and professional students to campus boards, thereby delegating the establishment of total campus enrollment capacity as well.

- *Appointments of senior officers.* A key question is whether presidents or chancellors of campuses would be appointed by the campus board, by the system board, or by the system board subject to the recommendation of the campus board. Established corporate practice is that a board appoints its own CEO; however that would remove the usual role of the system CEO in campus CEO appointments. It would, in any event, make sense to delegate the appointment of the next line of senior officers on a campus, that is, vice presidents or vice chancellors.

- *Construction and renovation projects.* Major projects are best managed close to the scene. For state-funded projects, it may be necessary to deal with approval mechanisms within the state government, in which case that function should probably be a responsibility of the system board and office, while actual oversight of the projects is delegated to the campuses. For privately funded projects it will make more sense to put them entirely at the level of the campus board and campus administration.

- *Endowment and investment.* In view of the public trust, state funds and tuition or fee money should probably be invested at the system level, under the auspices of the main system board. Private gifts, grants, and endowments, if given at the campus level, most logically should be managed at the campus level, so as to reflect campus objectives, needs, and circumstances. Campuses would be subject to audit to assure financial responsibility and prudence.

## CONCLUSION

As states as well as public college and universities look to address the changing dynamics in their political, social, and economic environments, there is a need to examine the existing university governance structures and identify ways to adapt or replace such structures so as best to enable institutions to respond to the rising challenges. At least part, if not all, of the public postsecondary education sectors in most states are multi-campus systems, governed by a central board. These systems were created during a time when the state was the primary funder of public institutions and was considered higher education's primary stakeholder. States now provide a minority of the funding needed to run these institutions, and many of the existing governance structures do not adequately enable institutions to pursue new funding possibilities. This chapter describes potential new sources of funding as well as alternatives to the existing system governance structures. It highlights, in particular, the options of mixed public/private membership of public boards and developing campus-level boards within a system structure. It also discusses how distributing authority between these two entities may be able to balance better the needs of the state and campuses.

## NOTES

This chapter is based on a working paper published by the Center for Studies in Higher Education (CSHE.16.12) in November 2012. The author has benefited from fruitful discussions with his coauthors on the University of California proposal—Robert Birgeneau, George

Breslauer, John Wilton. and Frank Yeary—as well as with colleagues at the Center for Studies in Higher Education, notably Patricia Pelfrey and John Douglass, and also others within the University of California.

1. The lowering of the percentage is attributable to increases in capacity and total budget as well as reductions in state funding.
2. Determined by consulting the websites of the individual institutions.
3. In 2011, New York City mayor Michael Bloomberg's administration announced that it was interested in hearing from educational providers from around the world to assist with the development of a science and technology campus. The city was willing to provide land and up to $100 million in seed money. The stated intention is to build New York City into a high-tech hub. Out of a set of international applications, Cornell was selected as the lead institution to build the new development on Roosevelt Island.
4. The University of Delaware board consists of 8 trustees appointed by the governor with the consent of the state senate and 20 other members who are appointed by a vote of the majority of the entire board. The University of Vermont Board has 25 members of whom nine are appointed by the legislature, three are appointed by the governor, nine are self-perpetuating, two are students, and the other two are the governor and the president of the university. Clemson University has a 13-member board of which six are political appointees and seven are self-perpetuating, a situation that reflects the will of Thomas Clemson. Of the 32 members of the Pennsylvania State University board, six are selected by the rest of the board (Kiley, 2012), typically for business expertise.
5. The 64 members of the Cornell board include 43 members at large elected by the board, eight alumni members elected by the alumni, two faculty members elected by the faculty, two student members elected by the students, and one staff member elected by the staff (56 in all), the eldest lineal descendant of Ezra Cornell, the president of the university, and six public members—the governor, the temporary president of the senate, the speaker of the assembly, and three trustees appointed by the governor subject to confirmation by the senate (bylaws of Cornell University, https://trustees.cornell.edu/docs/052612-cu-bylaws.pdf).
6. In a separate and previous paper (Birgeneau, Breslauer, King,

Wilton, & Yeary, 2012), we have addressed the specific needs of the University of California as a system, and have recommended alternative 2, with appointment of members of campus boards by the Regents of the University of California, and with recommendations being received from the campus boards.

7. More information about the delegation of authority in the UNC system can be found at http://unc.edu/depts/trustees/delegat. html. There is also an extensive discussion of the delegation of authority to boards in chapter 4.

## REFERENCES

Birgeneau, R., Breslauer, G., King, J., Wilton, J., & Yeary, F. (2012). Modernizing governance at the University of California: A proposal that the regents create and delegate some responsibilities to campus boards (Research and Occasional Papers Series No. CSHE.16.12). Retrieved from Center for Studies in Higher Education, University of California, Berkeley website: http://cshe.berkeley.edu/publications/docs/ROPS.Birgeneau%20et%20al.UC%20Gov.4.23.2012.pdf.

Browne, J., Barber, M., Coyle, D., Eastwood, D., King, J., Naik, R., & Sands, P. (2010). Securing a sustainable future for higher education finance: An independent review of higher education funding & student finance. Retrieved from UK Department for Business Innovation & Skills website: http://www.bis.gov.uk/assets/biscore/corporate/docs/s/10-1208-securing-sustainable-higher-education-browne-report.

Education Commission of the States. (2012). Postsecondary governance: Online database. Retrieved from http://www.ecs.org/html/educationIssues/Governance/GovPSDB_intro.asp.

Garland, J. C. (2009). Saving alma mater: A rescue plan for America's public universities. Chicago, IL: University of Chicago Press.

Harman, G. (2009). Australia's experiment: Tuition fees, student loans, and university income generation. In J. A. Douglass, C. J. King, & I. Feller (Eds.), *Globalization's muse: Universities and higher education systems in a changing world* (pp. 93–110). Berkeley, CA: Institute of Governmental Studies Press.

Kiley, Kevin (2012, July 25). Redefining the relationship. *Inside*

*Higher Ed.* Retrieved from http://www.insidehighered.com/news/2012/07/25/vermont-group-proposes-making-more-flag-ship-universitys-board-private.

Lane, J. E. (2008). Sustaining a public agenda for higher education: A case study of the North Dakota Higher Education Round-table. Boulder, CO: Western Interstate Commission for Higher Education.

List of colleges and universities in the United States by endowment. (2012). In Wikipedia. Retrieved from http://en.wikipedia.org/wiki/List_of_colleges_and_universities_in_the_United_States_by_endowment.

Morrill Land-Grant Act of 1862 (7 U.S.C. §301 et seq.).

Ottman, T. (2010). Forging SUNY in New York's political cauldron. In J. B. Clark, W. B. Leslie, & K. P. O'Brien (Eds.), *SUNY at sixty: The promise of the State University of New York* (pp. 29–38). Albany: State University of New York Press.

Regents of the University of California. (1976). Bylaw 5: Composition and Powers of the Corporation. Retrieved from http://www.universityofcalifornia.edu/regents/bylaws/bl5.html.

University of California. (2012). Budget for current operations. Retrieved from http://www.ucop.edu/operating-budget/_files/rbudget/2012-13-budget.pdf.

Zumeta, W., & Kinne, A. (2011). The recession is not over for higher education. In NEA 2011 almanac of higher education (pp. 29–42). Retrieved from National Education Association website: http://www.nea.org/assets/docs/HE/D-Zumeta_2011_23Feb11_p29-42.pdf.

# 8

## SYSTEMS, ECOSYSTEMS, AND CHANGE IN STATE-LEVEL PUBLIC HIGHER EDUCATION

### MARIO MARTINEZ AND BRANDY SMITH

ABSTRACT

Public higher education systems exist in an ecosystem comprised of people, processes, and structures. This ecosystem is in a constant state of change. Building on a three-tiered model of organizational change and drawing on higher education policy, innovation, and change literatures, this chapter presents a framework to examine how change in postsecondary higher education systems is influenced by the various actors, structures, and processes that constitute the ecosystem. The influence of state-level variables on postsecondary system change is the focus of this chapter, as examples from existing research and recent events suggest that variables at this level may disproportionately affect the change process. Propositions and implications are provided as a resource for higher education leaders and policy makers as they anticipate challenges, react to innovations, and implement their own change initiatives.

Postsecondary systems do not exist in isolation; each is situated in a complex and dynamic ecosystem. This *public higher education ecosystem* is comprised of three levels: the state policy level, the postsecondary system level, and the institution level. Continuous adaptation and innovation are natural components of evolutionary change across all three levels, causing postsecondary systems and their ecosystem to remain in a constant state of flux (Levy & Merry, 1986).

As postsecondary systems evolve and change, our research (Martinez & Smith, 2012) suggests it is the state policy level that exerts a disproportionate influence on that change. Therefore, postsecondary system leaders who understand their broader public higher education ecosystem and its various levels and components are in a better position to champion the changes they seek and respond effectively to changes that emerge from elsewhere in the ecosystem. A formal understanding of change and innovation within postsecondary systems logically starts with a description of those systems. Additional insight lies in understanding more about the different levels that comprise the postsecondary system's wider ecosystem and the interactions between and among the levels. Our analysis of research and recent events within the context of the public higher education ecosystem, which is presented in the form of propositions and affiliated implications, provides a starting point for such understanding.

Postsecondary systems themselves are complex organizational structures. *Postsecondary systems*, as we use the term, are organizational entities within higher education that develop policy for, oversee, and/or manage a family of public institutions. Postsecondary system offices provide centralized services to this family of institutions and address questions of program or administrative efficiency and effectiveness (Gerth, 2010), coordination, resource allocation, and policy development.

Recognizing that postsecondary systems exist within a broader public higher education ecosystem leads to a range of questions: How do the particular components of the ecosystem facilitate or inhibit change within the postsecondary system level? Regarding the state policy level, are there effective strategies that postsecondary system leaders can use to convey their support for or opposition to changes proposed by policy makers? How can postsecondary system leaders maximize cooperation or gain support for change and innovation?

This chapter provides insight into these questions by synthesizing existing literature and current events with our own research. From a research perspective, surprisingly little is known about the relationship between postsecondary systems and the different levels of the ecosystem in which they exist. We address this gap by focusing on the interaction between the state policy and postsecondary system levels as it pertains to change and innovation within postsecondary systems. We begin with a brief review of the literature on change and innovation to conceptualize the public higher education ecosystem, the different levels that comprise it, and how change and innovation happen within this environment. We then detail the placement of the postsecondary system level relative to the other levels of the ecosystem. Next we highlight the change dynamic primarily between the postsecondary and state policy levels, drawing on recent examples and past research. In the final two sections of the chapter we discuss propositions and implications for postsecondary leaders, which indicate how the different levels and components of the ecosystem interact to influence postsecondary level change and innovation.

## CHANGE AND INNOVATION

Change is "multilayered and complex," encompassing many characteristics and processes simultaneously (Van de Ven & Poole, 1995, p. 526). Different types (Kezar, 2001; Nordvall, 1982; Van de Ven & Poole, 1995) and magnitudes (Levy & Merry, 1986) of change are frequently discussed in the literature. Within a public higher education ecosystem, causes of change originating in the external environment are multiple and varied. For example, fiscal pressures and calls for accountability have increased for academic institutions as federal and state appropriations decrease, creating unprecedented resource constraint (Gumport & Pusser, 1997). Changes instigated internally at the organizational level are usually aimed at organizational revitalization, which is "a complex social process that involves a deliberate and self-conscious examination of organizational behavior and a collaborative relationship . . . to improve performance" (Bennis, 1966, p. 24).

Whether initiated internally or externally, innovation is essentially a type of change. Innovations include new ideas, objects, or technologies that may be adopted by individuals or organizations. The adoption and implementation of innovations are influenced by decision-making processes, system and cultural norms, and communication channels that exist within and between organizations and their broader environments.

Innovation scholars address how particular organizations, such as postsecondary systems, strategically maneuver within their ecosystem to manage change or stimulate innovation. Adner (2012) posited that organizations operate within an ecosystem that is ultimately tied to its success, although the success of an organization is not just a function of its innovativeness. Rather, success is also a function of how well the organization anticipates and manages the many inter-dependencies that exist between it and other elements of its ecosystem. Similarly, Christensen (2003) identified a value network, or the context within which a firm identifies and responds to customers' needs, solves problems, procures inputs, reacts to competitors, and strives for profit. Rogers's (2003) comprehensive review of innovation studies also found that people, communication channels, and information within a particular environment play central roles in the diffusion of innovation, but structural characteristics at the organizational level, such as the degree of centralization or decentralization, also influence the adoption of change or receptivity to innovation.

## Levels and Weights of Organizational Change

The Burke-Litwin Causal Model of Organizational Performance and Change (Burke & Litwin, 1992) provides insight into higher education environments. The model's concept of levels is useful to state (Martinez & Smith, 2012; Richardson & Martinez, 2009) and institutional (Smith, 2011) frameworks that examine policy dynamics and organizational change. The model is predicated on an open system approach and proposes three general, dynamic levels that influence the change process: system, group, and individual. The higher levels carry more weight, or influence, over other levels.

Conceptually, the three levels translate to a useful analog within the context of a state public higher education ecosystem, though at a more macro level. Figure 8.1 is our adaptation of the model for application to a state's public higher education ecosystem. The framework also shows, in general terms, different components (actors, structures, and processes) associated with the different levels, which we describe in more detail in the next section.

From a public higher education perspective, the state policy, the state postsecondary, and the institutional levels are equivalent to Burke's (2011) system, group, and individual levels, respectively. The top level—the state policy level—carries more weight than the two lower levels, thus asserting greater influence on them than they do on it.

Figure 8.1. Public Higher Education Ecosystem

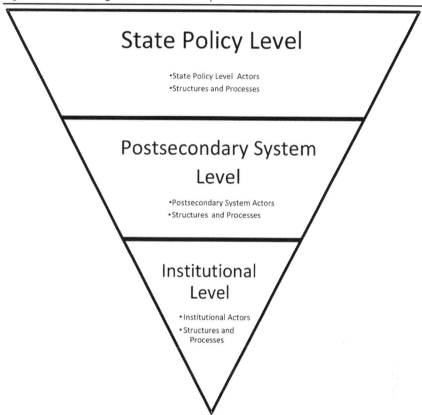

*Components of the Public Higher Education Ecosystem*

Similar to the Burke-Litwin Model (Burke & Litwin, 1992), each level of the public higher education ecosystem is comprised of components, such as actors, structures, and processes, which interact with each other and influence the other levels. These components are derived from a synthesis of the higher education, policy, and innovation literatures. For example, at the state policy level, higher education studies (McLendon, Hearn, & Deaton, 2006; Richardson & Martinez, 2009) draw attention to policy actors, structures (e.g., governance arrangements specified in statute), and processes (e.g., funding methods). The general components associated with each of the levels depicted in figure 8.1 provide a starting point for thinking about the many factors that comprise the public higher education ecosystem. Future research will unearth additional components, revise existing categories, or suggest how important certain components are relative to others in the context of managing change and innovation in higher education.

## POSTSECONDARY SYSTEMS

Postsecondary systems are positioned in the middle of the public higher education ecosystem, as shown in figure 8.1. Postsecondary system level actors include the chief executive officer of the system and associated office staff. System officers and staff members usually report to a governing board that has policy-making responsibility for and oversight of the system. Individual board members are also actors at this level, although the board might be thought of collectively as a group actor. Postsecondary system leaders play a critical role in negotiating with state policy level actors for resources, often influencing whether policy makers view the system and its institutions as one unified voice or a loose confederation of organizations.

The literature also points to a number of structural and process components that may influence how and if change happens at this level: system-level priorities and policies, organizational arrangements, methods for allocating funding from a system to its institutions, and reports and information generated by the system office. For example, with respect to organizational arrangements, Cantor and Courant (1997) advised that an appropriate balance is critical to any system's effectiveness. Specifically, decentralization without appropriate system-level capacity for coordination may lead to inefficiencies and inattention to broader, critical goals, while too much centralization may hamstring institutions and lead to missed opportunities at the local level.

Organizational arrangements also encompass postsecondary system-level governance. Many states have coordinating boards (state policy level) that are distinct from their postsecondary system governing boards. Postsecondary system governing boards are tasked with leading systems of public institutions, whereas coordinating boards are usually charged with coordinating, at a statewide level, all postsecondary education (Zumeta, Breneman, Callan, & Finney, 2012). Coordination takes place through mechanisms of planning, policy, and funding recommendations, all of which inform decision making at the state policy level. In some states, the distribution of responsibility between the postsecondary and state policy levels of governance is not always clear, particularly when a consolidated governing board has authority over all public institutions in the state or a family of institutions within the same sector (e.g., a consolidated board for four-year institutions). Consolidated boards may in practice simultaneously fulfill coordinating and governing responsibilities, producing an overlap between the state policy and postsecondary system levels.

The institutions that a postsecondary system-level board oversees may be within the same sector (i.e., two- or four-year) or a complex mixture of types (e.g., universities, community colleges, research centers). Many states have multiple postsecondary systems, each with its own mission and priorities, as well as its own governing board and executive staff. System-level staff members also typically oversee resource allocation among institutions and gather and analyze data related to individual institutions and the system as a whole.

New York, Texas, Louisiana, and Massachusetts are among the states that have multiple postsecondary systems. In New York, for example, the State University of New York (SUNY) is a 64-campus postsecondary system of universities, comprehensive colleges, healthcare centers, community colleges, and technology colleges that reaches across the state. The 19-campus postsecondary system of the City University of New York (CUNY) is focused in the New York City area. The SUNY and CUNY systems work with a state-level coordinating board that oversees all educational institutions (public and private) in New York, as well as with the legislature, which retains authority over institutional tuition rates and operational budgets. Policy makers and state-level coordinating board members are not system-level actors, however, and they are part of the state policy level shown in figure 8.1.

## State Policy Level

Decisions, actions, and reactions at the state policy level have the potential to reverberate throughout the public higher education ecosystem, particularly in the lower postsecondary and institutional levels. The state policy level is comprised of actors, organizations, and processes that operate at the state level and are therefore technically outside the direct control or influence of postsecondary or institutional leaders. State policy-level actors include governors, legislators, agency administrators outside of higher education (e.g., department of education and K–12 leadership), and state-level business and industry leaders. The state policy level may also include higher-education-related governing organizations, such as a state-level coordinating board (as opposed to a postsecondary system-level governing board). Such boards, whether advisory or regulatory, carry out their coordinating function in the name of the public interest, at the state level. In addition, higher education governance structures are typically articulated in state code, as are higher education funding mechanisms. State code is not easily altered, so postsecondary and institutional level leaders must negotiate governance and funding arrangements with state-level actors (primarily governors and legislators) if they wish to change them.

Many state policy-level components are not specific to higher education but still influence it. In a zero-sum funding environment, gubernatorial and legislative priorities for other state agencies, such as K–12 education and health and human services, may affect funding and policy for colleges and universities. Of course, governors and legislators may also articulate priorities directly focused on higher education. Once again, however, higher education leaders may need to negotiate with state-level actors if these priorities, or the means to achieve them, are not in sync. For example, in many states, funding for public colleges and universities is increasingly based on performance. State policy makers across the nation are adopting the recommendation of influential foundations and experts, who argue that institutions should be funded according to such performance-based criteria as student completion rates (in contrast to states that provide funds to incentivize reaching specified completion goals). Most higher education leaders consider both access and completion as core components of their mission, and while they have not argued against the adoption of performance-based funding, many do oppose the use of completion rates as a core element of funding decisions at the same time state funding is being decreased.

*Institutional Level*

Colleges and universities are the most familiar organizational forms within the public higher education ecosystem. Actors at the institutional level include administrators, faculty and staff members, and students. Institutional governing boards are also actors at this level since they are responsible for oversight of single institutions. In addition, groups such as faculty unions and alumni associations are institutional actors inasmuch as they may represent single institutional interests. Single institutions also have their own organizational arrangements, structures, and processes. For example, a university is comprised of colleges or schools, departments, and administrative units, and it has its own processes for such activities as internal funding allocation.

Institutional-level actors may produce localized change, but in general they lack the capacity to propagate change throughout the ecosystem without support from actors working at higher levels. For example, unlike the actions of a single institution's president, gubernatorial and legislative decisions tend to have consequences across a state's institutions or postsecondary systems. Specifically, executive orders and legislation related to higher education funding, student aid, and governance can be far-reaching and influence an entire state higher education ecosystem. That being said, actions by policy makers are not always simple, authoritative processes, as organized opposition by grassroots groups can have a disproportionate effect on decision making (Olsen, 1973) between or within levels of an ecosystem.

## INNOVATION AND CHANGE AT THE STATE POLICY AND POSTSECONDARY SYSTEM LEVELS

Our synthesis and content analysis of current events and prior research has identified a common theme: Significant changes in or to postsecondary systems and institutions involve policy makers. Specifically, legislators and governors become involved in higher education change in one of two ways. They either initiate change by offering their own recommendations, or they react to proposals from higher education leaders. Postsecondary system leaders who understand how state policy-level actors' relationship to change strengthen their own ability to manage changes that are mandated at the state policy level, as well as to champion within the state policy level the changes that they seek. To illustrate the role of change and innovation within the higher education ecosystem, in the following discussion we provide examples from different states.

## Initiating Change and Innovation

Many initiatives that policy makers propose for the postsecondary systems or individual institutions within their states are attempts to contend with changes external to higher education, such as state fiscal challenges. Other changes are responses to changing social, demographic, or economic conditions, such as the need to increase educational capacity to meet workforce demands. Even when proposals for change are unsuccessful, the discussions and debates that accompany them have the benefit of creating interactions among different actors within the public higher education ecosystem.

One example of policy makers' responding to changing environments is the establishment of Western Governors University (WGU) in 1997 as a means to provide a cost-efficient higher education alternative to students in a climate of increasing demand for higher education and decreasing state resources. WGU, a private, nonprofit institution, is an affordable option for a wide range of students through its competency-based, entirely online options. More recently, in 2010 the governors of Indiana and Texas successfully advocated for a partnership between their states and WGU, essentially creating a "state-branded" model. WGU-Indiana and WGU-Texas operate in cooperation with WGU's national institution but with additional benefits gained from the relationships with the states (e.g., eligibility for state student financial aid in the case of Indiana). WGU-Washington was also established, but initiated through the actions of state legislators rather than the governor.

More recently, declining state resources during the Great Recession served as a stimulus for many states to reexamine how they appropriated higher education funds. For example, facing a $4 billion deficit, Pennsylvania's deep reductions in higher education appropriations in 2011 were the result of the governor's desire to address state budget difficulties without raising taxes, a common practice in many state environments. In 2012, the Nevada legislature initiated an effort to revisit the state's public higher education funding formula, which had been in effect for decades.

Not all state-level proposals for change are strictly budget-driven. When the president of the Maryland state senate proposed in 2011 that the University of Maryland campuses in Baltimore and College Park merge, the idea was presented as an effort to enhance prestige and increase research and grant activity. The large undergraduate programs on the College Park flagship campus, combined with the strength of the medical and law programs at the Baltimore campus, would have created an institutional powerhouse. The Maryland Boards of Regents, however, dismissed the proposal as cost-prohibitive. In addition, stakeholders were concerned for the institutional identities of the two campuses. They also predicted that the merger would fail because it, unlike prior successful mergers (e.g., the 1982 merger of the Chicago and Urbana campuses of the University of Illinois), was initiated outside of the postsecondary system level (Carney, 2011).

Similarly, in 2011, the Louisiana Board of Regents was ordered by the governor to consider a merger of three institutions: the University of New Orleans (UNO), Southern University of New Orleans (SUNO), and a branch campus of Delgado Community College. Both larger institutions had faced difficulties rebounding in the aftermath of Hurricane Katrina. State-level leaders, with the findings and recommendations of a report from a consulting organization, believed that a merger would increase opportunities for students, improve degree-attainment levels, and more efficiently utilize existing resources. As was the case with the Maryland proposal, this merger plan threatened the institutional identities of the targeted campuses. The resistance in Louisiana was much more pronounced due to the potential implications for SUNO's status as a historically black university, which deeply resonated with the state legislature's black caucus. Even though the Louisiana merger was approved by the state's Board of Regents, the governor and speaker of the house pulled the bill in the legislature because of a lack of support.

Some state-level policy makers begin their tenure in office with aspirations of creating large-scale change in their state's higher education ecosystem. As calls for more graduates increase (e.g., Lumina Foundation, 2012), it is not surprising that first-term policy makers are taking notice and focusing on raising completion rates and meeting workforce demands. For example, when the governor of Ohio took office in 2007, he sought to transform higher education by calling for an overhaul of the entire state system as well as the appointment of a new chancellor. He commissioned a ten-year plan for higher education, which the new chancellor wrote, and which addressed the needs that the governor had identified: increasing access to and affordability of higher education for Ohio residents and meeting the economic development needs of the state. The governor vowed that appropriations to higher education would remain untouched, even with Ohio facing severe budget constraints.

Innovations that attract policy makers' attention may also be incremental or smaller in scale, such as three-year degree offerings. Three-year degrees typically allow undergraduates to apply a year's worth of Advanced Placement general education credits that they earned in high school to their college studies without requiring them to be enrolled at their institution for the traditional four-year term. They also aim to create a succinct path to completion by reducing duplicative courses. In addition to reducing the time to degree, three-year programs also significantly reduce the overall cost of a degree for a student (Keller, 2008; Zemsky, 2009). Several institutions are in various stages of adopting and implementing these programs, with state legislatures playing a key role. In 2011, the Washington legislature passed a bill specifically allowing three-year degrees. Although the legislation does not mandate the adoption of a three-year degree, it is significant that the four-year university leaders regard the option as a credible and viable innovation. Addressing the need for an educated workforce, state-level policy makers in Rhode Island and Ohio have also implemented three-year degree programs. In 2009, the Rhode Island legislature mandated that all public institutions must begin developing three-year degree options. As part of the Ohio governor's 10-year master plan for higher education, the Sophomore to Senior program encourages students to apply high school credits toward their college degree through dual enrollment in high school and undergraduate courses.

Change that comes from the state policy level is influenced by the degree of power that actors at this level possess, but existing policies, processes, and structural components at the system or institutional level may influence the success of prospective change. For example, the degree of centralization in higher education systems may affect leaders' ability to implement innovations. Prior research on state higher education policy has suggested that legislators in states such as Michigan (Martinez & Nodine, 1997) and New Mexico (Richardson & Martinez, 2009) find it difficult to achieve meaningful change because their efforts are inhibited by the highly autonomous and decentralized nature of institutions in their states.

## Reacting to Change and Innovation

Policy makers react to changes proposed by higher education leaders when they perceive that such changes have state-level implications (e.g., reorganization of governance structure, suggestions to change the funding formula) or a vocal constituent group successfully organizes its opposition or support for the change. In the midst of state budget cuts in 2011, the governor of Wisconsin reacted to postsecondary system-level leadership when he proposed the separation of the University of Wisconsin-Madison (UW-Madison) from the UW System and creation of a separate UW-Madison governing board. He noted that such a move would give the flagship campus the "tools it needs to remain a world leader in research and instruction—while continuing to be a driver of economic development for [the] state" (Stripling, 2011). This move was prompted, in part, by the chancellor of UW-Madison, who sought increased autonomy over traditionally bureaucratic processes and financial decisions, such as purchasing and tuition setting. The chancellor held that UW-Madison would be better able to accommodate decreased state funding with independence from restrictive state policies. The governor's proposal was halted in the legislature as a result of resistance at (1) the institutional level, where other Wisconsin institutions were cautious about the loss of stature as well as their similar desire for increased autonomy; and (2) the postsecondary system level, where the Board of Regents had concerns regarding the continued efforts of cooperation among institutions. Nevertheless, changes to the system subsequently emerged as a new, incremental plan, administered by the Board of Regents, provided concessions and some increased level of autonomy to all institutions.

In Arizona, a 2003 pitch initiated by system-level leaders to re-organize the postsecondary system in an effort to address population growth and decreasing state financial support to higher education eventually led to policy maker involvement. The Herstam plan, as it became known, was created by Board of Regents chair Chris Herstam, along with two powerful institutional presidents and an outside national figure. The proposal would have created three regional four-year universities focusing on bachelor's degrees, leaving Arizona State University and the University of Arizona to concentrate their efforts toward research. The proposal generated vocal resistance from college administrators, faculty, students, and alumni of several institutions as well as apprehension from lawmakers. The plan was replaced by the Board of Regents with one that addressed the access and cost issues with less controversy. State lawmakers, noticeably absent in the formulation of the plans, reacted by creating legislation addressing institutional budgets and workforce-related degree programs. The bill was eventually halted by the governor, paving the way for the more conservative Board of Regents plan to proceed.

Some policy makers react strongly to constituent groups who successfully organize in opposition (or sometimes in support) of a change. The SUNY Board of Trustees' plan for the traditionally independent institutions in the system to consolidate and share administrative resources is an example of a postsecondary system-level proposal for change that elicited policy maker reaction. The SUNY Board of Trustees directed system and institutional leaders to promote collaboration among its campuses in efforts to increase efficiencies through administrative cost savings, program realignments, and other strategic changes. Proposed changes included the consolidation of presidential positions for some merged campuses, a controversial transformational change for the system. Two prominent concerns were raised, and exemplified in protests from various stakeholders, including faculty, staff, advisory boards, and donors: (1) established institutional identities and missions may be compromised in a merger, and (2) a longtime, popular institutional president would be displaced. Reacting to the opposition by constituents, a state senator introduced a bill that would require each institution to have its own president, citing its relevance and ties to institutional identity, and strongly supported by city and local entities as well as the stakeholder communities. In the end, some institutional presidencies were consolidated, while others remained intact. The SUNY plan does demonstrate the importance of anticipating stakeholder reactions to postsecondary-level-initiated change, as such reactions could affect the timing of change or necessitate modification to it.

In some states, where goals are aligned and facilitating structures are present, the state policy, postsecondary system, and institutional levels work collaboratively toward change efforts. The Board of Regents in South Dakota successfully pushed for change in the state, in a move to reward institutions for outcomes more closely aligned with system and state priorities. Throughout this process, postsecondary system leaders constantly included policy makers and institutional presidents in discussions about goals and actively sought input from the governor's office and legislators (Martinez & Nilson, 2006). The executive director was adept at conceiving of and managing change, but he was also aided by a centralized structure, which meant institutions were responsive to the change.

## PROPOSITIONS

Recent and attempted changes in postsecondary systems across various states offer lessons to policy makers and higher education leaders. Five propositions emerged from an analysis of these changes as they are viewed and interpreted through relevant literatures and the ecosystem framework in figure 8.1. These propositions are preliminary statements that summarize key findings and capture lessons. Each proposition is stated individually, followed by brief points of evidence drawn from the chapter. In the best case, the propositions may provide reflections that postsecondary system leaders find helpful as they propose, advocate, or challenge a given change.

### Policy Makers

*Proposition 1:* Governors who have high personal power are most influential in facilitating changes they support or blocking those they are against. In states where the governor's personal powers are relatively low, proposed changes tend to happen through collective decision-making processes (which includes the legislature, the press, and other actors).

Beyle (1999) has created a categorization of gubernatorial power along two dimensions: institutional power and personal power. Institutional power is aligned with the formalized executive powers bestowed upon governors as given by their state laws. Personal power may, roughly speaking, be equated with a governor's past, current, and prospective popularity. The adoption of WGU as a state model across three states suggests that it is personal power that allows governors to make more authoritative, top-down decisions (Martinez & Smith, 2012).

Ohio's governor possessed high personal power during the time he was advocating for higher education changes in his state, which certainly facilitated receptivity to and adoption of several of his priorities. In cases where a governor lacks the ability or interest to push a change but where an agenda for change exists at the state level, it is often because an experienced legislator pushes for the change. This was the case in Nevada's investigation into a new funding formula and the adoption of WGU Washington. Literature in higher education policy (McClendon, Hearn, & Deaton, 2006; Richardson & Martinez, 2009; Richardson, Bracco, Callan, & Finney, 1999) confirms the central role of policy makers to system change. Innovation studies (Rogers, 2003) differentiate between collective vs. authoritative decision-making processes during the adoption and implementation of innovation, which aligns well with change driven by governors versus those that travel through a longer, collective legislative process.

*Proposition 2:* Policy maker reaction to postsecondary-level-initiated change largely depends on two things: (1) whether those policy makers felt apprised of the change, and (2) how policy makers' constituents view the change.

The cases of the 2011 SUNY consolidation plan and the 2003 Arizona Board of Regents reorganization proposal demonstrate that policy maker support is an important ingredient for launching system-level proposed changes. Governors and legislators may challenge change proposals that emanate from system-level leaders for a number of reasons, including a need to respond to constituent groups or perhaps to avoid a perception that they were not properly consulted during the construction of a plan. As demonstrated by the Arizona Herstam plan, policy makers are likely to react negatively to change driven by postsecondary-system-level actors if they feel left out of the conversation or there is a perception that they were not informed or "in the know."

## Outside Influences

*Proposition 3:* Decision makers often learn about innovations from sources (champions and information) that are outside the state or postsecondary system. Decision makers may also promote their own changes, but they still use outside champions and outside information to bring a perceived validation and credibility to the change.

Early studies in diffusion point to the central role of outside champions and outside information in creating initial awareness about an innovation or change. Coleman, Katz, and Menzel (1966) concluded that doctors' initial knowledge about new medical drugs came from salespeople and advertisements that they did not seek, with many of these same doctors subsequently seeking more information about the drugs. Gladwell's (2000) popularized work on social connectors detailed the impact of champions who are able to propagate ideas. Regarding information, Goldenberg, Mazursky, and Solomon (1999) made the case that comparative information is compelling and has stickiness—several influential national higher education reports containing state-by-state metrics serve as a good example of this principle.

True to the literature, policy makers and postsecondary system leaders do regularly draw on outside experts to champion a change or to provide evidence that substantiates the need for the change. The perception is that outside sources are objective and can credibly validate the change as applicable to a particular state or postsecondary system. The governor's efforts in Ohio were certainly buoyed by several national reports that pointed out challenges and problems across the states. Major foundations have also played an advocacy role in championing for change in states like Ohio, adding an element of credibility to policy-maker-driven initiatives.

Our synthesis also indicates that leaders at all levels often hire outside experts (i.e., consultants) to weigh in on such issues as governance and funding allocation. Consultants act as experts who provide information to decision makers. The Louisiana Board of Regents, which was legislatively charged with examining the higher education needs of New Orleans following Hurricane Katrina, hired consultants to evaluate the postsecondary system. The Nevada legislature (state-policy-level actor) hired one consultant to examine the state's higher education funding formula, while the Nevada System of Higher Education (postsecondary-system-level actor) hired another. Whatever outside information or outside champions decision makers pay attention to or solicit for help, it may be useful to heed Pfeffer's (1997) caution that people often use information and sources to retrospectively rationalize a decision they have already made. In matters of postsecondary system change, this tendency may be amplified when state-level officials have publicly committed to a position or the stakes are high.

## Resources and Structures

*Proposition 4:* In private enterprise, a surplus of organizational resources facilitates receptivity to and adoption of innovation; in public higher education ecosystems, decreasing levels of organizational resources facilitate receptivity to change and adoption of innovation.

Organizational slack can be thought of as a surplus of resources. The identification of organizational slack as an important variable in enhancing an organization's ability to innovate has a rich history of study (Bourgeois, 1981), and those organizations of greater size and greater levels of resources are assumed to be more innovative (Berry, 1994). In higher education ecosystems, much evidence suggests that decision makers are more likely to promote changes or increase their receptivity to new innovations when resources are scarce. Over the last five years, a number of states, including Georgia, Louisiana, and New Jersey, have proposed merging institutions in the face of fiscal difficulties. Depressed state resources have motivated some states to examine new funding methods or move toward performance funding as they search for efficiencies and cost savings. The evidence also is strong that policy makers have been increasingly receptive to new models for the delivery of education in the face of constrained resources.

*Proposition 5:* The adoption and implementation of change and innovation are facilitated by centralized organizational structures in higher education.

Characteristics of an organization's structural components affect its capacity for change. Rogers (2003) concluded that centralization (defined as power concentrated through various organizational mechanisms) facilitates the adoption or implementation of a change or innovation that leaders support. In higher education, postsecondary system structures influence the adoption and implementation of change and innovation. The South Dakota University System Board of Regents' ability to define policy priorities and implement a new funding methodology in the 1990s was facilitated by the highly centralized higher education structure in the state (Martinez & Nilson, 2006).

There are indications in other states that centralization facilitates change. For example, policy makers in Washington State were looking for new ways to increase higher education capacity in the face of increased demand and depressed funding, both of which coincided with the adoption of WGU as a state-branded institution. In Washington, the State Board of Community and Technical Colleges was able to work with WGU to draft transfer agreements for the entire 34-institution system—a centralized system. In Indiana, WGU officials were also able to work with two-year postsecondary officials, namely the board of trustees for the Ivy Tech Community College System, which governs all 31 of its campuses.

## CONCLUSIONS AND IMPLICATIONS

Our five propositions are predicated on a synthesis of existing literature and current events across different states, as viewed through the ecosystem framework. The propositions have implications for practice, which may help postsecondary leaders champion the changes they seek or manage those emanating from or advocated by those outside of the postsecondary-system level. The following implications draw on evidence from one or more of our propositions.

### Implications for Postsecondary System Leaders when They Are the Ones Driving Change and Innovation

First, awareness building (making others within the ecosystem aware of the change, articulating the reason for the change, highlighting its benefits, etc.) is critical to the success of a change initiative. Efforts toward awareness building should be strategic and targeted, starting with a state's governor, if that governor is popular within the state. Second, in states where the governor's popularity is relatively low or the governor lacks interest in higher education issues, awareness building might reasonably focus on influential legislators who are proven "players" in the state. This approach does not mean that other actors are not informed and consulted about the change, only that legislators may be the priority. Finally, postsecondary leaders who support and advocate a change might proactively anticipate constituents, at any level within the ecosystem, who oppose or support the change. Constituent reaction (at the institutional level, for example) to the change, if it is strong enough and organized, may evoke policy maker involvement that can derail the change. System leaders who take the lead on initiating dialogue and discussion with those who oppose or support the change proactively manage the change process.

### Implications for Practice when Postsecondary System Leaders Are Reacting to Policy-Maker-Driven Change and Innovation

Policy makers who push for change are influenced by innovation champions from outside the state and information produced outside the postsecondary system. Oftentimes, postsecondary leaders who oppose policy-maker-driven change will find their personal testimony or system-level-generated information only marginally effective, as policy makers will look at such evidence as self-serving. The incorporation of outside expertise and information builds credibility when raising concerns about a proposed change. Postsecondary leaders should seek outside experts to provide validation for or against a change. One final implication is that organized, grassroots opposition draws press attention and may be effective when raising concerns about a policy-maker-driven change.

One of the most complex and difficult tasks that postsecondary leaders face is that of managing change and innovation. With ever-increasing calls for improved performance and consistent pressure to remain competitive, all within the confines of limited fiscal resources, the process of change will only intensify. The interactions among the state policy, postsecondary system, and institutional levels influence the adoption and implementation of any change. The framework provided in this chapter is a starting point for conceptualizing the ecosystem as a whole. The cases, from current events and prior research, serve as real-life examples of actual interactions that occur between and among the levels that comprise the ecosystem. The subsequent propositions and implications bridge the theory to the practice and are intended to be initial guidelines that postsecondary leaders may want to consider as they manage external change or advocate for their own initiatives.

## REFERENCES

Adner, R. (2012). *The wide lens: A new strategy for innovation.* New York, NY: Penguin.

Bennis, W. G. (1966). Changing organizations. *Journal of Applied Behavioral Science, 2,* 247–263. doi:10.1177/002188636600200301.

Berry, F. S. (1994). Innovation in public management: The adoption of state strategic planning. *Public Administration Review, 54,* 395–329.

Beyle, T. (1999). The governors. In V. Gray, R. Hanson, & H. Jacob (Eds.), *Politics in the American states: A comparative analysis* (pp. 191–231). Washington, DC: CQ Press.

Bourgeois, L. J., III. (1981). On the measure of organizational slack. *Academy of Management Review, 6*(1), 29–39.

Burke, W. W. (2011). Organization change: Theory and practice, 3rd ed. Thousand Oaks, CA: Sage.

Burke. W. W., & Litwin, G. H. (1992). A causal model of organizational performance and change. *Journal of Management, 18*(3), 523–545. doi:10.1177/014920639201800306.

Cantor, M. C., & Courant, P. N. (1997). Budgets and budgeting at the University of Michigan: A work in progress. Retrieved from http://www.umich.edu/~urecord/9798/Nov26_97/budget.htm.

Carnevale, A. P., Smith, N., & Strohl, J. (2010). Help wanted: Projections of jobs and education requirements through 2018. Retrieved from http://www9.georgetown.edu/grad/gppi/hpi/cew/pdfs/FullReport.pdf.

Carney, G. (2011, October 10). University of Maryland seeks input on mergers. Elkridge Patch. Retrieved from http://elkridge.patch.com/articles/university-of-maryland-seeks-input-on-merger.

Christensen, C. M. (2003). *The innovator's dilemma*. New York, NY: Harper Business.

Coleman, J. S., Katz, E., & Menzel, H. (1966). *Medical innovation: A diffusion study*. New York, NY: Bobbs-Merrill.

Gerth, D. R. (2010). *The people's university: A history of the California State University*. Berkeley, CA: Berkeley Public Policy Press.

Gladwell, M. (2000). *The tipping point: How little things can make a big difference*. Boston, MA: Little, Brown and Company.

Goldenberg, J., Mazursky, D., & Solomon, S. (1999). The fundamental templates of quality ads. *Marketing Science, 18*(3), 333–351. doi:10.1287/mksc.18.3.333.

Gumport, P. J., & Pusser, B. (1997). Restructuring the academic environment. In M. W. Peterson, D. D. Dill, L. A. Mets, & Associates (Eds.), *Planning and managing for a changing environment* (pp. 453–478). San Francisco, CA: Jossey-Bass.

Keller, G. (2008, November 14). Why colleges should offer 3-year diplomas. *Chronicle of Higher Education*. Retrieved from http://chronicle.com/article/Why-Colleges-Should-Offer/3253.

Kezar, A. (2001). *Understanding and facilitating organizational change in the 21st century: Recent research and conceptualizations*. New York, NY: John Wiley & Sons.

Lattuca, L. R. (2001). *Creating interdisciplinarity: Interdisciplinary research and teaching among college and university faculty*. Nashville, TN: Vanderbilt University Press.

Levy, A., & Merry, U. (1986). *Organizational transformation: Approaches, strategies, theories*. New York, NY: Praeger.

Lumina Foundation. (2012). A stronger nation through higher education. Retrieved from http://www.luminafoundation.org/publications/A_Stronger_Nation-2012.pdf.

Martinez, M. C., & Nilson, M. (2006). Assessing the connection between higher education policy and performance. *Educational Policy, 20*(2), 299–322. doi:10.1177/0895904805285017.

Martinez, M. C., & Nodine, T. (1997). Michigan: Fiscal stability and constitutional autonomy. In P. M. Callan & J. E. Finney (Eds.), *Public and Private Financing of Higher Education* (pp. 137–168). Phoenix, AZ: ACE/Oryx Press.

Martinez, M. C., & Smith, B. D. (2012, November). Adoption and implementation of innovation in state higher education systems.

Paper presented at the 12th annual Council on Public Policy in Higher Education Pre-Conference Forum, 37th annual Association for the Study of Higher Education, Las Vegas, NV.

McLendon, M. K., Hearn, J. C., & Deaton, R. (2006). Called to account: Analyzing the origins and spread of state performance accountability policies for higher education. *Educational Evaluation and Policy Analysis, 28*(1), 1–24.

Nordvall, R. C. (1982). *The process of change in higher education institutions.* Washington, DC: American Association for Higher Education.

Olsen, M. (1973). *The logic of collective action.* Cambridge, MA: Harvard University Press.

Pfeffer, J. (1997). *New directions for organizational theory.* New York, NY: Oxford University Press.

Richardson, R. C., Jr., Bracco, K. R., Callan, P. M., & Finney, J. E. (1999). *Designing state higher education systems for a new century.* Phoenix, AZ: Oryx Press.

Richardson, R. C., Jr., & Martinez, M. (2009). *Policy and performance in American Higher Education: An examination of cases across state systems.* Baltimore, MD: Johns Hopkins University Press.

Rogers, E. M. (2003). *Diffusion of innovations.* 5th edition. New York: Free Press.

Schmidt, K. (2011, April 18). Governor Chris Gregoire signs bill to create three-year bachelor's degrees. *The News Tribune.* Retrieved from http://blog.thenewstribune.com/politics/2011/04/18/gov-chris-gregoire-signs-bill-to-create-three-year-bachelors-degrees/.

Smith, B. D. (2011). A case study of organizational change: College restructuring in response to mandated department eliminations. (Doctoral dissertation). Retrieved from ProQuest dissertations and theses database (Document ID 922418703).

Stripling, J. (2011, March 1). Governor would cut University of Wisconsin's flagship campus loose. *The Chronicle of Higher Education.* Retrieved from http://chronicle.com/article/Governor-Would-Cut-U-of/126549.

Van de Ven, A. H., & Poole, M. S. (1995). Explaining development and change in organizations. *Academy of Management Review, 20*(3), 510–540. doi:10.1177/0170840605056907.

Zemsky, R. (2009). *Making reform work: The case for transforming American higher education.* Piscataway, NJ: Rutgers University Press.

Zumeta, W., Breneman, D. W., Callan, P. M. & Finney, J. E. (2012). *Financing American higher education in the era of globalization.* Cambridge, MA: Harvard Education Press.

# 9

## SERVING PUBLIC PURPOSES

*Challenges for Systems in Changing State Context*

AIMS C. MCGUINNESS JR.

ABSTRACT

The economic and political pressures of the Great Recession and 2010 elections forced a fundamental rethinking of the characteristics of effective systems for the next decade and beyond. The challenges came from many directions. Several major public research universities launched campaigns to separate from systems and establish their own governing boards or to be given increased autonomy within systems. At the same time, state leaders looked to systems as the means to achieve significant economies of scale and to implement system-wide initiatives to improve the alignment of higher education with state goals (a "public agenda"). This chapter reviews the cases of Oregon and Wisconsin and discusses the arguments for and against local boards within systems. Finally, the chapter summarizes actions that systems must take to redefine their mission and core functions to meet the challenges of the next decade and beyond.

The changing dynamics of state policy in the post–Great Recession and economic recovery period have far-reaching implications for public higher education systems and their capacity to serve public purposes. In many states there has been growing division and turmoil in state politics, making efforts to gain consensus on statewide goals and policies related to higher education exceptionally difficult. These conditions contributed to the unprecedented turnover in executives of state higher education agencies and systems.[1] Governors have taken aggressive actions aimed at reducing costs, improving productivity, and getting a stronger connection between higher education and state priorities. Some of these initiatives were direct actions to propose massive restructuring and place statewide coordination under the control of the governor; others were indirect actions to gain greater control of system governing boards through board appointments and control of the appointments of system executives.

Moreover, the dramatic cuts in state funding and the resulting decline in the percentage of institutional budgets from state appropriations (especially at major research universities) is intensifying the pressure on institutions to obtain other revenue—especially from tuition increases. While in earlier times the principal competition among institutions was for state appropriations (and this tendency certainly continues), the main competition now is for tuition-paying students, wherever they may be found. Faced with state policies that limit tuition increases for in-state students, public institutions are increasingly competing for out-of-state and international students, thereby drawing institutions away from historic commitments to serve their own state's students.

In the search for new and sustainable revenue sources, some systems have begun to do an "end-run" around systems to gain political support to raise tuition and gain independence from system policies. Declining resources have also led to efforts to create economies of scale through centralization, especially of functions related to technology, human resources, and purchasing. System-wide rationalization has also resulted in the elimination of unnecessary duplications of academic programs, promotion of more inter-institutional collaborations, closures and mergers of campuses, and development of more cost-effective modes of program and service delivery.

Finally, sharp cuts in the budgets of state higher education coordinating boards and university systems has caused a significant reduction in state- and system-level capacity for policy leadership and other state-level functions. Many systems have been confronted with reduced staff sizes and increased accountability expectations. This situation has resulted in many states' focusing on day-to-day administrative business and leaving little capacity to engage in policy and planning initiatives.

## PROPOSED RESTRUCTURING OF SYSTEMS

Perhaps the most controversial proposals during this time of transition have been to restructure existing systems by increasing the autonomy of research universities within systems or even separating these institutions from their systems. Oregon and Wisconsin are among the most debated examples of these proposals.

The variations among states in the degree of regulatory authority retained by the state government versus the authority of a consolidated system board affect these debates about increasing institutional autonomy. Oregon and Wisconsin remain among the states in which the state government retains significant regulatory control of higher education. In essence, these states continue to treat universities as state agencies, not as separate legal entities (e.g., a corporation organized to carry out public purposes) with a degree of autonomy from state financial and procedural regulation (McGuinness, 1996). Several other states with large university systems such as the State University of New York and the University of North Carolina also retain significant regulatory control in state agencies, not the system governing board.

Although the details vary greatly among states, the most common regulatory controls relate to human resources, purchasing, facilities construction and renovation, and budgetary and expenditure controls. In many states, university and college personnel are treated as state employees, subject to state civil service restrictions; pay scales; fringe benefit programs; and, in periods of economic crisis, statewide requirements for temporary furloughs or pay cuts. Many states also restrict the purchasing powers of campuses, requiring them to use existing negotiated state contracts or comply with other purchasing restrictions, many of which do not account for the complicated scientific and other purchases that an academic institution must make.

State oversight of and intervention in public academic organizations also includes construction and renovation of facilities as well as the collection and disbursement of tuition and fees (Lane, 2007).

Some states require that capital projects, including in some cases those that are privately financed, be planned, designed, and/or supervised through a state general government agency, and they impose other requirements that apply to university buildings as "state-owned" assets. A final significant form of state intervention comes in the area of finances (see also chapter 5). Some states allocate appropriations to colleges and universities in broad line items (e.g., salaries and benefits), separated from other expenditures and allowing only limited transfers among funding lines. In the past, states have also required that tuition revenue (and non-state revenue in general) be deposited in the state treasury and then reappropriated by the state legislature. The cases of Oregon and Wisconsin illustrate how a drive for increased autonomy concerns regulatory controls established by the state legislature and state agencies as much as, if not more than, controls exercised by the system.

## WISCONSIN

The chancellor of the University of Wisconsin-Madison (UW-Madison), Carolyn "Biddy" Martin, proposed in 2010 a New Badger Partnership that would separate the campus from the system and grant it substantial autonomy from state government. Martin stated that the UW-Madison, as one of the top 20 research universities in the world, contributes significantly to the state as a global talent magnet and job creator. But, she argued that the university could not remain competitive and contribute to the state if it were continued to be run as though it were another state agency. Her basic premise was that increased regulatory and financial flexibility would allow UW-Madison to add greater value to the state, enhance institutional revenues, and manage its most urgent needs for teaching, research and outreach. The New Badger Partnership asked the state to make a commitment to (1) continue to fund the state's share of the university's current operations, and (2) adopt a new business model that provides greater flexibility to become more efficient and cost effective. This new business model would apply to a broad range of functions such as procurement, compensation and hiring, tuition and financial aid, and construction and building projects. In return the university would commit to providing: (1) greater quality, efficiency, access and affordability, (2) more graduates from Wisconsin, (3) new revenue for Wisconsin from outside the state, (4) research that spurs innovation and supports jobs, and (4) enhanced accountability and transparency for the flexibility the university was afforded (Martin, 2010b).

Beyond the issue of UW-Madison's relationship with the State of Wisconsin was the university's relationship to the UW system administration. UW-Madison argued that the system failed to give appropriate attention to the unique role and mission of the Madison campus and was an ineffective advocate for the kinds of operational flexibilities essential for the competitive positioning of UW-Madison. Others argued that splitting Madison away from the system would have negative consequences for the other campuses and unleash the destructive competition and unnecessary duplication that the system was intended to curb when it was established in 1971. Still others agreed with Martin on the need for increased operational flexibility but argued that these should be applied to the university system as a whole, not just UW-Madison (Letterman, 2011; Pleger, 2011).

Governor Scott Walker introduced a similar idea as a provision of the 2011–2013 biennial budget bill. It would have created UW-Madison as a public authority independent of the UW system's Board of Regents and governed by its own board of trustees. If adopted by the legislature, the governor's version of the budget bill would have granted UW-Madison substantial operational flexibility compared to current law (Wisconsin Legislative Fiscal Bureau, 2011).

Following the introduction of the governor's budget, the UW System president, Kevin Reilly, established the President's Advisory Committee on the Roles of the UW System Administration. The advisory committee's report (2011) made recommendations to President Reilly for changes in several areas that could reduce the amount of regulation with which each campus had to contend. These changes included delegation to the campuses of some responsibilities for academic program review, clarification of delegations to chancellors, and streamlining the functions and staffing of the system administration (President's Advisory Committee on the Roles of UW System Administration, 2011; Reilly, 2011). The Board of Regents of the University of Wisconsin System endorsed the Wisconsin Idea Partnership, a proposal that would have extended operational flexibilities to all UW institutions without creating UW-Madison as a public authority independent of the Board of Regents.

The Wisconsin legislature deleted all budget provisions related to the establishment of UW-Madison as a public authority independent of the UW System. The biennial budget act did extend some operational flexibility to the UW System and UW institutions, most notably the creation of block grant appropriations and the authority to establish new personnel systems for all UW employees that would be separate from the state personnel system. The biennial budget act also created a Special Task Force on UW Restructuring and Operational Flexibilities (Wisconsin Legislative Fiscal Bureau, 2011). Parallel to the work of the Special Task Force, President Reilly established the Ad Hoc Work Group on UW System Governance and Structure, which examined the need for additional changes within the system, including the issue of establishing campus-level boards (Smith et al., 2012).

The Special Task Force report (2012) recommended increased flexibility from state regulation for the UW System in the areas of personnel, construction planning, and procurement. It also considered but rejected the proposal that a local board with some governing authority be established for each UW campus. Instead, the task force recommended that the Board of Regents retain primary responsibility for governing the UW system and be authorized to establish an advisory board for each campus at the discretion of its chancellor (Special Task Force, 2012). At the time of this writing, the governor and legislature had not yet acted on these recommendations.

## OREGON

The governance debate in Oregon extends back to the early 2000s and involves the state's multifaceted higher education governing and coordinating structures. The Oregon University System (OUS) is governed by the Board of Higher Education, but the State Board of Education provides state-level oversight of the locally governed community colleges and provides the overall coordination of the education system from preschool through higher education. Much of the national attention on Oregon within higher education circles focused on a controversial proposal by then-president of the University of Oregon, Richard W. Lariviere (University of Oregon, 2010), to establish his institution as an independently governed university under a board of trustees outside the Oregon University System. He also proposed to establish a new financial model of a public endowment that would provide sustained support for the university largely independent of the state.

While national attention focused on the University of Oregon proposal, state leaders were examining how to achieve the most ambitious goals in the country for increasing the educational attainment by the state's population. The Postsecondary Quality Education Commission, appointed by the governor and co-chaired by the presidents of Oregon State University and Lane Community College, proposed that Oregon set a goal (the "40-40-20 goal") that by 2025 40% of the population have at least a bachelor's degree, 40% have an associate's degree or postsecondary education credential, and the remaining 20% have attained a high school diploma (Postsecondary Quality Education Commission, 2008).[2] The legislative assembly formally established these objectives as state goals through legislation enacted in 2011 (Or. Rev. Stat. Ann. § 351.009, 2011).

As the University of Oregon lobbied for its proposal with substantial support from wealthy alumni, the legislative assembly, governor, and Oregon University System (OUS) were concentrating on broader reforms designed to realign system leadership and coordination with the 40-40-20 goal. As early as 2009—before the University of Oregon proposal—the State Board of Higher Education, the governing body for OUS, established a Committee on Governance and Policy to explore restructuring the system to grant significantly increased autonomy to the institutions within the framework of system coordination and governance (Oregon University System, 2011). In 2011, the OUS proposed, and the legislature adopted, far-reaching reforms in Senate Bill 242 to grant increased autonomy and management flexibility from state government to the OUS and through the OUS to institutions. New autonomy was granted in key procedural areas such as allowing institutions to retain tuition revenue instead of having revenues deposited into the state treasury and used to fund non-higher-education functions, carryover of tuition revenue from one fiscal year to the next without affecting the state funding, development of a retirement system independent of the state, and risk management (Oregon Senate Bill 242, 2011). In the same legislation (Senate Bill 242), the legislative assembly established a statewide coordinating entity, the Higher Education Coordinating Commission, charged with statewide planning and coordination of all postsecondary education, including OUS institutions and the community colleges. The legislative assembly rejected proposals to establish an independent board and financing scheme for the University of Oregon. Also in 2011, the legislative assembly enacted a proposal from newly elected Governor Kitzhaber to establish the Oregon Education Investment Board, an overarching body for all levels of education charged with developing strategies to create a seamless zero to 20 education system that is integrated, efficient, and accountable (Oregon Senate Bill 909, 2011). Throughout 2012, the Oregon legislature worked to implement these new laws, including efforts to resolve ambiguities in the division of responsibilities between the Oregon Education Investment Board, the new Higher Education Coordinating Commission, and OUS.

Meanwhile, the issue of whether the University of Oregon or any other institution within OUS should have a local board continued to be debated. Some argued that the universities should have local boards but remain within the OUS; others argued that the universities should be separated entirely from the system and placed under their own separate boards. The president of the University of Oregon continued to make the university's case to the State Board of Higher Education (Berdahl & Kyr, 2012). Portland State University joined the University of Oregon in arguing that it, too, should have its own board while other institutions—most notably, Oregon State University—argued against having local boards (Portland State University, 2009; Ray, 2012). In July 2012, the State Board of Higher Education adopted the report of the Oregon University System's Committee on Governance and Policy, which recommended giving increased autonomy to the seven universities in the system and the opportunity for institutions to develop local boards with limited powers within the overall governing system authority of the State Board of Higher Education (Oregon University System, 2012). At the time of this writing, a joint committee of the legislative assembly, the Joint Committee on University Governance, was at work on proposed legislation for the 2013 session.

## REASONS FOR INCREASING INSTITUTIONAL AUTHORITY

These cases illustrate several themes that reflect both long-standing concerns and comparatively new social and economic realities. The flagship campuses in both cases were convinced that they would be better able to carry out their missions and meet their state's goals if they were granted increased autonomy. Three common themes that seem to be driving these proposals are the perceived disconnect between the system board and campus activities, a desire to decrease state oversight in relation to decreased state financial support, and the need for institutions to pursue alternative forms of funding.

Since system boards oversee a large number of campuses, the attention of the board members, by necessity, is spread among multiple campuses. This arrangement can create a perception of distance between the system board and the campuses, resulting in a perception that the system board does not fully understand the uniqueness of each institution's mission and, in particular, the complexity of the research university's mission. Consequently, the view is that the system board is not prepared to be an effective advocate for each institution's interests.

Moreover, as the amount of funding from state government declines, there are increasing calls to decrease the state's role in governing public colleges and universities. In the extreme, the argument is that since the state is no longer funding the university, the university should be able to pursue its own goals much as a private, nonprofit, independent institution would. In the two cases, the advocates argue that the institutions should still be accountable to the state through their newly established governing boards but be granted significant relief from state oversight and regulatory requirements.

Finally, there is increasing pressure for institutions to increase non-state revenue, especially student tuition and fees. Each of the proposals seeks significantly increased authority for individual institutions to increase tuition and to recruit students from out-of-state markets. Recognizing that many states will continue to limit tuition increases for in-state undergraduate students, colleges and universities are seeking greater independence to increase tuition for out-of-state and foreign students and to increase the proportion of enrollments from these sources. Institutions share a need for regulatory relief on matters that constrain the ability of the universities to compete in the global knowledge economy for faculty members, graduate students, non-state funding, research funding, and other areas. Of course, there are sometimes occasions when state government regulations may be perceived as system requirements. In Oregon and Wisconsin, most of the regulatory barriers of concern are related to the state government, not the system administration per se. The system administration may be the target primarily because it is the agent for implementing policies of a state department of administration.

## REASONS AGAINST INCREASED
## INSTITUTIONAL AUTHORITY

The proposals discussed here may seem beneficial when viewed from the institutional perspective. However, from the state and system perspectives, these ideas present serious problems. The proposals focus primarily on what is good for a single university, not the state or other institutions in the system. While couched in language about enabling universities to be "better able to serve the state," they raise basic questions about institutions' continuing commitment to basic state priorities related to affordability, access, and opportunity for state residents. From the state perspective, the proposals fail to answer two questions: Will increased autonomy advance the state's goals (such as the 40-40-20 goal in Oregon)? Will the proposal contribute to the quality and cost effectiveness of the system as a whole, or just the single institution?

Critics argue that the proposals will undermine states' capacity to implement system-wide initiatives and will counteract the economies of scale achieved via the system approach. System-level coordination can facilitate student transfer among various institutions, create linkages with P-20 reform, and foster statewide approaches to economic development. Also, separating one of the largest institutions with the most powerful alumni network and lobbying base from the system could undermine the competitive position of smaller member institutions.

Finally, systems were created to provide coherence among a decentralized group of institutions with diverse demands and missions. Separating institutions from their system would unleash the negative, centrifugal forces that caused the state originally to create the system, such as negative competition for public funds and students, unnecessary duplication, and barriers to student transfer. In addition, the ability of higher education institutions to make a coherent case for support to the governor and state legislature often depends on a united front and the combined political influence of all the institutions (Boatright, 1999; Lee & Bowen, 1971).

## THE PRESSURE FOR LOCAL BOARDS

The Oregon and Wisconsin proposals call for establishing local or campus-level governing boards either within systems or as newly independent public entities separated from the systems. The proposition that university systems should include campus-level boards is not new. Lee and Bowen (1971) noted that systems that had local boards with some degree of governing authority are most often an artifact of the systems and institutions that were consolidated to form the new system. However, it is interesting that Clark Kerr, who had been chancellor of the University of California-Berkeley campus and president of the University of California system, which is governed by a single system-wide board, recommended the establishment of such boards in his foreword to the 1971 Lee and Bowen study.[3] In his recommendations for the operation of multi-campus systems, Kerr (1971) suggested that systems "Decentralize to the maximum extent possible . . . [and] create local boards with final authority in the maximum number of areas like grounds and buildings, faculty appointments and promotions, student disciplinary actions, and so forth" (p. xiii).

As noted in chapter 3, states such as Iowa, North Dakota, and Oregon deliberately eliminated local boards in the early 1900s and consolidated all institutions under a single board to counter concerns about entanglement of local boards with regional politics and patronage. Generally, systems have been reluctant to establish local boards with governing authority, except within clearly defined policies of delegation and accountability to the central boards in key areas such as advice in the appointment, evaluation, and dismissal of campus presidents; decisions regarding major new academic programs and capital developments; and in developing new campus sites.

Only six systems currently allow local boards with a degree of delegated governing authority within the overall authority of the system board: the University System of Florida,[4] the State University of New York,[5] the University of North Carolina,[6] the Pennsylvania State System of Higher Education, the institutions within the governing jurisdiction of the Massachusetts Board of Higher Education, and the Utah System of Higher Education (Smith et al., 2012). Consistent with Lee and Bowen's (1971) observation, in each of these states, the institutions or systems that were consolidated to form the new system had local boards prior to the consolidation, and the continuing existence of local boards tends to be an artifact of the governance of the institutions and systems prior to establishment of the new system.

Two other states, Maine and Maryland, have local boards with advisory powers carefully specified by the system board. The University of Maine System established boards of visitors with advisory powers delegated by the system Board of Trustees. The University System of Maryland authorizes institutions within the system to establish boards of visitors at the request of the institution's president, subject to approval of the system Board of Regents. Other systems, such as the University of Wisconsin System, have policies that authorize campuses to establish advisory bodies, but the implementation of this option varies among the campuses.

The arguments for and against local boards are being widely debated in Oregon and Wisconsin. The report of the University of Wisconsin Ad Hoc Work Group on UW System Structure and Governance (2012) summarizes the arguments in that state. The arguments for and against campus-level boards are summarized in table 9.1.

The debate in Oregon is more far-reaching than in Wisconsin because the alternatives are not only for local boards within the system but for the University of Oregon to be removed from the oversight of the State Board of Higher Education and placed under the authority of a new governing board only for that institution. The ultimate impact of some of the proposals pending in Oregon would be to change the Oregon State Board of Higher Education from a statewide governing board to a statewide coordinating entity for a system of institutions, each with its own governing board. How new boards, if established, would relate to the OUS or another state entity has yet to be resolved.

Table 9.1. Arguments for and against Campus-Level Boards in Wisconsin

| Arguments for | Arguments against |
|---|---|
| Enhance advocacy for the institution with the public, business community, legislature, and governor | Add another board to whom chancellors must report, which may create confusion regarding lines of responsibility and accountability |
| Increase attention on the unique aspects of each institution | Potentially diminish the authority, control, and autonomy of campus chief executive officers |
| Give greater opportunity for citizen involvement to support and obtain more flexibilities | Add a layer of bureaucracy at a time when the UW System is trying to reduce bureaucracy |
| Provide more accountability, closer to the institutions | Create a risk of institution-level board members attempting to micromanage an institution |
| Encourage greater engagement of an institution with the community, promoting better understanding of the campus culture and environment | Be time consuming and potentially costly because of the need to staff a board and manage board relations |
| | Promote competition for resources among institutions |
| | Be unhelpful to smaller institutions or areas of the state with lower populations and fewer representatives in the legislature |
| | Create an opportunity for local politics to influence institutional decisions |

## ESSENTIAL ACTIONS FOR EFFECTIVE SYSTEMS

As the country emerges from the Great Recession, challenges to the future of systems are likely to continue. In several respects, statewide consolidated systems could contribute to the capacity of public institutions to advance state priorities and ensure the institutions' future sustainability and competitiveness. To lead in this new environment, however, systems must act to:

- Shape and gain consensus around a long-term public agenda linking higher education to the state's future economy and quality of life. The agenda should *not* be just a public relations façade for an appeal for more state funding. The agenda should be about the state, not institutions. Systems cannot pursue development of a public agenda alone. Most systems function in states with two or more systems and a wide array of public and private higher education providers. Where there is no public agenda, system leaders must take the initiative to shape an agenda working with the other systems (if any) and higher education providers and in collaboration with the governor, state legislature, and business and civic leaders.
- Decentralize governing and operational responsibilities to the institutional level to the maximum degree possible *within a system-wide framework of accountability.* Institutional leaders should be held accountable and rewarded for performance in relationship to system goals as well as goals relevant to their institution's mission.
- Redefine the system mission to *lead change* for a sustained, multiyear action agenda—statewide, region by region, and institution by institution—to achieve measurable improvements in quality and performance at significantly reduced costs to students and the state.
- Focus on system-wide issues that are *between and among* campuses and sectors
  - Between and among campuses: articulation and transfer, joint and collaborative programs
  - Linking the system and the institutions to P-20 reform
  - Linking the system to statewide and regional economic development
- Shift from the mentality of an inwardly focused system organized to serve the interests of constituent institutions and help them compete for students (and tuition revenue) with other providers, to a more outwardly focused system in which the role of the system is to make the system more than the sum of its parts in serving a broader public interest and to facilitate partnerships and strategic alliances both

within the system and state as well as with national and global partners.

- Differentiate policies to reflect differences in mission and institutional size and complexity. One-size-fits-all system policies and processes that fail to recognize the complexity of major research university campuses are a major source of the recent turmoil in some consolidated governing systems. Failure to recognize the uniqueness of the community college mission in multi-level, multi-mission systems can have the same negative consequences.
- Innovate in the delivery of shared services and traditional system-wide functions related to human resources, procurement, capital planning, and information technology. There is little tolerance for centralized bureaucracies that are not held accountable for performance, cost effectiveness, and innovation.
- Use finance policy aligned with the system goals and the public agenda to leverage and provide incentives for change and improved performance.

Several systems stand out for their leadership in the transition to a new vision and mission for systems. The recently completed master plan for the State University of New York is an excellent illustration (SUNY, 2012). Despite the recent controversies discussed earlier, both Oregon and Wisconsin also stand out for their leadership in shaping system strategic directions aligned with a public agenda and in fundamental rethinking of the mission and functions of the system board and central offices. In both cases, the changes predated the controversies caused by the breakaway efforts of the major research university campuses, but there is no doubt that the external threats accelerate the process of change. However, these cases illustrate the forces at work to undermine the ability of systems to carry out this leadership role.

As state funding continues to decline and institutions become increasingly dependent on tuition and other non-state revenue sources, institutions will shift to out-of-state and global markets. Consequently, there will be fewer incentives for these institutions to focus on state priorities. The state and system finance policies will have to be redesigned to provide incentives for public institutions to respond to state and regional needs.

The major research university campuses can use their prestige and the power of alumni and major private donors to pursue their own priorities without regard to the impact on the system as a whole. Actions by the presidents of the major research universities to circumvent the system leadership by going directly to the state's political leaders for special governance arrangements threaten to tear the systems apart. Moreover, an "anti-bureaucracy" culture is likely to lead to additional targeted cuts in funding of system offices, limiting their capacity to provide policy leadership for the state and system and to pursue system initiatives. Unlike their member institutions, systems have never had "constituencies."

In both Oregon and Wisconsin, several forces converged to prompt a fundamental rethinking of the mission of the system, including the internal structure and policies. The imperative to link the university system to a public agenda focused on increasing the educational attainment of the state's population and the competitiveness of the state's workforce and economy. There were severe economic constraints and budget cuts, and both the governor and state legislature were putting significant pressure on higher education to embrace reform.

In response to these pressures, the systems have been engaging in transformative activities. In Wisconsin, these include a combination of some proposals in the New Badger Partnership and actions to redesign the system by the Board of Regents and president on the recommendations of system task forces (President's Advisory Committee on the Roles of UW System Administration, 2011; Reilly, 2011). In Oregon, the reforms include continuing efforts to deregulate and decentralize as the OUS implements the recently enacted provisions of Senate Bill 242 and full commitment of the State Board of Higher Education and chancellor to the state's 40-40-20 goals. Changes at the University of Wisconsin are likely to lead to a more dynamic, effective system. It is too early to predict the outcome of the Oregon debate, but the leadership of the Oregon University System (OUS) on behalf of the people of Oregon and the future of the universities will have a long-term impact.

Other systems across the nation are taking steps to redefine their role, but the reality is that many systems are not making the transition to new modes of leadership and operations. The priorities of their governing boards and the day-to-day operations of their offices have changed only marginally over the past decade. Since these systems encompass such a large portion of the nation's higher education capacity, their failure to make needed changes could have severe consequences for the nation's future.

## NOTES

1. Almost half of the system heads had been in office less than two years. Almost one quarter of the system heads had been in their positions for one year or less. As of December 2012, 13 (25%) of the 51 system heads in the National Association of System Heads (NASH) directory were appointed in 2012, another nine in 2011, three in 2010, 12 in 2009, and five in 2008. Only nine had been appointed before 2008.
2. As of 2010, Oregon educational attainment was at 30/18/42, with the remaining 10% of adults being high school dropouts.
3. At the time of this writing the University of California system was also debating the creation of campus boards, more than 30 years after Clark Kerr argued for their creation. See Birgeneau, Breslauer, King, Wilton, and Yeary (2012).
4. As noted earlier, in 2001 Florida enacted legislation abolishing the Board of Regents for the University System of Florida and establishing a governing board for each of the public universities. In 2003, the state enacted a constitutional amendment to reconsolidate the universities under the Board of Governors, but institutions retained their local boards. Determining the authority of the Board of Governors in relationship to the campus boards has been an ongoing challenge since 2003.
5. The university councils within SUNY institutions are primarily advisory but have authority to recommend candidates for president to the system chancellor and Board of Trustees.
6. Among these six systems, the policy statement *Delegations of Authority and Powers to Boards of Trustees*, established by the Board of Governors of the University of North Carolina, is widely viewed as the most carefully drawn division of authority and responsibility between the system and campus-level boards. The UNC system has operated under the provisions of this document

since the system was established in 1971 (University of North Carolina Board of Governors, 2009).

## REFERENCES

Berdahl, R., & Kyr, R. (2012, January 20). *University of Oregon independent governing board.* [Memorandum to Matthew W. Donegan]. Retrieved from http://www.ous.edu/sites/default/files/state_board/meeting/dockets/UOltrsRegardingInstBds.pdf.

Birgeneau, R., Breslauer, G., King, J., Wilton, J., & Yeary, F. (2012). *Modernizing governance at the University of California: A proposal that the Regents create and delegate some responsibilities to campus boards* (Research and Occasional Papers Series No. CSHE.4.12). Retrieved from Center for Studies in Higher Education, University of California, Berkeley website: http://cshe.berkeley.edu/publications/docs/ROPS.Birgeneau%20et%20al.UC%20Gov.4.23.2012.pdf.

Boatright, K. J. (1999). Many voices, one choice: Managing external affairs. In G. H. Gaither (Ed.), *The multicampus system: Perspectives on practice and prospects* (pp. 21–39). Sterling, WV: Stylus.

Kerr, C. (1971). Foreword. In E. C. Lee & F. M. Bowen, *The multicampus university: A study of academic governance* (pp. xi–xvii). New York, NY: McGraw-Hill.

Lane, J. E. (2007). Spider web of oversight: Latent and manifest regulatory controls in higher education. *Journal of Higher Education, 78*(6), 1–30. doi: 10.1353/jhe.2007.0038.

Lee, E. C., & Bowen, F. M. (1971). *The multi-campus university: A study of academic governance.* New York, NY: McGraw-Hill.

Letterman, D. (2011, February 28). Flexibility—But for (and from) whom? *Inside Higher Ed*, February 28, 201. Retrieved from: http://www.insidehighered.com/news/2011/02/28/wisconsin_debates_whether_madison_should_stay_within_university_system#ixzz2F3wogkbj.

Martin, C. A. (2010a, September). Bucky in the new millennium. *Madison Magazine*. Retrieved from http://www.madisonmagazine.com/Madison-Magazine/September-2010/Bucky-in-the-New-Millennium/.

Martin, C. A. (2010b, December). New Badger partnership [Power

Point presentation]. Retrieved from University of Wisconsin System website: http://www.uwsa.edu/news/2010/12-2010/New-Badger-Partnership.pdf.

McGuinness, A. C., Jr. (1996). A model for successful restructuring. In T. J. MacTaggart & Associates (Eds.), *Restructuring higher education: What works and what doesn't in reorganizing governing systems* (pp. 203–229). San Francisco, CA: Jossey-Bass.

Oregon Senate Bill 909. (2011). An act relating to education; appropriating money; and declaring an emergency. 76th Oregon Legislative Assembly. Regular Session.

Oregon Senate Bill 242 (2011). Relating to education; creating new provisions. 76th Oregon Legislative Assembly. Regular session.

Or. Rev. Stat. Ann. § 351.009. (2011). Higher education generally.

Oregon University System. (2012, June 1). Regular meeting of state board of higher education (#856). [Meeting Minutes].

Pleger, T. (2011, September. 19). Understand the history of UW System. *Wisconsin State Journal*, September 19, 2011. Retrieved from http://host.madison.com/news/opinion/column/guest/article_df5b5a90-e0cb-11e0-8dae-001cc4c03286.html.

Portland State University. (2009). Restructuring PSU's relationship with the state: The case for change (Draft Discussion Paper). Retrieved from Oregon University System website: http://www.ous.edu/sites/default/files/dept/communications/files/RestructuringPSUsRelationshipwiththeState.pdf.

Postsecondary Quality Education Commission. (2008). *Postsecondary Quality Education Commission Report*. Retrieved from Oregon University System website: http://www.ous.edu/sites/default/files/factreport/psqec/PSQECfinal2008.pdf.

President's Advisory Committee on the Roles of UW System Administration. (2011). A new model for change within the University of Wisconsin System: Report of the President's Advisory Committee on the Roles of UW System Administration. Retrieved from http://www.wisconsin.edu/uwsa-roles-committee/Roles/Report-of-Presidents-Advisory-Committee.pdf.

Ray, E. J. (2012, March). *In consideration of local governance for Oregon public universities*. [Statement presented to the Oregon State Board of Higher Education]. Retrieved from Official Oregon State website: http://www.oregon.gov/gov/oeib/docs/ooray.pdf.

Reilly, K. P. (2011). President Reilly's response to the report of the President's Advisory Committee on the roles of the UW System Administration. Retrieved from PROFS website: http://profs.wisc.edu/wp-content/uploads/2011/09/Reilly-Response-September-2011.pdf.

Smith, B., Crain, J., Levin-Stankevitch, B., Lovell, M., Richards, A., Pruitt, C., & Wells, R. (2012). Report of the Ad Hoc Work Group of UW System Structure and Governance. Retrieved from: http://profs.wisc.edu/wp-content/uploads/2012/02/Report-of-Ad-Hoc-Work-Group-on-UW-System-Structure-and-Governance.pdf.

Special Task Force on UW Restructuring and Operational Flexibilities. (2012). Report. Retrieved from state of Wisconsin website: http://legis.wisconsin.gov/lfb/UW_Task_Force/Documents/Task%20Force%20Report.pdf.

State University of New York. (2012). *2012 master plan: Delivering on our promise.* Retrieved from http://www.suny.edu/sunynews/MasterPlan2012.pdf.

University of North Carolina Board of Governors. (2009). Delegations of duty and authority to boards of trustees. *The UNC Policy Manual,* The Code 100.1, Appendix 1, pp. 42–47, revised as of October 9, 2009. Retrieved from: http://www.northcarolina.edu/policy/index.php?pg=dl&id=s10866&inline=1&return_url=%2Fpolicy%2Findex.php%3Fpg%3Dvb%26tag%3D100.1

University of Oregon. (2010). *Preserving our public mission through a new partnership with the state* (White Paper). Retrieved from: http://newpartnership.uoregon.edu/blog/2010/05/12/the-white-paper-introduction-and-oregons-public-responsibility-regarding-higher-education/index.html.

Wisconsin Legislative Fiscal Bureau. (2011). *Create UW-Madison Authority* (Paper No. 690). Retrieved from University of Wisconsin-Madison Budget Office website: http://www.mbo.wisc.edu/biennial/bienn1113/LFB690-Create%20UW-Madison%20Authority.pdf.

# Part III

## EMERGING ROLES
## FOR SYSTEMS

# 10

## THE CHANGING ROLE OF SYSTEMS IN ACADEMIC AFFAIRS

JAN M. IGNASH

ABSTRACT

This chapter describes the changing roles of academic affairs within higher education system offices over the past decade or so and makes the case for more intentional steering of higher education. The system role in academic affairs today goes beyond approving new programs, reviewing existing ones, and avoiding unnecessary duplication. Today, there is an increasing need to build and maintain connections among multiple stakeholders: K–12 education, public and private two- and four-year institutions, business and industry, legislators and various executive offices, as well as the media. Academic affairs offices at the system level need to demonstrate whether connections among all entities are succeeding and suggest improvements to steer higher education institutions in the right direction if they are not. System offices now find themselves devoting more attention to academic policy, very broadly interpreted, than to the review of academic programs. Academic affairs systems must successfully manage this expanded role or risk unwise intrusion into academic policies and programs.

The system role in academic affairs today goes well beyond approving new programs, reviewing existing ones, and avoiding unnecessary duplication. Previously, academic affairs staff primarily dealt with colleagues inside higher education institutions and, to a lesser extent, with counterparts in the K–12 education sector. Today, however, the degree to which staff needs to develop and maintain good relationships with all stakeholders—including legislators, governors, and the press—has increased. These new relationships also bring increased demands for data to inform policy and decision making.

Systems offices have traditionally devoted considerable attention to academic programs first, and then to academic policy, very broadly interpreted, but that role has changed over the past 10 or more years. These changes raise a series of questions that academic administrators should consider: How has it changed? Are the changes positive, showing maturity and growth in our thinking and practices? What do we do well? What can we do better? The thesis of this chapter is that today there is less emphasis on the traditional functions of program approval and program review in academic affairs administration and considerably more emphasis on broad policy, strategic planning, and data collection and analysis.

Some of the major policy responsibilities occupying academic affairs offices today include conducting regional and state-level strategic planning; raising statewide educational attainment; demonstrating student success and student learning outcomes; promoting successful transitions among all educational levels and sectors; documenting academic "productivity"; and aligning workforce needs with academic programs, costs, and locations. Academic affairs systems must successfully manage this expanded role or risk unnecessary intrusion into policies and programs.

Before delving into an examination of this expanded role for academic affairs, I begin by describing the four broad steering functions of higher education systems identified by Richardson, Callan, Bracco, and Finney (1999). With this backdrop, I then explore the evolution of the major functions of academic affairs administration.[1] The chapter ends with a discussion of whether higher education systems have matured regarding academic affairs policies and practices, and whether the changes we see are evidence of intentionality in steering higher education in a defined direction rather than a reaction to external forces on an ad hoc basis.

## THE "STEERING FUNCTION" OF HIGHER EDUCATION GOVERNANCE

In *Designing State Higher Education Systems for a New Century*, Richardson and associates (1999) developed a dynamic model that wove together state policy roles and system structures in a continuum of governance designs. According to the model, systems can engage in four broad functions: providing resources, regulation, consumer advocacy, and steering. While the model can be applied to advisory, coordinating, and governing boards, the focus of this chapter is specifically on the governance and management of multi-campus systems.

The model presented by Richardson and his colleagues (1999) was founded upon the concept of "market forces," which they defined as

> the broad array of interests and influences that are external to the formal structures of both state government and higher education institutions. . . . It does include economic influences, such as competitive pressures, user satisfaction, cost and price, and student demand. But it also includes noneconomic forces, some of which are quantifiable, such as demographic characteristics and projections; and some of which are less quantifiable, such as political pressures, public confidence, and the availability of new technologies. (p. 12)

Richardson et al. (1999) built upon Clark's Triangle of Tensions (1983) and Williams's (1995) dynamic model for understanding higher education finance to develop their four-tiered description of state governance roles. In the first role, the state subsidizes higher education, and the system, in turn, allocates funding to its institutions without much regard for market influences. In the regulator role, the system or state defines the relationship between institutions and the market by controlling price, limiting institutional discretion in using resources, and eliminating or weakening incentives for efficient operations. If the state fulfills this role, then it is up to the system to enforce these policy decisions. As consumer advocate, the system or state supports demand for higher education and redirects dollars to students, thus increasing the influence of their choices on institutional behavior. In the steering role, the system or state steers higher education by structuring the market for higher education to produce outcomes aligned with governmental priorities. Examples of such steering activities might include the recent reemergence of performance-based funding, which rewards institutions for achieving certain goals set by the state or system.

## UNPACKING THE ROLES OF SYSTEM-LEVEL ACADEMIC OFFICERS

Academic affairs is at the core of the higher education enterprise. At institutions, academic work is carried out mostly by faculty members in classrooms, and institution-level academic administrators tend to engage in activities that directly affect faculty and students. However, academic administration at a system office can look much different. System-level academic affairs offices lead and provide support across multiple institutions, managing competing demands among institutions, identifying areas of critical need for the entire state, supporting public policy decision makers, and attempting to conserve limited resources. More specifically, major responsibilities of academic affairs system offices include: approval of new programs; review of existing programs; alignment of high school exit/college entry admissions standards for students; oversight of teacher education, alternate pathways, and professional development; transfer and articulation; information gathering and management, including the development and maintenance of data systems; and regional and statewide planning to meet workforce demand for graduates.

By their very nature, system-level academic officers are caught between demands of politicians and the general public and the expectations and desires of their constituent campuses. These tensions often center on the approval or dissolution of academic programs. However, the roles of the system office in regard to academic administration have been evolving for some time, and the pressures caused by the Great Recession have intensified the external demands on system officials. It is these external demands that have played a critical role in the recent transformation of the work of academic affairs at the system level.

The activities that trigger external oversight and calls for reform have not changed dramatically over the last two decades. According to McGuinness (1994), the common irritants that can result in calls for reorganization or expanding the mission of academic affairs include:

- Actual or potential duplication of high-cost graduate and professional programs;
- Conflict between the aspirations of two institutions located in the same geographic area;
- Legislative reaction to institutional lobbying;
- Frustrations with barriers to student transfer and articulation;
- Inadequate coordination among institutions offering one- and two-year vocational, technical, and occupational and transfer programs;
- Proposals (and related opposition) to close, merge colleges or universities, or to change institutional missions.

These conflict areas are not new. What *is* new, however, is stakeholders' unwillingness to wait very long for resolutions to conflicts. The blogs, quasi-news websites, social networks (e.g., Twitter and Facebook), smart phones, and other instant messaging devices allow legislators, governors, the media, and the public to learn about potential problems quickly after they occur and, as a result, to expect quick responses and resolutions. The following sections examine the expanding role of academic affairs as triggered by these rising external pressures. I then argue why it is more important than ever for system offices to engage in steering functions to guide the academic development of their constituent institutions.

### Program Approval, Duplication, and Review

Almost every system has the authority to approve and review new programs. The system role in this area has changed in recent times to include a stronger emphasis on the following concerns: (1) the quality of new and existing programs, especially in the face of major funding cuts; (2) the role of the market and discussion of "necessary" versus "unnecessary" duplication; (3) a "consumer" focus; (4) the role of distance learning from within and outside the system; and (5) the role that technology plays in providing data for program approval and review processes.

Although there are no data specifically about the role of systems in academic reviews, a recent study by Barak (2007) provides some insights into state-level activities from which we can extrapolate. Barak reported that 45 of 48 state boards responding to his survey conducted approval of at least some new programs at some institutions in 2006. The number of states conducting program approval was exactly the same in 2006 as in a 1991 study—45 states. Approval, however, can vary considerably, from "advisory" only to formal system recognition before an institution may offer a degree. Major purposes for program approval cited by survey respondents concerned quality improvement/maintenance, the need and/or demand for a program, the consistency of mission/role, and avoiding duplication. The least popular reasons, cited by just a few states, were consistency with plans (institutional and/or state), maintaining a coordinated system, and attention to workforce needs.

A major reason that systems and states have retained authority to approve new programs has been to avoid unnecessary duplication. The potential for conflicts over new program development within the same area by two or more institutions is even more likely today than 20 years ago, as more providers are delivering academic degrees. Out-of-state and even out-of-country online degree programs are now delivered everywhere via distance learning. In addition, community and technical colleges in some states have been granted the authority to offer baccalaureate degree programs, creating competition where mission differentiation once forbade it.[2] In many states, clear collaborative processes for approving new baccalaureate programs offered by predominantly two-year institutions have not been established. This expansion of mission can pit institutions against each other if a clear process for addressing unnecessary duplication is not implemented.

While the role of system boards can be to reduce duplication and make sure that state resources are not wasted on unneeded programs, the potential for unwise or unproductive intrusion remains. In Utah, for example, an institution that wanted to offer an engineering program was told that there was not sufficient need for the program, based upon analysis conducted during a review process that also included external evaluators. The institution's president was able, however, to persuade the governor that the program was necessary, and the program was approved (P. Safman, personal communication, August 24, 2012). This experience is not an unusual occurrence, and academic affairs staff in systems offices who raise concerns about the educational and economic viability of a program may find that campus proponents go around them to appeal directly to their elected representatives to introduce legislation that provides statutory language establishing the new program—and often direct funding to support it.

Another difficulty in program approval today is that systems must prove their efficiency to an increasingly skeptical public that sees higher education as wasteful. Higher education leaders are arguably better at defining "unnecessary duplication" than defining "necessary duplication." Typically, unnecessary duplication becomes a concern when a new program is proposed that is expensive and already offered by one or more institutions in the area. In the past, examples have usually been applied professional programs, such as medical or dental schools, which most states need (although not seven of them). In today's environment, in which higher education budgets are being cut by millions of dollars during successive legislative sessions, *any* new program is scrutinized, including those that most colleges and universities must offer to provide student access, to fulfill institutional mission, or to offer courses that fit professional association and accreditation learning outcomes or standards. A recent dust-up in Florida over anthropology programs is a case in point (Anderson, 2011). In 2011, the governor of Florida, like a number of public officials nationally, announced his intention to shift more funding to science, engineering, technology, and mathematics (STEM) programs. To do so, however, would result in other programs' receiving reduced support. The governor asked, "Is it a vital interest of the state to have more anthropologists? I don't think so" (Wallace, 2011).

The review of existing programs has also been a long-standing interest among state government officials to insure against the waste of taxpayer money. Almost 20 years ago, the State of Minnesota Office of the Legislative Auditor reported, we identified many baccalaureate programs with relatively high costs or small size that should be reviewed—particularly in the state university system. While some inefficient programs are necessary to fulfill institutional missions or provide student access, others should be restructured or eliminated. (Alter, Jacobson, & Vos, 1993, p. 12).

In his 2006 study, Barak (2007) reported that 41 states conducted some form of program review, with 33 states reporting that they reviewed all programs covered under their policies on a regular cycle, such as every five to seven years. Other states also reviewed programs based upon "triggers," such as low productivity, high cost, state need, and duplication. Survey respondents reported that the top reason for evaluating existing programs was to improve program quality. As one academic affairs official noted, "Program review is a proxy for academic quality. Institutions improve the quality of new programs over time. They don't start out as quality programs, typically" (P. Safman, personal communication, August 24, 2012). Other important reasons cited for program review included to improve student learning, teaching, overall accountability, and to identify weak programs for improvement or elimination (Barak, 2007).

Thirty states indicated that program review practices had changed in the five years just before the 2006 study, a level of change that the author cited as "unprecedented" (Barak, 2007). Mirroring trends seen in the program approval process, some states expanded or tightened the review process, and others delegated some or all the responsibility for reviews to institutions. Drivers for change included cost as well as technological advancements, such as searchable academic program inventories or databases where institutions could simply load updated information about programs onto a website.

Utah is an example of a system that has designed quality program review processes. The system office conducts reports on programs that were approved three years earlier so that there is feedback on how the program is doing. In cases where programs do not remain viable because of demand, for example, the Utah Board of Regents can recommend termination of a program, although typically the institution will do that itself and teach out the program, allowing currently enrolled students to finish their course of study. Utah also conducts five- and seven-year program review reports, with metropolitan universities to be reviewed every five years and research universities every seven years. All institutions need to secure outside evaluators for the reviews (P. Safman, personal communication, August 24, 2012).

Ultimately, institutions are responsible for the quality of the programs they deliver. Nevertheless, as legislators and governors challenge the value of a college degree and explore performance-based funding measures that attempt to include assessments of learning, systems do get involved. What is new today is an increasing emphasis on codifying and measuring outcomes. In Florida, for example, all institutions must file Academic Learning Compacts with the Board of Governors' office and make them available online for students so that there is a public record of what students in various majors should know and be able to do.[3] Student learning outcomes must be assessed in three areas: discipline-specific knowledge; skills, attitudes, and behaviors; and communication and critical thinking (State University System of Florida Board of Governors, 2007).

Among the contemporary concerns regarding program approval and program review is that time accorded to deep analysis has been reduced—in some cases, dramatically. Staff members engaged in system-level program approval and review over the past decade have reported a reduction in both staff and time devoted to analysis and review. In Florida, for example, board staff members were responsible for summarizing institutional reviews at the state level and then conducting system-wide reviews. The board staff was decreased, however, from over 100 to 43, a reduction that made this kind of intensive review impossible (R. Stevens, personal communication, August 24, 2012). In Illinois, as in other states, an especially rigorous and thorough version of program review was conducted during the 1980s and early 1990s in which outside consultants were hired for three-day on-campus retreats to conduct intensive reviews of all doctoral programs. This practice was abandoned, however, because it was deemed too expensive.

Finally, the question of who should have responsibility for ultimate program approval has arisen amid ongoing debates by public colleges and universities about the tradeoffs of accountability and flexibility. Several states have experienced both devolution *and* a reinstitution of state control (also called *dirigisme*) in their program approval processes. In 2001 in Florida, bachelor's, master's, and specialist's degree approvals were "devolved" to the universities, with general approval criteria set by the then-Department of Education. In contrast, the state of Washington provides at least a short-lived example of evolution in program approval. In Washington, the former Higher Education Coordinating Board (HECB) approved all levels of degree programs—bachelor's, master's, and doctoral. Working with the State Board for Community and Technical Colleges, the staffs of the two boards developed a collaborative process to approve new applied baccalaureates (B.A.S.) offered by the state's two-year colleges. The community colleges were required to complete a single joint application to be reviewed at the same time by both boards. When the HECB was abolished in July 2012 and became the Council for Student Achievement—a cabinet-level state agency responsible to the governor and guided by an advisory body of nine legislators and business, industry, and education leaders—the collaborative review of B.A.S. degrees offered by two-year colleges was altered so that the two-year board held sole approval authority. A staff member from the former coordinating board was still invited, however, to participate in the peer review process (Washington Student Achievement Council, 2012; R. Spaulding, personal communication, September 4, 2012).

## Strategic Planning

Strategic planning has become a mainstay of higher education. At the system level, particularly for academic affairs offices, these efforts often consist of some form of rational planning and political strategy. Wildavsky (1979) summarized well these tensions:

> The criterion of choice in planning is obvious—the one policy known to be right—but what is the correct criterion for politics? That there is no correct criterion. Does this mean that whatever is done is right? Hardly. It does mean that short of agreement no one is authoritatively able to say another alternative is better. (p. 17)

The context for planning within a system office can shift from more of an emphasis on planning to greater consideration of the political landscape. An understanding of both is often necessary for any plan to be successful and receive broad support.

In strategic planning, a number of questions, spurred by interest from various executive offices, have dominated system higher education offices in recent years. For example:

- What are our goals for increasing educational attainment?
- How many degrees—and at what levels and in what majors—should we be producing over the next decade or more?
- Where are the bottlenecks in the system regarding student persistence and success?
- What obstacles exist for expedient approval (or denial) of new academic degree programs?
- How do we balance access and quality?
- Where is the system ineffective? How do we put resources invested in these areas to better use?

Strategic planning has always been a significant part of the work of academic affairs professionals. The luxury of being able to dedicate large amounts of time to a strategic planning assignment, however, has been eroded in recent years not only by the faster pace of work but also by the growing focus on performance and accountability regarding degree production as *the* dominant strategic planning issue. As an academic affairs system director in California observed, "Once you are at capacity and turning students away, you have to turn each enrollment into a degree" (K. O'Donnell, personal communication, September 14, 2012). In this case, once enrollments were maximized, the planning efforts had to focus on making sure enrolled students were able to complete their degrees.

## Data Management and Analysis

An increasing emphasis on degree production has resulted in demands from legislators and other external stakeholders for more accurate and comprehensive student tracking information. Jane Wellman, executive director of the National Association of System Heads, has suggested: "Expectations for data about performance—beginning with information about not just student flow but student success—have grown enormously. This is part of the whole trend toward data-driven accountability" (personal communication, July 22, 2012). The ability to know where to find accurate and appropriate state and national data, as well as to manage the data expertly to inform policy, is a key component of the work of academic affairs professionals today. However, data systems are complex, and it is challenging to keep up with the variables, their definitions, their limitations, and their applicability to policy and planning questions. It can take as long as a year or two for academic affairs staff who *already* have considerable knowledge of national databases, such as Integrated Postsecondary Education Databases (IPEDS) and statistical software, to efficiently pull data, design reports, and analyze results that successfully address key policy questions. In a fast-paced, politically charged environment, academic affairs staff members are challenged to develop clear guiding questions targeted to inform policy and planning. As databases have become more sophisticated and better populated, the challenge has become to avoid "fishing expeditions" where staff reports descriptive data because they can—not because the data are necessary to answer critical policy and planning questions.

*Managing Quality*

There has been an increasing focus on the attempt to measure the quality of student learning at colleges and universities. This trend has resulted in a greater demand for metrics that can be used by elected officials and institutional leaders to assess the learning outcomes of students at public colleges and universities. System officials often hear questions such as: "What are students really learning in college?" "How can student learning outcomes be measured?" "What is the common core that *all* students should have as a result of a college education?" The latter question was included as part of an omnibus higher education bill in Florida during the 2012 legislative session, Florida House Bill 7135, in which faculty panels representing all two- and four-year colleges in the state were required to identify up to five courses within the five broad discipline areas of math, communications, natural sciences, social sciences, and humanities. The legislative intent of the bill was to reduce the amount of choice and provide clear direction to lower-division students in their general education experience and to reduce wasteful inefficiencies that resulted from an endless array of single course choices at some institutions that fulfilled general education distribution requirements. The goal was to make institutions accountable for what students learn in their general education programs.

Demonstrating the quality of the education students receive in college has never been an easy task, but that is no longer accepted as an excuse. Several systems and state officials noted the promise of the Degree Qualifications Profile as a way to demonstrate what students know and are able to do as a result of their college education. The Degree Qualifications Profile "proposes specific learning outcomes that benchmark the associate, bachelor's and master's degrees . . . regardless of a student's field of specialization" (Lumina Foundation, 2011, p. 1). The challenge in documenting the quality of a college education lies in finding metrics that are "clear, consequential and consistently applied" (O'Donnell, personal communication, September 14, 2012). Any demonstration of the quality of student learning must capture what faculty and content experts identify as learning benchmarks, but external stakeholders must also be able to understand them.

Other accountability efforts have focused on developing more accurate means of calculating the cost of inefficiencies. A recent example is a national study to quantify attrition, putting dollar amounts on inefficiencies in the system when students in their junior and senior years of college do not finish (Johnson, 2009). Results of studies such as these can be used by academic affairs staff to examine the attrition rates in their systems and to explore interventionist policies that address the leakages.

## Collaborating across Sectors and Stakeholders

Much of the work of academic affairs professionals involves collaboration across sectors and stakeholders in program approval and review, P-16 coordination, strategic planning, workforce education, and so forth. The work of collaboration in academic affairs units in systems and state offices has arguably changed, too, over the past decade. A primary impetus is the transformation of higher education itself, in which institutional missions are expanding and changing. More community colleges are offering four-year programs, with questions being raised about the potential for duplication of the same programs at four-year colleges and universities. Collaborations within and across sectors are also necessary in high-demand fields, such as health, in which competition for space for students in clinical sites can be fierce among institutions in the same area or across a broader region of the state because of distance learning options. Distance learning provides additional need for collaboration with higher education providers, especially those that span states and even countries. Existing campuses are setting up more sites and centers, in part because of the continuing need for access to college by a growing population in a number of states as well as the scarcity of capital dollars to build new main and branch campuses.

The need for greater collaboration with external stakeholders is fueled by the accountability movement, which has become a fixture within higher education. The popularity of accountability "dashboards" by governors in states such as Washington and Michigan has also opened up university systems to greater scrutiny where "report cards" show graduation and retention rates, student debt, and other metrics by institution (State of Michigan, 2012; State of Washington, 2012).

Other important stakeholders in higher education are state workforce and labor departments. The work of academic affairs staff has typically included analysis of state, regional, and local employment demands. It is not possible to project state needs for graduates in various fields and majors without working closely with workforce and labor. The difficulty has been, however, that education and labor do not speak the same language, particularly in the realm of data collection. For example, the National Center for Educational Statistics collects information about academic degree programs using the Classification of Instructional Programs (CIP). The data classifications used in this database are very different than that used by the Bureau of Labor Statistics in the Standard Occupational Classification (SOC) System or the Census Bureau's North American Industry Classification System (NAICS). Cross-walking between these databases remain difficult and many states are still struggling with projecting demand for graduates for the state's future workforce needs in terms that both communities understand.

Legislators and governors have lost patience, however, with the difficulties that education and workforce have traditionally had in communicating with each other. To conduct effective program approval and review as well as state and regional demand analyses, academic affairs professionals must speak both languages—education and workforce/labor—because the ability to project a state's need for graduates in various disciplines and fields depends very much upon a real understanding of how terms are defined and how cohorts and demand are measured. Without deep understanding, it is easy to present a partial or inaccurate picture of what a state's needs for future graduates are.

Collaboration between system and institutional academic affairs offices also deserves comment. Tension between system offices and campuses has always existed. Some tension is healthy, but too much can prevent effective working relationships. College and university faculty members and academic officers who have served as faculty members may dismiss system academic affairs staff as bureaucrats who add little academic value. Conversely, system officers may assume that institutional academic affairs officers—provosts, deans, vice presidents for academic affairs, and college and university presidents—are not capable of understanding the system-wide perspective on academic affairs issues. A reasonable tension between system and campus can be healthy, but it must be managed for the good of both the system and its member campuses. External stakeholders can be quick to criticize system offices that appear to be cheerleaders for their member institutions and reluctant to assert the public interest in program approval, transfer and articulation, transitions between college and work, and other traditional academic affairs areas.

## THE CHALLENGE OF "STEERING" HIGHER EDUCATION FOR ACADEMIC AFFAIRS

This chapter began with a discussion of the "steering role" in higher education and two questions regarding the role of academic affairs in systems offices: "Have higher education systems matured regarding academic affairs policies and practices?" and "Do the changes we see show evidence of intentionality in steering higher education in a defined direction (as opposed to being ad hoc reactions to external forces)?"

First, I reviewed the question of whether higher education systems have matured regarding academic affairs policies and practices. The traditional program approval and review functions continue to be important responsibilities, as shown in the recent study by Barak (2007) in which he reported that 45 of 50 states continue to conduct some form of program approval, and 41 of 50 conduct some type of academic program review. My findings from purposeful interviews of selected state- or system-level academic affairs officers affirmed the central role that program approval and review still hold. Strategic planning also continues to be a central responsibility of academic affairs offices, with arguably even more emphasis placed on it because of the increased power of state, system, and national databases to respond to questions from legislatures, governors, and the media. The ability of system staff to develop and use state, system, and national databases assists in steering higher education by allowing system leaders to set goals, including specific degree targets, and assess how well systems are achieving these goals.

What has changed regarding academic affairs offices, however, is the amount of concentrated time that staff can devote to any issue. The traditional functions of program approval and program review, although still key activities, are often given less time and focus among the major work assignments of academic affairs staff. The pace of work has also accelerated, with less time to complete detailed analyses and more interruptions by the media, and legislative and governor's office staff members who want instant responses to requests for information and to crises that emerge within the 24-hour news cycle. This is not an insignificant change. It takes time and focus to design studies, analyze campus plans and policies, and craft regional and statewide goals for the future. Attention and focus encourage intentionality.[4]

The answer to the next question is also, I believe, a qualified yes: "Do the changes we see show evidence of intentionality in steering higher education in a defined direction (as opposed to being ad hoc reactions to external forces)?"

Efforts to intentionally steer higher education to respond to market forces have been evident at national and state levels for some time. Recently, most states have adopted aggressive goals to increase degree production, such as the Lumina Foundation's Big Goal to increase the percentage of Americans with high-quality degrees and credentials to 60% by the year 2025 (Lumina Foundation, n.d.). Richardson and his colleagues (1999) warned that there is a danger, however, in structuring the market for higher education to encourage more students to enroll in college and, at the same time, to over-regulate institutions in a climate that is resource poor. We do not have abundant resources, which limits higher education's freedom to respond to market forces. In most systems and states, those market forces today are demanding that higher education expand capacity—and do so with greater efficiency.

Perhaps most importantly, the stakes are higher today for students and for institutions. Over the last century and a half, the United States has established a commitment to providing higher education for all who are willing and able to attend. Federal policies such as the Morrill Land Grant Acts of 1862 and 1890, the G.I. Bill (Serviceman's Readjustment Act of 1944 and its successors), and the Higher Education Act of 1965 (and creation of federal student aid) greatly expanded access to higher education. So too did the creation of junior and community colleges to help prepare students for success in four-year institutions or careers not requiring a baccalaureate degree. However, the current economic situation has put many institutions in the position of turning away large numbers of students who want to go to college—and would be successful there. Competition for public funding in all but a few states (e.g., North Dakota and Alaska) is intense, and our public higher education system is still predominantly driven by enrollments. Institutions in some states find themselves in the difficult position of having to provide incentives for sufficient numbers of students to enroll in college, to complete in a timely fashion, and to pursue majors that will provide them with jobs in a very tight job market. These choices are not entirely within institutional hands.

## CONCLUDING THOUGHTS

Have higher education systems matured regarding academic affairs policies and practices? Are the changes we see evidence of intentionality in steering higher education in a defined direction or rather a reaction to external forces on an ad hoc, less-defined basis? Two key ideas surfaced from the higher education policy leaders who were interviewed for this chapter: (1) there is less time to do academic affairs work today, even with our technological advantages, and (2) the stakes are higher than a decade or more ago because we are actually in danger of turning away students who are able to benefit from a college degree. In a resource-poor environment, where information travels quickly and the power of external actors has grown, it is more difficult than ever to steer higher education systems with intentionality and in defined directions.

This chapter has described ways in which academic affairs systems office roles and responsibilities have changed over the past decade or so. The system role in academic affairs today goes well beyond approving new programs, reviewing existing ones, and avoiding unnecessary duplication. The connector role has become even more prominent than it was in previous decades, when academic affairs offices at the state and system levels primarily managed connections among educational entities—K–12 to higher education, two- to four-year institutions, and, to a lesser extent, between public and private institutions, business and industry, and legislatures and governors' offices. Today, the degree to which attention must be paid to *all* stakeholders has increased.

Academic affairs systems offices need to use data effectively to demonstrate whether connections among all entities are succeeding and suggest improvements to steer higher education in the right direction if they are not. Performing regional and state-level strategic planning; raising statewide educational attainment; demonstrating student success and student learning outcomes; promoting successful transitions among all educational levels and sectors; documenting academic "productivity"; and aligning workforce needs with academic programs, costs, and locations are some of the major policy functions occupying academic affairs today. Academic affairs systems must successfully manage this expanded role or risk unwise intrusion from legislators and governors into academic policies and programs.

## NOTES

1. To help inform this portion of the chapter, I interviewed four former and current senior-level academic affairs state and systems

office directors. For their insights and expertise, I would like to thank Kathleen Kelly, former deputy director, Illinois Board of Higher Education; Ken O'Donnell, senior director, Student Engagement and Academic Initiatives & Partnerships, California State University Office of the Chancellor; Richard Stevens, director, Academic and Student Affairs, Florida Board of Governors, State University System; and Phyllis "Teddi" Safman, assistant commissioner for academic affairs, Utah System of Higher Education.

2. In 2012, there were 48 public and 82 independent two-year colleges that offered bachelor's degrees in 13 states (American Association of Community Colleges, 2012).

3. For an example, please see University of Central Florida's College of Arts and Humanities Academic Learning Compacts, available at http://oeas.ucf.edu/alc/alc_students_cahum.htm.

4. A full discussion of intentionality is beyond the scope of this chapter, but using the three basic kinds of intentionality of vision, belief, and knowledge in the work of Le Morvan (2005), higher education must be transparent in its intentionality and not merely opaque.

## REFERENCES

Alter, J., Jacobson, D., & Vos, J. (1993). *Higher education programs.* Retrieved from Minnesota Office of the Legislative Auditor website: http://www.auditor.leg.state.mn.us/ped/1993/93-03.pdf.

American Association of Community Colleges. (2012). 2012 community college fact sheet. Retrieved from http://www.aacc.nche.edu/AboutCC/Documents/FactSheet2012.pdf.

Anderson, Z. (2011, October 10). Rick Scott wants to shift university funding away from some degrees. *Sarasota Herald-Tribune.* Retrieved from http://politics.heraldtribune.com/2011/10/10/rick-scott-wants-to-shift-university-funding-away-from-some-majors/.

Barak, R. J. (2007). *Thirty years of academic review and approval by state postsecondary coordinating and governing boards.* Retrieved from State Higher Education Executive Officers website: http://www.sheeo.org/academic/Barak%20final.pdf.

Clark, B. R. (1983). *The higher education system: Academic organization in cross-national perspective.* Berkeley: University of California Press.

Florida House Bill 7135. (2012). Provided for requirements for planning for system and institution goals and objectives.

Johnson, N. (2009, May). What does a college degree cost? Comparing approaches to measuring "cost per degree." Retrieved from Delta Cost Project website: http://www.deltacostproject.org/resources/pdf/johnson3-09_WP.pdf.

Le Morvan, P. (2005). Intentionality: Transparent, translucent, and opaque. *The Journal of Philosophical Research, 30,* 283–302. doi:10.5840/jpr20053039.

Lumina Foundation. (n.d.) The Big Goal: To increase the proportion of Americans with high-quality degrees and credentials to 60 percent by the year 2025. Retrieved from http://www.luminafoundation.org/goal_2025.html.

Lumina Foundation. (2011). The Degree Qualifications Profile. Retrieved from http://www.luminafoundation.org/publications/The_Degree_Qualifications_Profile.pdf.

McGuiness, A. C., Jr. (1994). The changing structure of state higher education leadership. In A. C. McGuiness, Jr., R. M. Epper, & S. Arredondo, *State postsecondary education structures Handbook 1994* (pp. 1–45). Retrieved from the Florida State University DigiNole Commons website: http://diginole.lib.fsu.edu/ecs/4.

Morrill Land-Grant Act of 1862 (7 U.S.C. § 301 et seq.).

Morrill Land-Grant Act of 1890 (26 Stat. 417, 7 U.S.C. § 321 et seq.)

Richardson, R. C., Jr., Bracco, K. R., Callan, P. M., & Finney, J. E. (1999). *Designing state higher education systems for a new century.* Phoenix, AZ: Oryx Press.

Servicemen's Readjustment Act of 1944 (P.L. 78-345, 58 Stat. 284m).

State of Michigan. (2012). Michigan education dashboard. Retrieved from http://www.michigan.gov/midashboard/0,4624,7-256-580 84---,00.html.

State University System of Florida Board of Governors. (2007). 8.016 academic learning compacts. Retrieved from http://www.flbog.edu/documents_regulations/regulations/8_016_Academic_Learning_Compacts.pdf.

State of Washington. (2012). Education dashboard final 05-05-12. Retrieved from Government Management Accountability and

Performance website: http://performance.wa.gov/Education/Ed05 1215/Pages/Default.aspx.

Wallace, J. (2011, October 10). Rick Scott no fan of anthropology. *Herald Tribune.* Retrieved from http://politics.heraldtribune. com/2011/10/10/rick-scott-no-fan-of-anthropology/.

Washington Student Achievement Council. (2012). About the council. Retrieved from http://www.wsac.wa.gov/AboutTheCouncil.

Wildavsky, A. (1979). *Speaking Truth to Power: The Art and Craft of Policy Analysis.* New York, NY: Little, Brown and Company.

Williams, G. L. (1995). The "marketization" of higher education: Reforms and potential reforms in higher education finance. In D. D. Dill & B. Sporn (Eds.), *Emerging patterns of social demand and university reform: Through a glass darkly* (pp. 170–193). Tarrytown, NY: Elsevier Science.

# 11

## WORKFORCE DEVELOPMENT AT COMMUNITY COLLEGES

*Can Systems Make a Difference?*

DAVID F. SHAFFER

ABSTRACT

Amid growing concerns about a "skills gap" between the nation's workforce and its projected future job openings, business and political leaders are counting on community colleges to prepare workers for jobs that require more than a high school education. A key question is the extent to which states' varying educational governance and coordinating structures are up to the task of aligning community colleges to meet these needs. This chapter explores experiences in four states that are leveraging system-level powers and resources to try to improve their workforce development efforts: North Carolina, which has revamped a large part of its career-oriented curriculum; Georgia, which uses central system resources for its largest training programs; Virginia, which has put its community colleges at the lead of its overall workforce development system; and Massachusetts, which has enacted legislation to strengthen the state government's control of the system. Their experiences suggest that as states strive to meet their workforce needs, they will increasingly turn to more "system" direction for their community college systems. Culture and leadership, as much as formal legal controls, may be key to states' ability to pursue new policies in this direction.

On August 16, 2012, the North Carolina Community College System announced that it had completed a broad curriculum restructuring, consolidating 77 curriculums into 32, adding 21 new majors, eliminating 16, and revising more than 50 others. The changes, to be applied across the system's 58 campuses, reshaped about one-third of its programs. Full implementation of the new curriculum was mandated to occur by the fall of 2014.

North Carolina's announcement occasioned wide interest among followers of workforce development and community colleges. Much of the commentary focused on how the curriculum revisions could enhance North Carolina's already well-regarded use of its two-year college system in preparing its citizens for employment. For example, Jennifer McNelly, president of the Manufacturing Institute (an affiliate of the National Association of Manufacturers), remarked that the new curriculum "provides flexibility and adaptability to meet changing market demands. It aligns to industry standards, ensuring students enter the workforce with national certifications with labor market value" (Hoenk, 2012).

The action came as governmental and business leaders were voicing ever higher expectations for the contributions that community colleges should make to workforce development and the nation's economic competitiveness. These two-year schools prepare people for so-called middle skill jobs (those requiring more than a high school education but less than a four-year degree) that many employers, trade groups, and analysts say are going unfilled (Jacobs, 2012). Even at the trough of the Great Recession, 32% of manufacturers, who generally pay higher-than-average wages, reported that jobs were going unfilled because they could not find workers with the right qualifications (Manufacturing Institute, 2011).

Amid the commentary about the outcome of the North Carolina reform effort, however, some called attention to a different factor: the specific institutional and governance characteristics that made this rapid, statewide curriculum update possible in the first place. Shanna Smith Jaggars, assistant director of the Community College Research Center at Teachers College, Columbia University, noted in an interview that a strong, centralized system enabled North Carolina to "create a more coherent policy, and (one) more comprehensive" (Fain, 2012). Jaggars's assertion prompts a question about the nature of community college systems. Specifically, can community college systems, *as systems*, make a difference in what their constituent institutions deliver for their students and their communities? To a surprising degree, the two-year college systems across the nation differ widely in how they operate, how they are funded, and how they are governed—that is, in the degree to which they are, in fact, systems.

The layperson might reasonably assume that all community colleges are pretty much the same. After all, they tend to be lower-cost institutions where people of any age beyond high school may enroll on a full- or part-time basis for courses in anything from the liberal arts to specific job skills to personal interests such as cooking. Moreover, they are generally close enough to home that one may attend without living on campus. Two-year colleges prepare students for transfer to four-year colleges, produce associate's degree holders in fields that do not require four-year degrees for licensure (e.g., occupational therapy assistants), offer two-year degrees or shorter-term certificates in skills ranging from auto repair to clean-room management, remediate high school graduates who are not prepared for college-level work, and offer short-term (often noncredit) courses requested by employers who want workers to receive training in a very specific work process or piece of equipment (Hendrickson, Lane, Harris, & Dorman, 2013).

These traits are basically consistent among community colleges across the country, yet they mask many differences, sometimes significant ones, in how states govern and coordinate these institutions. Some state governments pay most of the cost, but other state governments divide the costs with localities (Boswell, 2000). Some states give top priority to workforce development, others less so. In some states, two-year institutions are under direct control of the state government, while in others institutional governance is shared with, or even dominated by, local governments. Some states allow each two-year institution to determine its own curriculum, some have a mandated statewide curriculum, and some have a statewide "core" of courses while allowing local additions and variations (Tollefson, Garrett, Ingram, & Associates, 1999).

What has not been explored in the literature on this topic is the extent to which the existence or operation of higher education systems affects how a particular state approaches workforce development issues, particularly in relation to community colleges. At the time of this writing, North Carolina was the only state to have undertaken a sweeping, career-focused, statewide reform of its community college course offerings in recent years, and it has one of the strongest central system processes for developing and enforcing its curriculum. Given this example, is there a connection between systemness and how states address their workforce development needs? An observation from one recent influential report on community colleges and workforce development in Massachusetts would suggest that the answer to this question is "yes."

> States with community colleges that are known to be highly successful workforce and economic development entities—including Kentucky, North Carolina, Virginia and Washington—all operate through strong, centralized, state-run community college systems that are governed separately from other higher education institutions. (Alssid, Goldberg, & Schneider, 2011, p. 13)

There does not, however, appear to be a strong correlation between the quality of a state's workforce and the *formal* structure, at least, of its community college system. In CNBC's 2012 survey of state business climates, for example, only two of the states—Colorado and Virginia—that were rated in the top 10 for the quality of their available workforce were also among the top 10 states in terms of the centralization of their formal community college governance systems, as ranked in a comprehensive study of community college governance structures across the country (Garrett, 1999).[1]

## SYSTEM APPROACHES TO WORKFORCE DEVELOPMENT IN COMMUNITY COLLEGES

To examine in more depth how a system approach, whether formal or informal, may enhance a state's ability to upgrade its workforce, this chapter explores efforts in North Carolina and three other states, Georgia, Virginia, and Massachusetts. The specifics among the four states vary widely enough to enable a broad exploration of the various connections between system governance and the engagement of community colleges in workforce development:

- North Carolina has revamped its curriculum across the entire system.
- Georgia has a centralized system-level service for delivering specialized job training programs at major employer locations.
- Virginia has turned over the stewardship of almost all its federal workforce training funds to its community college system, and has created a single structure to coordinate its diverse training providers.
- After a heated political dispute over state versus local control, Massachusetts enacted legislation to move its community colleges from a largely decentralized system to one with stronger state oversight and a more direct mission of workforce development.

The developments in all four states reflect the fact that today two-year colleges across the country are hearing calls from the White House on down for a strong focus on teaching job-relevant skills.

## NORTH CAROLINA

The North Carolina Community College System has emphasized workforce from its outset. The system was created in 1963, pulling together a loose grouping of six community colleges and 25 industrial education sites into a single system under the State Board of Education (Lancaster, 1999). It currently reports for-credit enrollment of over 335,000 (on a nonduplicated headcount basis). At its beginning, its statutory mission declared, "The major purpose of each and every institution . . . shall be and shall continue to be the offering of vocational and technical education and training" (N.C. Gen. Stat. ch115D § 1, 1963). The statute designates the community college system's central office as "the primary lead agency for delivering workforce development training, adult literacy training, and adult education programs in the State."

In addition to a broad for-credit curriculum with heavy emphasis on job-related skills, the North Carolina system institutions offer customized, generally not-for-credit programs tailored to the specific needs of a new or existing employer—without charge to the company

(Shaffer & Wright, 2010). The system reported that in 2009–2010 this program provided customized training to more than 16,000 workers at almost 600 employers (North Carolina Community College System, 2012b). In the business press and among industry groups, the state is regularly praised for its overall workforce development programs. For example, *Forbes* magazine (Badenhausen, 2011) and CNBC (2012) have both ranked North Carolina in the top three states for the quality of its available workforce, while *Business Facilities* magazine (Rogers, 2010) ranked it in the top five states for workforce development.

Each of North Carolina's community colleges, of which there are now 58, is operated by a local board of trustees with 13 members (four selected by the governor, eight by local governments, and one by students). However, the state government provides about two-thirds of the funding, with localities contributing 12% (Fiscal Research Division, 2011). The overall system is governed by a 21-member State Board of Community Colleges, which operates the formula that divides the state funding among the individual colleges, approves admissions policies and the curriculum, and gives final approval to the appointment of each college's president upon recommendation from the local board (N.C. Gen. Stat. 115D-2.1 & 12, 1963; 23 NCAC 02C.0201, 1976).

Given the role of the local boards, the North Carolina system has been rated as only "moderately decentralized" in comparisons of community college governance systems across the 50 states (Garrett, 1999). However, the State Board of Community Colleges and its system office exercise a strong role in the heart of the educational process—the development of the curriculum. This role is not the norm among two-year systems. In keeping with the general practice at four-year colleges and universities, many community colleges and systems have traditionally left the development of courses and curricula in the hands of the faculty at individual institutions (though generally with some form of after-the-fact state approval).

In 1995 North Carolina's General Assembly required that the State Board of Community Colleges develop what is now called a "common course library" across the entire system. Teams totaling 1,200 faculty members across the system worked for two years to write descriptions for 3,800 courses (Lancaster, 1999). Any North Carolina community college that offers, for example, an introductory course in aquaculture must follow the system's guidelines for that course. The guidelines are general enough to allow some flexibility (and a statewide course description is limited to three sentences), so variations from one campus to another do occur. Still, the basic principle is one of a common, statewide curriculum.

Since 1995, the system has made repeated use of what it calls its Curriculum Improvement Process (CIP), in which faculty teams from various campuses review and revise various aspects of the course library. In January 2010, North Carolina's Association of Community College Presidents asked for a broader than usual CIP—a total revamping of entire sectors of the system's technical education programs, with a special emphasis on programs relevant to the rapidly evolving fields of energy and sustainability.

This Code Green Super CIP, as the system named it, was launched in August 2010 to review more than 80 of its curricula. Faculty members and administrators at particular campuses took lead roles following a statewide bidding process and subsequently revised specific parts of the curriculum. Faculty members from multiple campuses collaborated on each team, and the teams also had outside advisory groups, including employer representatives. System administrators monitored their progress but did not interfere in the work, according to Sharon Morrissey, the system's senior vice president for academic services. "Once it's in the hands of the faculty we back off and say, 'It's yours now,'" according to Morrissey (S. Morrissey, personal communication, October 22, 2012).

The new curriculum classifies the affected course offerings by "career cluster" (such as manufacturing, or transportation, distribution, and logistics), each with several potential majors. Course requirements are laid out for each of several potential majors within a cluster. For example, under architecture and construction technology there are six potential program majors: architectural technology, carpentry, building construction technology, masonry, construction management, and plumbing. For all those majors there are recommended general education and technical education cores, coupled with courses specific to the major.

In this process some 21 new majors programs were also added, in such fields as equine business technology, environmental management technology, and geospatial mapping. More than 50 majors were revised, including programs as varied as fish and wildlife management, landscape gardening, automation engineering, and outdoor leadership. Sixteen majors were "archived," meaning they were either merged into other similar programs or, in some cases, phased out altogether (North Carolina Community College System, 2012a).


## GEORGIA

Most states struggle to strike a balance between two principal missions of their two-year colleges: academic programs that enable students to transfer to four-year colleges, on the one hand, and career-focused programs that prepare students for jobs that regional employers need to fill, on the other. Georgia developed an unusual solution to this dichotomy, creating two different systems, one for each mission.

First, there are 16 institutions called "state colleges," offering mostly certificates and two-year associate's degrees. Second, Georgia has an entirely separate system of 25 institutions in its Technical College System, providing technical education programs as well as customized training for employers. That system started with two institutes in 1943 and added 20 more during the 1960s. Originally the institutes were governed by local boards, under the supervision of the Georgia State Board of Education, but beginning in 1984 the state began to merge them under the Georgia State Board of Technical and Adult Education. The 22 members of the latter board are appointed by the governor; each institution also has a local board, appointed by the state board, with the power to approve budgets and programs (Walton, 1999).

The system reports enrollment of over 180,000 and says 40% of its students are enrolled in programs related to one of the six industries that the state's economic development plan has identified as priorities: aerospace, health care, life sciences/biotechnology, agribusiness, energy and the environment, and logistics and transportation (Technical College System of Georgia, 2011). In the CNBC study of state business climates, Georgia ranked first in the quality of its workforce.

As is common in community college systems, each individual technical college offers customized training and other workforce help to employers within its region. But on top of that, Georgia has a centralized, system-based approach that is unique in the country. Rather than relying solely on individual colleges to develop and provide training, Georgia's renowned Quick Start program uses central system staff and other central resources to design and implement large-scale and sophisticated employer-specific training.

Similar to customized training programs at community colleges in some other states,[2] Quick Start's services are free for qualifying employers—including new employers and existing companies that are increasing employment and/or making substantial upgrades in plant and equipment. The difference is that the Georgia program is centralized, rather than run by individual colleges, on the premise that only a centralized operation can marshal the skills and resources to meet sophisticated training needs.

Quick Start employs industrial specialists trained to dissect a manufacturing process from beginning to end and then design specific training for each job. It uses specialized equipment and staff to develop, for example, a training video for a biopharmaceutical company that needs to show its workers what a process that they are learning to manage looks like from *inside* the sealed laboratory equipment. More dramatically, Quick Start will recruit and train the workforce while a new plant is under construction so that production can start the day the doors open.

The state created Quick Start in its current form in the 1990s after finding that competitors were undermining Georgia's traditional cost advantage. State leaders concluded that complete training services were a way to get back a competitive edge. Since then it has conducted over 6,000 projects involving some 800,000 trainees.

When qualifying employers ask, Quick Start assigns teams of analysts to investigate the process or workflow in question. Often they travel to a company's other locations, including overseas, if necessary. They develop a customized program, complete with handbooks, presentations, videos, online lessons, or other training materials, all produced by in-house specialists. Quick Start can prescreen potential hirees for the company, using the knowledge it has acquired of the production system to identify candidates who are likely to learn the skills required. The training is then deployed at the company's location, at one or more of the technical colleges, or at one of five Quick Start facilities around the state. The team providing the training may include central staff, faculty from the host technical colleges, faculty from other institutions, and specialists retained on a project-by-project basis.

In June 2009, for example, NCR Corporation, a computer hardware and electronics company, announced that it would move its headquarters from Dayton, Ohio, to Georgia. NCR also built a new plant in Georgia to manufacture ATMs—eventually bringing 3,000 jobs to the state. Quick Start had been working closely all along with the team of Georgia economic developers who were negotiating with NCR, so even before the announcement it had prepared a first draft of a training program, built a simulated NCR production line using actual NCR equipment, and begun prescreening job applicants. Within a week of the official announcement, Quick Start sent a team to study an existing NCR plant in Hungary to ensure that the training plan would work properly. A revised training program was then delivered to hirees even as the plant was under construction. It paid off; the first ATM for delivery rolled off the production line in Georgia only eight weeks after the announcement.[3]

## VIRGINIA

*Silos* is a word commonly used to describe the disparate, overlapping, and often uncoordinated job training and workforce development programs existing in every state. Training programs are dependent on federal funds, so states' delivery structures often mirror specific federal funding streams. Those streams, in turn, tend to be organized not around labor market needs, but around defined categories of workers (for example, veterans, youth in need, or those displaced by overseas competition). The Education Commission of the States (2007) summarized the problem this way:

> With few exceptions, the nation's education and training systems operate in relative isolation from broader economic development efforts, largely because state policies governing adult and postsecondary education, workforce and economic development, and social and human services are designed and implemented with few meaningful connections. As a result, these systems do not effectively work together to produce the kinds of skilled workers needed in today's changing economy.

More recently, Anthony Carnevale, director of the Georgetown University Center on Education and the Workforce, testified before Congress that fixing the mismatch between job openings and training programs will require breaking down the "silos between our postsecondary education and training programs, job openings, and career pathways" (Carnevale, 2010, p. 1). Robert G. Templin Jr., president of Northern Virginia Community College, testified at the same hearing that training providers often work in isolation, without coordination and without a shared understanding of what skills are needed in the job market, and often provide only entry-level training skills that do not result in a "portable and market-valued credential" (Gonzalez, 2010).

To address this issue, the commonwealth of Virginia embarked in 2006 on a unique attempt to pull all its workforce programs under one umbrella—and gave its community college system the lead in taking on the task. Virginia had created its community college system 40 years before, in 1966 (and at the same time enacted the state's first sales tax to pay for it). The first two colleges opened that year, and by 1972–1973 the current system, with 23 colleges, was fully in place (Graham, 1999). From its outset, the Virginia system was defined as a "comprehensive" one, meaning that it was to offer both career-oriented and transfer-oriented programs.

Since its inception, the Virginia system has been state funded and under strong, central state control. The system is governed by a 15-member State Board of Community Colleges, whose members are appointed by the governor. The board, in turn, appoints a system chancellor; the presidents of the individual local colleges report to the chancellor. Each college has a local board, but its role is officially described as advisory. In the Garrett (1999) study, the system was ranked 11th in the nation for degree of centralization. The system reports for-credit enrollment of about 285,000.

Virginia has a strong reputation for its overall business climate; it ranked first in the nation, for example, in the 2012 CNBC survey. Virginia's workforce's reputation, however, is not quite as stellar; for that it ranked eighth in the CNBC index. By the early 2000s, according to Elizabeth Povar, vice president for business and ally services at the Virginia Economic Development Partnership, the state's leadership had begun to worry that its workforce strategy was not contributing as it should to the state's ability to attract businesses. "Where we had a problem," she said, "was in demonstrating that our workforce development system was strong, flexible, and reliable" (Workforce Strategy Center, 2012).

So Virginia turned to the Workforce Strategy Center (WSC), a small think tank in Rhode Island that had been working on a way to bypass the "silos" problem. In 2002, the center had published a report arguing that states should create regional "career pathways" systems that would assess job market needs by region and then link various entities that had often failed to work together, including "workforce agencies, community-based organizations, and social service organizations." Community colleges, WSC argued, were best suited to lead these efforts because of their role in teaching skills above the level of basics and because of the regional nature of their territories (Alssid et al., 2002, pp. 3–6).

"Career pathways," as the Education Commission of the States summarized the concept in 2007, "are helpful frameworks for making systemic changes that fill gaps in education and workforce training systems by addressing the complementary goals of student and worker advancement, and regional economic development" (Education Commission of the States, 2007). In September of 2006, then governor Thomas Kaine released a strategic plan for Virginia's economic development in which he called for "a world-class workforce system that is both responsive to employer and worker needs and focused on regional markets." In 2007 he adopted the WSC's career pathways construct, with an executive order creating a Workforce Sub Cabinet to coordinate the efforts of the state agencies for commerce, education, human resources, and the community college system.

In July 2008 the Virginia Community College System was given authority over the administration of the Virginia Workforce Council, as well as the fiscal stewardship of Virginia's federal Workforce Investment Act funding. The council was directed to set up regional task forces that would assess the needs of their regional labor markets and align some 34 separate workforce development programs, ranging from adult education to the Manufacturing Extension Partnership to the Trade Adjustment Assistance Program (Workforce Strategy Center, 2008, pp. 4, 8, 9).

When Governor Robert McDonnell, a Republican, succeeded Governor Kaine, a Democrat, in 2010, he embraced the Virginia Career Pathways system and elevated a senior official, Elizabeth

Creamer, to supervise it. As of this writing, the effort remains a work in progress. But all the agencies involved had started working and planning together, treating Career Pathways as "a lever for systemic change . . . and not a 'program,'" as Creamer puts it (Workforce Strategy Center, 2012). Three (out of a planned 15) regional collaborations have been established as pilots, for the peninsula region east of Chesapeake Bay, the Southside region south of Richmond, and the southwest corner of the state. As a result, "The Virginia Career Pathways Initiative has taken hold in the Commonwealth," the Workforce Strategy Center said in a September 2012 progress report. "The initiative has shown results with respect to putting the framework in place to meet the changing needs of the Commonwealth's businesses and residents" (Goldberg & Alssid, 2012, p. 13).

## MASSACHUSETTS

Massachusetts has 15 community colleges, with for-credit enrollment of about 127,000 students. The state provides an annual appropriation to the colleges; there is no contribution from local taxes. The colleges have, nonetheless, functioned with a fair degree of local autonomy. In 2012 the commonwealth embarked on an effort to determine if stronger, central control of the system could lead to better results in workforce development.

The creation of Massachusetts's community college system was authorized by the legislature (the General Court) in 1958, and initially the colleges were all governed by a State Board of Regional Community Colleges, which was brought under the umbrella of the Massachusetts Higher Education Coordinating Council in 1965. In 1996 that council was superseded by the Massachusetts Board of Higher Education, the separate board for community colleges was abolished, and Massachusetts moved from a system of central state control to one in which most decision making was vested in each college's individual board.

Since 1996 the Massachusetts Board of Higher Education, with 11 members appointed by the governor, has approved educational programs and other broad policies for the community colleges (as well as for the state's four-year institutions, other than the University of Massachusetts). The individual campuses' boards of trustees, with eight members appointed by the governor, select each institution's president and oversee operations. The mission of the community college system, as articulated by the Higher Education Coordinating Council in 1992, listed associate's degree programs for transfer to four-year colleges as the first responsibility, followed by career-oriented education (Motta, 1999). State funding for community colleges has been appropriated by the General Court on a college-by-college basis, and not, as in some states, appropriated to the system board for reallocation to individual institutions.

Workforce development may not have been designated officially as a high statewide priority in 1992, but individual colleges offered extensive job-oriented courses, on both for-credit and noncredit bases, and enrolled tens of thousands of trainees each year in special courses designed to meet the needs of individual employers. For example, Bunker Hill Community College, the state's largest with over 16,000 students, operates a Workforce Development Center that has offered customized training programs for over 100 Boston-area employers.[4]

Individual college administrators and trustees argued that local governance enabled them to respond more nimbly to the particular needs of employers and job markets in their regions (Motta, 1999). In the business, civic, and political communities in Massachusetts, however, there were emerging concerns that the two-year college system was not keeping up with other states in terms of the kind of workforce development needed to attract and support employers. This culminated in the creation of a Coalition FOR Community Colleges, spearheaded by the Boston Foundation, which in November of 2011 published a report entitled The Case for Community Colleges: Aligning Higher Education and Workforce Needs in Massachusetts.

The report was authored jointly by the Workforce Strategy Center and MassINC, a Boston think tank. It said that there was "a continuing and growing concern about the mismatch between the middle-skilled jobs that are going unfilled in the Massachusetts economy and the opportunities offered by higher education to prepare workers to fill these needs" (Alssid, Goldberg, & Schneider, 2011, p. ii), and it recommended that the commonwealth:

- Clarify the community colleges' mission, giving priority to meeting labor market needs
- Strengthen governance to make the colleges more accountable to state officials

- Adopt state performance goals, with colleges provided more, or less, autonomy depending upon their performance. (Alssid, Goldberg, & Schneider, 2011, pp. 32–33)

About two months after the Boston Foundation report was published, Governor Deval Patrick announced in his 2012 State of the State address that he would propose a "unified" community college system for the state. His office cited estimates that there were 120,000 job openings in the state going unfilled for lack of qualified workers—or about one for every two residents who were unemployed (Patrick, 2012). The governor's subsequent budget proposal[5] included provisions that would have:

- replaced the college-by-college system of appropriations with a formula, to be developed by the Board of Higher Education, "with a specific focus on the colleges' role as regional work training and skill development centers";
- given the state's Board of Higher Education the authority to appoint (and remove) the presidents of community colleges, stripping the local boards of that power;
- required the state board to determine salary and other terms of employment of each president—again, removing that power from the local boards; and
- permitted the governor to name the chairperson of each community college board, a power hitherto possessed by the local board itself.

The governor's budget proposal prompted strong opposition from numerous community college presidents and board members. "The true intent of this legislation? To render our community colleges as glorified vocational schools," protested the chair of one local board of trustees (Grady, 2012). Leaders of the legislature reacted cautiously. Less than a week after Governor Patrick made his proposal, Senate president Therese Murray said that she had

> concerns about taking the local control away and putting it all under the Board of Higher Ed in Boston. Does Boston know what the Berkshires need? Does Boston know what the Cape needs and the business needs of the Cape? I think we need to go a little bit slower. (Cheney, 2012)

By April, the House Ways and Means Committee had drafted a proposal to continue the school-by-school appropriations system and to leave the appointment of presidents in the hands of the local boards, while adding incentive grants for workforce programs (Welker, 2012).

The final 2012 state budget embodied a compromise that generally followed Governor Patrick's direction, while retaining more local control. Its provisions:

- Give the governor the power to appoint the chairperson of each college's board of trustees.
- Leave the power to select and remove college presidents with the local boards. (However, the state board is now required to "establish and issue guidelines and procedures" for the search and appointment process, for compensation, and for the evaluation and removal of the presidents. The state board is also now required to appoint one voting representative to serve on the local board during any search for a new president.)
- Continues the college-by-college appropriation for the 2013 fiscal year, but requires the state board to develop a new formula, and new performance metrics, for future years.
- Creates a new "Office of Coordination" in the Department of Higher Education to "establish a clearinghouse for all training opportunities provided by public higher education institutions."
- Establishes a Community College Workforce Advisory Committee to develop recommendations for distributing up to $12 million a year in workforce training grants to individual community colleges. (Mass. Gen. Laws 2012)

## IMPLICATIONS FOR THE FUTURE

What can the developments reported in this chapter tell governmental and education leaders and others about how to shape and direct the evolving role of community colleges and systems in workforce development? One takeaway is simply that there *will* continue to be pressure on community colleges to change. That pressure, in turn, will fall on systems and will require system responses. Of the three key roles of two-year colleges (transfer, remediation, and workforce), it is the workforce role that is attracting more and more attention from national and state leaders, from the White House down. Responsible state leaders will inevitably turn to their systems, as systems, to respond, if only because that is their best point of leverage over the individual colleges. They will do so regardless of whether their existing systems are highly centralized or not; systems are likely to be asked to act as systems, whether that has been their past practice or not.

The cases of Massachusetts and Virginia illustrate the point. Massachusetts has had a highly *de*centralized system. When Governor Patrick felt the need to upgrade the community colleges' performance on workforce development, his approach was to strengthen central system powers. Virginia, on the other hand, has had a highly centralized community college system from the outset—yet when former governor Kaine wanted to improve his state's workforce development, his response was to turn to still more "systemness," giving the community college system a leadership role in coordinating the state's other training providers.

The initiatives in both Virginia and Massachusetts are works in progress, too new for us to know how well they will work out. The Quick Start program in Georgia, by contrast, is a long-established success story, but it is also unique enough that its lessons may not be applicable elsewhere. The key insight behind Quick Start's creation was that a strong, central resource serving an entire state system could provide assets for urgent, large-scale employer training needs that could not be matched by individual technical colleges working on their own. Quick Start's niche, however, is quick turnaround on training for significant business expansions and for major new manufacturers coming to Georgia, which is a "problem" that not every state has.

The case of the curriculum change in North Carolina is perhaps most germane to the challenges facing other state systems. It leads to our second takeaway, which is that change can be achieved through a process of collaboration that is facilitated, but not necessarily dictated, by a central system administration. North Carolina's curriculum change was initiated not by the system administration, but in response to a request from the presidents of individual colleges. It was developed by teams led by faculty from individual colleges, each with participants drawn from both faculty and employers across the state. The central system sought to support the process rather than dictate it, but once the work was complete, the state board mandated the resulting changes statewide. These are not the marks of a "top-down" system. They are, however, the marks of a *system*—one that works in unity.

"If you don't do that—if you just say, 'this is the way it's going to be'—you get resistance," stated Shanna Smith Jaggars, of Columbia University's Community College Research Center. Centralized direction of community college systems "works best when it is subtle," she adds. An effective central administration will "use collaboration . . . to strike a balance between pushing their networks of colleges in the same direction, while letting all the colleges contribute to the change" (S. Jaggars, personal communication, October 25, 2012).

This point ties in with a third and final takeaway, which is that formal, on-paper structures of control will not necessarily determine how systems behave in reality. To illustrate, compare Massachusetts and North Carolina.

Massachusetts started in 1958 with a state-controlled system but then reorganized in 1996 into largely regional governance (in a move toward *de*centralization that was intended in part to make the colleges more attuned to the workforce needs in their own particular regions). The 2012 legislation shifted the balance back to more state control, again in the name of workforce development. The role of system administration in North Carolina's successes was cited as one reason.

On the books, however, from 1996 on the Massachusetts system *already had* a governance structure much like that in North Carolina. The centralization index developed by Garrett ranked North Carolina as the 24th most centralized system; Massachusetts was 29th (Tollefson et al., 1999). Both states' systems are largely state funded, both allowed local boards to choose their college president and otherwise control most operations, and both employed an umbrella state board to approve policies and curriculum.

The real difference may simply be that North Carolina *behaves* like a system. The state board in Raleigh in effect took the position, for example, that its legal authority to "approve" curricula allowed it to decline to approve anything that would not fit in the statewide course catalog. Massachussetts never tried anything like that.

Perhaps the conditions prevailing when the two systems were starting up in the early 1960s influenced their respective cultures. North Carolina was a relatively poor state that was hungry to attract business. Its state leadership gave top priority to workforce development, and the system never looked back. Massachusetts at the time was more prosperous, and its leaders focused on academic programs that would send people on to four-year colleges.

The degree of systemness in community college systems, therefore, may depend upon culture and leadership at least as much as—if not more than—it depends upon legal and historical factors. Whether laws are changed or not, perhaps the key to *being* a system is simply to *act* like one.

## NOTES

1. The governance study (Garrett, 1999) based its index of centralization on the authority of the state-level board and the state and local shares of funding, among other criteria. The CNBC ranking was based on "the relative success of each state's worker training programs in placing their participants in jobs," as well as on overall education levels and other criteria (CNBC, 2012).
2. See Shaffer and Wright (2011) for an extensive discussion of customized training programs in other states.
3. Quick Start publishes a quarterly newsletter that is full of stories of cases like NCR—most of them small or medium sized, but others quite large, including a 2,500-worker Kia plant that opened in 2008.
4. See http://www.bhcc.mass.edu/corporatetraining for details.
5. See www.mass.gov/bb/h1/fy13h1/os_13/h30.htm.

## REFERENCES

Alssid, J. L., Goldberg, M., & Schneider, J. (2011). The case for community colleges: Aligning higher education and workforce needs in Massachusetts. Retrieved from Boston Foundation website:

http://www.tbf.org/~/media/TBFOrg/Files/Reports/Community-College_Nov2011.pdf.

Alssid, J. L., Gruber, D., Jenkins, D., Mazzeo, C., Roberts, B., & Stanback-Stroud, R. (2002). Building a career pathways system: Promising practices in community college–centered workforce development. Retrieved from Workforce Strategy Center website: http://www.workforcestrategy.org/images/pdfs/publications/Career_Pathways.pdf.

Badenhausen, K. (2011, November 22). The best states for business and careers. *Forbes*. Retrieved from http://www.forbes.com/special-report/2011/best-states-11_land.html.

Boswell, K. (2000). State funding for community colleges: A 50-state survey. Retrieved from Education Commission of the States website: http://www.ecs.org/clearinghouse/22/86/2286.pdf.

Carnevale, A. P. (2010). Summary of written testimony before the Senate Committee on Health, Education, Labor, and Pensions: A stronger workforce investment system for a stronger economy. Retrieved from http://cew.georgetown.edu/uploadedfiles/Carnevale_summary_testimony_2.24.10.pdf.

Cheney, K. (2012, February 1). Senate leader hits Patrick proposal on community colleges. *Boston Globe*. Retrieved from http://www.bostonglobe.com/metro/2012/02/01/mass-senate-president-therese-murray-questions-patrick-community-college-proposal/a2cUZP5YqCCbXlC9eCjPLJ/story.html.

CNBC. (2012). America's top states for business 2012: A CNBC special report. Retrieved from http://www.cnbc.com/id/46414199/Top_States_for_Business_2012.

Education Commission of the States. (2007). The progress of education reform 2007: Economic and workforce development. Retrieved from http://www.ecs.org/clearinghouse/75/67/7567.pdf.

Fain, P. (2012, September 12). When statewide pays off. *Inside Higher Ed*. Retrieved from http://www.insidehighered.com/news/2012/09/12/ncs-community-colleges-big-green-jobs-curriculum-shift.

Fiscal Research Division. (2011). NC Community College System base budget. Retrieved from North Carolina General Assembly website: http://www.ncleg.net/documentsites/committees/JointAppropriationsEducation2011/2011-02-09%20Meeting/FRD_NCCCSBaseBudget_2011-02-09.pdf.

Garrett, R. L. (1999). Degrees of centralization of governance structures in state community college systems. In T. A. Tollefson, R. L. Garrett, W. G. Ingram, & Associates, *Fifty state systems of community colleges: Mission, governance, funding and accountability* (pp. 15–22). Johnson City, TN: Overmountain Press.

Goldberg, M., & Alssid, J. L. (2012). Taking root: The Virginia career pathways system. (p. 13) Retrieved from Virginia's Community Colleges website: http://www.vccs.edu/LinkClick.aspx?filetic ket=FAv9OkLwIgA%3D&tabid=76.

Gonzalez, J. (2010, February 4). Obama's job-creation goals spur interest in renewing law that covers training programs. *Chronicle of Higher Education*. Retrieved from http://chronicle.com/ article/Job-Creation-Goals-Spur/64366/.

Grady, J. (2012, June 7). Myths about Mass. governor's proposal for community colleges. *Community College Times*. Retrieved from http://www.communitycollegetimes.com/Pages/Opinions/Myths-about-Mass-governors-proposal-for-community-colleges.aspx.

Graham, J. S. (1999). Virginia. In T. A. Tollefson, R. L. Garrett, W. G. Ingram, & Associates, *Fifty state systems of community colleges: Mission, governance, funding and accountability* (pp. 421–444). Johnson City, TN: Overmountain Press.

Hendrickson, R. M., Lane, J. E., Harris, J. T., & Dorman, R. H. (2013). *Academic leadership and governance of higher education: A guide for trustees, leaders, and aspiring leaders of two- and four-year institutions.* Sterling, VA: Stylus.

Hoenk, M. (2012, August 16). State board makes history with approval of curriculum changes. Retrieved from North Carolina Community College System website: http://www.nccommunity-colleges.edu/pr/newsreleases/2012/SBCC_August_NewsRelease_FINAL.pdf.

Jacobs, J. (2012). The essential role of community colleges in rebuilding the nation's communities and economies. In J. E. Lane & D. B. Johnstone (Eds.), *Colleges and universities as economic drivers: Measuring higher education's contributions to economic development* (pp. 191–204). Albany: State University of New York Press.

Lancaster, H. M. (1999). North Carolina. In T. A. Tollefson, R. L. Garrett, W. G. Ingram, & Associates, *Fifty state systems of community colleges: Mission, governance, funding and accountability* (pp. 327–342). Johnson City, TN: Overmountain Press.

Mass. Gen. Laws ch. 139, § 46 et seq. An act making appropriations for the fiscal year 2013 for the maintenance of the departments, boards, commissions, institutions and certain activities of the commonwealth, for interest, sinking fund and serial bond requirements and for interest, sinking fund and serial bond requirements and for certain permanent improvements. July 8, 2012.

Manufacturing Institute. (2011). Roadmap to education reform for manufacturing. Retrieved from http://www.themanufacturinginstitute.org/~/media/736409933C084EECB2A307E0814DF757.ashx.

Motta, J. C. (1999). Massachusetts. In T. A. Tollefson, R. L. Garrett, W. G. Ingram, & Associates, *Fifty state systems of community colleges: Mission, governance, funding and accountability* (pp. 213–2121. Johnson City, TN: Overmountain Press.

N.C. Gen. Stat. ch115D art. 1§1 et seq., *Community colleges.* 1963

North Carolina Community College System. (2012a). Code Green Super Curriculum Improvement Project (CIP), new/revised/archived program major titles, approved by State Board of Community Colleges on 08/16/2012 [PDF document]. Retrieved from North Carolina Community College System website: https://www.nccommunitycolleges.edu/programs/docs/Curric_Standards/00%20Cluster%20Stds_Green%20Super%20CIP/Crosswalk.pdf.

North Carolina Community College System. (2012b). Get the facts [HTML document]. Retrieved from North Carolina Community College System website: http://www.nccommunitycolleges.edu/pr/Get_The_Facts/.

Patrick, D. (2012, January 24). Governor Patrick's call for unified community college system receives support from Mayor Menino and business leaders. Retrieved from Governor of Massachusetts website: http://www.mass.gov/governor/pressoffice/pressreleases/2012/2012124-community-college-proposal-support.html.

Rogers, J. (2010, July–August). 2010 rankings report. *Business Facilities.* Retrieved from http://www.businessfacilities.com/Rankings/BFJulAug10_STATE_RANKINGS.PDF.

Shaffer, D. F., & Wright, D. J. (2010). A new paradigm for economic development: How higher education institutions are working to revitalize their regional and state economies. Retrieved from Nelson A. Rockefeller Institute of Government, University at Albany website: http://www.rockinst.org/pdf/education/2010-03-18-A_New_Paradigm.pdf.

Technical College System of Georgia. (2011). Fast facts and college directory, 2011–2012. Retrieved from https://tcsg.edu/download/Fast_Facts_2012.pdf.

Tollefson, T. A., Garrett, R. L., Ingram, W. G., & Associates. (1999). *Fifty state systems of community colleges: Mission, governance, funding and accountability.* Johnson City, TN: Overmountain Press.

Walton, B. B. (1999). Georgia technical institutes. In T. A. Tollefson, R. L. Garrett, W. G. Ingram, & Associates, *Fifty state systems of community colleges: Mission, governance, funding and accountability* (pp. 15–22). Johnson City, TN: Overmountain Press.

Welker, G. (2012, April 12). House panel rebuffs Patrick's plan to overhaul community colleges. *Herald News.* Retrieved from http://www.heraldnews.com/news/x1830126520/BCC-others-oppose-Patricks-plan-to-overhaul-community-colleges.

Workforce Strategy Center. (2008). Bridging business and education for the 21st century workforce: A strategic plan for Virginia's career pathways system. Retrieved from Virginia's Community Colleges website: http://www.vccs.edu/LinkClick.aspx?fileticket=oQCG7Czxv60%3D&tabid=76.

Workforce Strategy Center. (Producer). (2012, October 24). Taking root: The Virginia Career Pathways System [Webinar]. Retrieved from http://www.workforcestrategy.org/media/webinars/124.

# 12

## THE SYSTEMNESS OF INTERNATIONALIZATION STRATEGIES

*How Higher Education Systems Are*
*Aiding Institutions with Globalization*

JASON E. LANE

ABSTRACT

Higher education systems in the United States have historically been domestically focused entities. Very little attention has been given by scholars or practitioners to the role of systems in activities related to the internationalization of higher education. A small number of systems have been quietly engaged in the organization and operations of student exchange and study abroad programs for their constituent campuses since the 1960s and 1970s. However, the growing importance, and associated liabilities, of international activities has prompted a number of systems to create new programs and policies in this area. This chapter reviews five primary areas (i.e., planning, promotion, programs, policies, and policing) in which systems are engaging in internationalization activities and discusses the associated tensions between the system and constituent campuses.

Higher education institutions are being transformed by globalization, which has been increasing the interconnectedness of the world's economies, cultures, governments, and social institutions. Globalization is not a new trend for higher education institutions, which have long supported the flow of students and scholars across borders. Moreover, their core product, knowledge, has rarely been constrained by geopolitical borders, particularly in the era of the Internet. Not all colleges and universities have emerged as international actors; some simply attempt to react to the buffeting winds of change. Others have emerged as key agents in facilitating and harnessing globalization. Indeed, colleges and universities are critical components of social, cultural, and economic development. As the economic and political competition between nations becomes more critical, countries have increasingly turned toward their colleges and universities to help facilitate the movement across borders of people, knowledge, data, technologies, products, and economic capital.

In fact, in many nations, governments have become much more active in promoting and supporting the international activities of their colleges and universities. They have gone so far as to link higher education development to their long-term economic development strategies (Lane & Owens, 2012). They have also increasingly turned to academe as a tool in public diplomacy, to gain influence among nations (Lane, 2013). In the United States, for example, the U.S. Departments of Commerce, Education, and State have become engaged, at varying levels and degrees, in broadly promoting the internationalization of higher education (Hendrickson, Lane, Harris, & Dorman, 2012).[1] Curiously, almost no attention has been given to the role of state governments or their higher education system offices in supporting such international activities by public colleges and universities.

While the federal government has become involved in some internationalization efforts in the United States, primary responsibility for higher education resides within the halls of state capitals. In most states, public higher education institutions are organized into one or more systems intended to help coordinate and regulate the activities of the constituent campuses (see chapter 1). These systems have long been viewed as domestically focused entities, designed to carry out the needs of the state government in regard to regulating, coordinating, and funding the public higher education system. Such structures were generally envisioned as quasi-state agencies, intended to create a bureaucracy that could carry out the desires of elected officials while simultaneously protecting colleges and universities from undue political influence.

Despite this domestic orientation, a growing number of systems have been involved in various international activities for decades.

Both the California State University and the University of California systems created international program offices in the 1960s to coordinate study abroad opportunities for all students in their respective systems (Gerth, 2010). In the 1970s, Oregon's system office assumed responsibility for some multi-institutional study abroad programs. System-level international activity is not limited to study abroad programs, however. The last decade or so has seen an increasing trend toward more systemic engagement in a broad range of activities under the internationalization umbrella. For example, the State University of New York (SUNY) system, which also began system-level study abroad programs in the 1960s, recently launched SUNY-Korea, a system-level initiative to provide constituent campuses the opportunity to deliver some of their academic programs in South Korea (see Back [2012] for the history of SUNY's international engagements).

This recent evolution seems to be propelled by a combination of policy maker concerns about the risks of international engagements, recognition of the economies of scale that can be achieved by system-level coordination, and acknowledgment of the critical link between internationalization and economic development. There remains, however, a glaring gap in the literature on this topic. Those who have written about the formal state system structures have neither addressed, nor acknowledged, the internationally oriented work of systems.

In considering the future of higher education systems and the concept of systemness, one would be remiss if no attention were given to the effects of globalization and what role systems are playing and might yet play in an increasingly interconnected world. The purpose of this chapter is to examine the historical and emerging efforts by higher education systems in the U.S. to deal with globalization, particularly how systems interact with the internationalization activities of constituent campuses. The chapter begins with a brief examination of the literature on systems. A description of system offices and the potential tensions with institutional-level initiatives is discussed. It then examines five primary areas where systems have been engaged in internationalization efforts and concludes with an assessment of the opportunities and obstacles associated with such involvement at the system level.

## SYSTEMS: A DOMESTIC ORIENTATION

Many of the founders of higher education systems likely never envisioned the extent to which globalization would transform the academic enterprise. In fact, most higher education systems in the United States were created long before colleges and universities became significantly involved in international activities and before terms such as *globalization* became part of the vernacular. As McGuinness (chapter 3) observes, the origins of systems are multifaceted, but systems were created to serve very common roles: coordinators, regulators, and allocators. Their attention was to be given mostly to academic programs, ensuring that taxpayer money was wisely invested and unnecessary duplication of programs avoided. As time passed, systems evolved. Some assumed more authority, some less. Recently, though, their general focus and areas of responsibility have expanded.

This is not to suggest that higher education systems were meant to be entirely inwardly focused. They were not. By their very nature, systems were designed to be bridges between the state government and public postsecondary educational institutions. In their study of multi-campus systems, Lee and Bowen (1971) dedicated an entire chapter to the external engagements of higher education systems. However, for them, external engagement largely ended at the state borders, acknowledging that some policy issues will attract system officials all the way to Washington, DC. There was no mention about the world beyond the United States, neither in terms of how international trends may affect systems or that systems may someday have to deal with the international engagements of their constituent campuses. The same omission occurred in their follow-up study on managing the multi-campus system (Lee & Bowen, 1975).

For Lee and Bowen (1971, 1975), external engagement constituted three primary areas: public relations, government relations, and alumni affairs. At the time of their study, the argument for system engagement in such efforts was twofold. First, if system leadership took responsibility for lobbying and public relations, campus heads were freed to focus on the academic core of their institution. Second, if the system took the lead in how issues were presented to the external public, it allowed the system to present a unified vision or argument, rather than legislators and the public having to hear the cacophony of individual requests and arguments from varied campus officials.

As Lee and Bowen (1971) observed, "a university system can—in theory—present a more comprehensive, coordinated account of the programs and problems of its campuses to both political and public audiences than would result from the independent pronouncements of a number of autonomous universities" (p. 329).

Clearly, the world changed after Lee and Bowen (1971, 1975) conducted their studies of state higher education systems. By the 1990s, one would have been hard pressed to find a campus president that was not extensively involved in a wide range of external affairs, including alumni relations, fundraising, community engagement, and lobbying at the state and federal levels. In fact, it is the increasing external engagements at the institutional level—in a broad array of areas—that have been fostering change at the system level. The core of system work remains in the areas of coordination, regulation, and allocation, but the focus has moved out of the academic core. A handful of authors (Johnstone, 1999; McGuinness, 1991; McGuinness, Epper, & Arrendono, 1994) would examine these changing roles of systems, but through a domestically oriented lens.

Nearly 30 years after Lee and Bowen (1971), two new volumes (Gaither, 1999; Richardson, Bracco, Callan, & Finney, 1999) took up the task of examining the development of higher education systems. In the introduction to Gaither's (1999) volume *The Multicampus System*, Lee and Bowen (1999) observed that, in regard to higher education systems, the more things change, the more things stay the same. Their observation was a broad one, but it holds true for the area of internationalization. Inasmuch as their study lacked reference to internationalization activities, so too did the writings of the varied authors included in these latest works. Boatright's (1999) chapter on external affairs was quite similar to that written by Lee and Bowen (1971) nearly three decades earlier, focusing mostly on state-level engagement, though also acknowledging the expanding federal influence with which systems must engage. In a chapter on strategic planning, Norris (1999) recognized the growing pressures being placed on systems by a global knowledge economy. Though, in large part, the chapter focused on online learning modalities, not discussing any type of substantive international engagement.

The lack of recognition of the international activities of systems is likely largely due to the historic lack of engagement of systems in this area. However, as explored throughout this volume, the work of systems is evolving in response to changing economic, political, and social demands. As explored in other chapters, systems are now, more than ever, supporting the work of their campuses in a wide range of areas not discussed in the literature on higher education systems, including economic development and public engagement. Such coordination has also occurred in the area of internationalization. While some systems have operated international program offices since the 1960s, there seems to be a renewed interest in such activities among many state higher education systems.

## SYSTEM OFFICES: TENSIONS AND FUNCTIONS

It seems that systems are perpetually in organizational flux, with administrative offices and programs being added and deleted. This trend is no less true with international programs. At the time of this writing, at least eight state higher education systems had formal international programs offices. This count does not include several other systems that were engaged in coordinating or convening campus international officers, but did not have an official office dedicated to international programs. As can be seen in table 12.1, there is no consistency in what these offices are named. Some take a more functional description in the label, such as international programs or Oregon Abroad. Others capture the tie to the academic program, calling themselves international education offices. A set also uses more modern terms such as *global affairs* and *international relations*, which seem to reflect a broader mission of engagement, reaching beyond academic matters.

Likewise, the areas of responsibility vary considerably among offices. Some offices have a fairly narrow mission, focusing mostly or exclusively on study abroad and international student exchanges. A growing number also seem to be identifying system-level responsibility for supporting or leading international recruitment initiatives. Responsibilities also include facilitating campus coordination in areas of research and academics, promoting the internationalization of the curriculum, and supporting international collaborations by campus faculty.

Any discourse about higher education system offices usually trends toward the tensions between the system and its constituent campuses. In this case, these tensions tend to reside between those

Table 12.1. Sample of System-Level International Offices and Selected Functions

| System | International Office | Selection of Functions |
|---|---|---|
| California State University | International Programs | International Exchange/ Study Abroad |
| Oregon University System | Oregon Abroad | Campus Coordination International Exchange/ Study Abroad |
| State University of New York | Office of Global Affairs | Campus Coordination International Exchange/ Study Abroad International Recruitment International Collaboration Outreach |
| University of California | Education Abroad Program | International Exchange/ Study Abroad |
| University of Massachusetts | International Relations | Campus Coordination Collaboration Outreach Promotion |
| University of North Carolina System | Global Readiness and International Programs | Campus Coordination International Exchange/ Study Abroad Outreach |
| University of Wisconsin System | International Education and Engagement | International Exchange/ Study Abroad |
| University System of Georgia | International Education | Campus Coordination International Exchange/ Study Abroad International Recruitment |

responsible for international activities at each level. Historically, these tensions have not been the same as those in the other areas of academic affairs, as systems have not sought to control or regulate the international activities of the campuses—at least not until recently, and those issues will be addressed later in the chapter. Instead, the tensions tend to have existed in the potential duplication of responsibilities, competition to provide certain programs, and rising demands among smaller campuses for the system to provide the types of programs that only larger institutions can afford to provide on their own.

It seems that there are three primary reasons for systems to become involved in internationalization activities. First, many academic leaders recognize the importance of internationalization in enhancing the intercultural knowledge and appreciation of students. Systems can play an important role in helping campuses become more internationally engaged. Second, systems can provide a level of expertise and an economy of scale that many institutions cannot achieve on their own. Third, governing boards, including those at the system level, are acknowledging the growing risks and complexities of operating internationally and are implementing policies to reduce liability in this area.

As many colleges and universities developed their internationalization strategies without system involvement, the growing engagement of systems in this area can be disconcerting to some institutions, particularly those that believe themselves to be successful in this arena without system engagement. Consequently, systems need to be careful of being overly directive in how institutions should be pursuing internationalization strategies. Moreover, some campuses, particularly the larger ones, have likely developed productive revenue streams via their international engagements and may fear system-level programs that compete with their existing programs. Finally, any new regulations in this area that limit institutional engagements or add another level of oversight, often interpreted as undue bureaucracy, are prone to create tension between institutions and their system office.

While there may be a handful of campuses within a system that have had a long and successful history with internationalization, most campuses are less likely to have the resources to provide the same level of programming or engage in the same type of due diligence that those with more extensive resources might be able to do. Indeed, many smaller campuses are looking to systems to provide study abroad and international exchanges for their students. They may also value having experts to consult as they look to develop their own international engagements. There are a growing number of examples of campuses that agreed to international partnerships without fully being aware of the associated liabilities and eventually needed system assistance in handling problematic situations. Thus, what might look like undue meddling by one campus might be welcomed as added, and needed, support at another.

To be certain, in the same way that alumni are most associated with the ivy walls of their alma mater and not the hallways of a system office, most international engagements are pursued by the faculty and students of the campuses, not the staff of the system office. International students come to attend classes at a campus, not a system. Students who study abroad are augmenting their campus degree. The work of research collaboration occurs between faculty members located at campuses, not between system-level administrators. The internationalization of curriculum is intended to impact student learning, which takes place at the campuses. Thus, while systems may be playing a more active role in supporting and directing internationalization strategies, this involvement must be balanced against the fact that most of the work occurs at the campus level. System engagement in internationalization seems to occur in five primary areas: planning, programs, promotion, policies, and policing.[2]

## Planning, Steering, and Coordination

An important role of system leaders is to provide opportunities for multi-campus coordination and to help steer institutions in a similar direction. As discussed throughout this chapter, in many systems, internationalization activities evolved at the institutional level, resulting in significant overlap among institutional offerings. Moreover, in a time of fiscal austerity, it has become more difficult for institutions and systems to support a large variety of international activities. Systems recognize these issues. Those that have acknowledged the growing importance of internationalization have also realized that the system can play an important role in harnessing the collective efforts of individual institutions in ways that can reduce costs but enhance productivity. To do so, two tools available to systems are the development of advisory or coordinating councils/committees and strategic planning initiatives.

Many systems already have coordinating or advisory councils/committees for discussing a whole host of issues such as distance learning, disability services, and finances. Another topic that is of increasing concern for inter-institutional collaboration and coordination is international programs. In some systems these councils are coordinated by the international programs office; in others they operate in the absence of an international programs office. They tend to be populated by the chief international officer on each campus and provide these leaders with the opportunity to network and collaborate as well as to provide advice to system-level leadership. Such entities can also be a useful way for system-level officers to communicate rationales for system-level decisions regarding internationalization activities.

The existence of a specific office or advisory council oriented toward internationalization activities is not the only way in which a system can influence or help steer the internationalization of its constituent campuses. Many systems have initiated strategic planning efforts. While not all such planning initiatives have focused on issues of internationalization, some have begun to do so. In a review of 38 system-level strategic plans, 12 included a substantive reference to internationalization activities.[3] However, there was no consistency in how these plans engaged with the topic. Two approaches covered by the various plans were system-level international recruitment efforts and enhancing study abroad opportunities (discussed in more depth in the following sections).

While the number of system-level strategic plans that mention internationalization as a priority remains limited, the fact that some acknowledge its importance is another piece of evidence suggesting that there is a growing interest among systems to engage in and support these international programs. Those plans that did include such a focus tended to address student recruitment, student exchanges, and internationalizing the curriculum. Some did include specific goals such as the number of new international students desired to be recruited or the percentage of students to have study abroad experience. The focus largely remains general, but that is mostly a reflection of the purpose of such plans to steer multiple campuses rather than engaging in institutional management.

*Programs: Student Exchanges and Study Abroad*

The movement of students among nations is a key aspect of internationalization. Among the system strategic plans that referenced international activities, providing system students with the opportunity to study in a foreign country is the most common theme. For example, SUNY, the University System of Georgia, and the University of North Carolina (UNC) System all indicated that improving the study abroad opportunities for their students was a priority for the system. USG set forth a specific goal of having at least 25% of their students engage in a study abroad experience by 2012 (at the time of this writing, it was not clear if the goal would be met). SUNY indicated a desire to increase the number of students studying abroad and developed financing programs to help support several thousand students to study abroad annually. Finally, internationalization has been a strategic priority for the UNC system since at least 2007, recognizing the "global readiness" of students to be of importance to the university and the state and recommending that the system "enhance the global competitiveness of its institutions and their graduates" (University of North Carolina, 2007, p. 11). One of the strategies put in place to help students achieve global readiness was to enhance the opportunities to study overseas.

The two primary strategies for systems to support their students to study in another country come from the development of programs such as international student exchanges and other forms of study abroad and providing financing to students to support their studying abroad. Developing student exchange programs is not a new endeavor for systems. Many of the systems in the western part of the United States have engaged in domestic student exchanges, particularly in professional fields such as medical and dental education, where access to such programs does not exist in every state. However, facilitating the recruitment of foreign students and supporting study abroad activities are other key areas of student exchange where systems can use their economy of scale to aid institutional efforts. Foreign student enrollment has been the most active area of international engagement for many systems.

Already, a handful of system efforts are underway in this area. They tend to be designed in two different ways. First, some system offices have created system-level study abroad offices that are designed to support students at all constituent campuses to pursue any number of different opportunities to study outside their home country. One of the oldest such programs, created in 1963, is the International Programs (IP) office of the California State University (CSU) system.

Since its inception, CSU has provided more than 15,000 system students with the opportunity to study abroad in 18 different countries. The system office coordinates with campus-level international offices, with the system office organizing year-long programs while the institutional offices primarily focus on shorter-term options. The Oregon University System operates a similar office, Oregon Abroad. Unlike the CSU programs, which are geared only toward system students, Oregon Abroad is available to any student in the state, regardless of whether the student attends a public or private institution. Oregon Abroad also provides a wide range of programs, including overseas internship opportunities that have placed more than 1,500 students in internships in 82 countries since 1996.[4]

A second approach is for systems to establish system-to-system or state-to-state (or country) exchange programs. For example, the University of Maine System (UMS) established the Partnership Maine-France to facilitate the exchange of both students and faculty among the seven UMS campuses and eight French institutions.[5] This program supports Maine students to engage in academic and research activities in France and enables French students to study in Maine. California State University has an agreement with the German state of Baden-Württemberg that facilitates the movement of students among the 23 CSU campuses and the 21 colleges and universities in Baden-Württemberg. Similarly, in 2001, SUNY entered into an agreement with the Turkish Higher Education Council (YOK), which allows Turkish students to pursue dual-degree programs by taking courses at their home institution in Turkey and one of the SUNY campuses.[6]

In terms of funding, a few systems have adopted funding mechanisms to help students study abroad. The University System of Georgia created the Students Abroad with Regents' Support (STARS) program, which provides matching grants to institutions to hire students on campus to help fund their study abroad experience. In a second example, the University of Maine System and Maine Community College System established the George J. Mitchell Peace Scholarship to honor the former U.S. senator from Maine and provide students with financial support to pursue part of their studies in Ireland. SUNY has developed a model to pool institutional resources to help disadvantaged students pursue study abroad opportunities. With their Global Reinvestment Fund, SUNY campuses that choose to participate in the system recruitment plan (discussed later) agree to contribute 18% of their first year of tuition revenues generated from the students recruited via system initiatives to provide funding for disadvantaged students to study overseas.

## Promotion, Research, and Recruitment

As institutions look to expand their global engagements, systems can provide an important function in helping to promote and market the system and constituent campuses in overseas markets as well as provide infrastructure to support campuses' international recruitment efforts. Some campuses, particularly those considered flagships, already have expansive reputations and international engagements and may see little benefit in being part of a system. However, for some campuses, particularly those that may not have widespread international reputations or engagements, being part of a system with a well-recognized name (e.g., University of California, University of North Carolina, or the State University of New York) can enhance their recognition among potential international partners. Potential partners may not have specific knowledge about their campus, but the system association can help attract attention and enhance legitimacy.

In addition to this more passive associational benefit, systems have also taken three more active approaches to promoting the system in the international context: membership with international organizations, outreach offices and partnership frameworks in foreign countries, and provision of recruitment infrastructure. The international education marketplace is becoming increasingly complex, and it is nearly impossible for any one institution or system to be fully aware of all the changing dynamics in different countries. Governments constantly change regulations and begin and end various funding programs. There are now several international organizations that provide research and analysis in international contexts as well as opportunities for international networking. The membership cost of many of these organizations is often quite expensive, and it may be difficult for any one institution to join these groups. Rather than leaving it up to the individual campuses, some systems now cover the cost of the membership, allowing their campuses to benefit from their resources and meetings/conferences. For example, the Observatory for Borderless Higher Education in the United Kingdom does research for its members on various forms of cross-border higher education around the world. Systems can also join the Organisation for Economic Co-operation and Development's (OECD) higher education program (Institutional Management in Higher Education [IMHE]). IMHE members get access to all the research and data collected by the OECD as well as reduced costs for attending their conference and workshops. These are only two of a myriad of organizations that systems could join to provide additional research and networking resources to campuses.

A second option is for systems to establish outreach offices in or create partnership frameworks with foreign countries. More than supporting the exchange of students, these initiatives are a way to promote the system in the foreign country and provide campuses with a framework for engaging in a wide variety of international partnerships. For example, the University of Massachusetts System has created partnership frameworks in China, Germany, Liberia, and South Africa. Each framework is country specific but allows for campuses and the faculty to engage and collaborate with faculty at institutions in each partner country. Another approach, which has been adopted by SUNY, is to establish outreach offices in strategic locations around the world (e.g., Mexico, Russia, and Turkey). These offices are intended to help develop and sustain a wide range of academic and research partnerships for the system and constituent campuses.

Finally, recruitment of students has been an area of much concern, but little activity, of most system offices. It has been largely left to the purview of the individual campuses. However, the international marketplace is vast and increasingly competitive. To provide support for campuses with limited recruitment budgets and to help campuses navigate the complexities of international recruitment, many systems are developing support structures to aid their campuses. For example, both the University of Colorado System and SUNY have implemented specific plans to increase the number of international students on their campuses. *The Power of SUNY*, the system's strategic plan, suggests that "By internationalizing the campus environment and the classroom, and by making the opportunity for education abroad available to all, we will send out 'global-ready' graduates whose efforts over the course of their careers will effectively secure New York State's central role in the global economy" (State University of New York, 2012, p. 42). The plan sets a goal of increasing the number of international students studying in the system by several thousand within five years. To achieve this goal, the plan set forth a series of exchange programs, promotional campaigns, and other initiatives to support the recruitment efforts of campuses.

Recognizing a one-size-fits-all approach would not work in the SUNY environment, the Office of Global Affairs established an opt-in recruitment program. The system agrees to identify and vet recruitment agents in overseas student markets to help campuses increase their international student recruitment. In return, the participating campuses agree to return 18% of each new international student's first-year tuition to the system. That money is then used to pay the agent fees and to reinvest in the system's international support infrastructure. As the complexities of international recruitment continue to expand, it is likely that more systems will develop mechanisms to support the international recruitment of students.

## Policies and Policing

Regardless of the level of or motivation for internationalization, such activities come with a long list of potential risks—from threats to quality of academic programming to financial losses to the safety and health of students, faculty, and staff traveling overseas. The final two areas of system engagement in internationalization activities, therefore, are policy development and the policing of the international activities of constituent campuses. While two distinct functions, it is difficult to discuss policies and policing separately. A traditional role of systems has been to provide oversight of the activities, particularly those within the academic core, of the constituent campuses. The authority of systems varies significantly in this respect, ranging from reviewing and commenting on new academic program proposals to having final approval of new programs and being able to review their long-term viability. However, the premise remains that a core function of systems remains oversight of the academic offerings across the state. The attention that systems have paid to this area of responsibility has long been bereft of international engagements. At times, such programs have operated under the radar and out of sight of system officials. At other times, systems have not established any policies relating to international engagements, particularly as such efforts have historically accounted for only a very small fraction of institutional activities.

Over the last two decades, these arrangements have begun to change significantly, with two high-profile events drawing the issue to the attention of the public (and system administration). In early spring of 2012, two very complicated situations brought a new focus to the role of systems in overseeing the international activities of their component institutions. First, Dickinson State University, part of the North Dakota University System, was slighted in an audit for operating a diploma-mill-like program for hundreds of international students (Donovan, 2012). The audit determined that the institution awarded degrees to these students without having completed all official degree requirements. Indeed, many did not even have a basic level of English proficiency. In a second example, which caught media attention just a week later, the *New York Times* raised several questions about the overseas activities of SUNY's Empire State College (Guttenplan, 2012).[7] The article reported that Empire State was partnering with the University of New York, Tirana (a privately held company in Albania) to offer degree-granting academic programs to students in Albania. The investigation by the *Times* suggested that the students may have been misled by advertising, some faculty were not approved by Empire State, and some of the courses were of poor quality. The truth behind these situations is likely far more complex than has been reported, but the actions of these institutions, both part of public, multi-campus systems, raise questions about the appropriate role of systems in overseeing the international activities of institutions.

Risks are an inherent part of most internationalization activities. Whether the activity involves study abroad, opening an overseas campus to serve foreign students, supporting faculty in international collaborations, or operating educational outposts overseas, institutions assume some form of liability. This liability varies from personal safety of those involved to assuring the quality of the programs and services being offered. In many systems, the international activities of constituent campuses have often happened below the radar. In fact, most institutions are not even aware of the full scope of the international engagements of their faculty and various offices.

At present, system-level oversight seems to be occurring in three main areas. First, systems may regulate the travel of students and staff abroad. In some cases, policies may pertain only to mandating the type of insurance needed for the students and staff traveling abroad. Such requirements are meant to protect the travelers should something go wrong while overseas. Some systems also provide evacuation insurance for the entire system, should anyone on campus or system business be caught in a dangerous situation. Some regulations may go so far as to limit the location of study abroad engagements. For example, the California State University does not allow programs in countries where the U.S. Department of State has issued a travel warning. Some policies may also specify that institutions must notify local officials and comply with local regulations where the programs are held.

Second, systems are also interested in how campuses handle international students studying within the system. Systems will often establish policies related to the cost of tuition and fees for international students as well as some minimum requirements such as the type of previous academic study or the level of English proficiency. The State University System of Florida has mandated that children of illegal immigrants may not be eligible for in-state tuition rates, although this may be amended following a recent court ruling (Weaver, 2012).

Third, there is a growing interest in the quality assurance of international programs. For example, systems such as Florida's State University System, SUNY, and the California State University all require that the system review and approve the offering of degree programs in a foreign country. Operating overseas programs can be complicated and difficult (Lane & Kinser, 2011). The reason for such system-level oversight is recognition of the growing number of international activities and the fact that many constituent campuses do not have the staffing or expertise to fully vet the potential dangers of extensive international engagements such as student exchanges and opening offshore academic programs. The expertise at the system level can help spot potential dangers and help institutions get out of difficult situations.

## CONCLUSION

While a very few system have had international programs offices since the 1960s and 1970s, the past two decades have witnessed an expansion in the system-level engagement in international affairs. These engagements are largely in the areas of planning, programs, promotion, policies, and policing. While some systems have gone so far as to create the system-level international programs offices, others have only engaged in policy development or supporting coordinating councils or committees.

There are many reasons why a system may be involved in internationalization. Rather than have many individual institutions provide largely duplicative programs, systems can benefit from an economy of scale that may allow them to provide programing at per-student cost lower than what institutions can manage. In times of fiscal austerity when campuses are looking for ways to reduce costs, systems could be an answer in the area of internationalization. However, this is not to argue that all campuses will want to give up their programs to a system office; but those that do could see some financial benefits. Moreover, the world is becoming an increasingly complex and risky place to engage internationally. Systems may be able to provide the expertise, support structures, and stability that allow campuses to safely pursue their international engagements. Concerns about liability and threats to quality control have also led some systems to implement policies expanding their oversight of such endeavors. And, it is very likely that systems will become increasingly engaged in internationalization efforts.

This growing system engagement, however, must be balanced against the real fact that most international activities occur at the campus level. In fact, the internationalization of higher education in the United States has largely been a grassroots-led phenomenon. And, it is an increasingly widespread phenomenon. All institutions, from community colleges to large research universities, are being affected by the increasing economic, political, cultural, and academic interconnectedness of the world. Some institutions struggle to respond to their environments while others are purposefully planning ways to expand their global footprint by creating outposts in foreign countries. Faculty and students are at the heart of most international engagements, and systems need to be wary that their efforts not curtail or quash such efforts.

## NOTES

The author would like to thank Leo Van Cleve, California State University; Paul Primak, Oregon University System; Mitch Leventhal and Sally Crimmins Villela, State University of New York; and Jan

Ignash, Florida State University System, for their insights about system engagements in international activities. Patrick Ziegler provided critical research support. Any errors or omissions remain the sole responsibility of the author.

1. Internationalization of higher education is "the process of integrating an international, intercultural, and global dimension into the purpose, functions (teaching, research, services) and the delivery of postsecondary education" (Knight, 2003, p. 2).
2. Thanks to Leo Van Cleve, director of international programs at California State University, for suggesting some of these labels for system functions. These areas are described in more depth in the following sections.
3. Arizona Board of Regents, 2010; California State University System, 2008; City University of New York, 2008; Colorado State University System, 2005, revised 2010; Idaho State Board of Education, 2010; Iowa Board of Regents, 2010; Kansas Board of Regents, 2010; Louisiana State University System, 2011; Minnesota State College and Universities, 2010; Mississippi Institutions of Higher Learning, 2011; Montana University System, 2012; Nevada System of Higher Education, 2010; North Dakota University System, 2009; Oregon University System, 2006; Pennsylvania State System of Higher Education, 2010; Rhode Island Board of Governors for Higher Education, 2005; Southern Illinois University System, 2012; State University of New York, 2012; State University System of Florida, 2011; Tennessee Board of Regents, 2010; Texas A&M University, 2009; University of Alaska System, 2003, revised 2009; University of Colorado System, 2010; University of Hawaii System, 2002, reaffirmed 2008; University of Louisiana System, 2011; University of Maine System, 2004, revised 2006; University of Nebraska System, 2010; University of North Carolina, 2004, revised 2006; University of North Texas System, 2011; University of Tennessee System, 2012; University of Texas System, 2006; University of Wisconsin System, 2009; University System of Georgia, 2010; University System of Maryland, 2010; University System of New Hampshire, 2011; University System of Ohio, 2008; Vermont State Colleges, 2008; West Virginia Higher Education Policy Commission, 2007.
4. The program is called IE$_3$ or International Education, Experience, and Employment global internship program.

5. University of Angers, University of Maine in Le Mans, University of Nantes, University of Western Brittany, Le Mans Fine Art School, the Teacher Formation Institute for the Lille Region and for the Loire Region, and Theories-Didactique de la Lecture-Écriture (THÉODILE)—an Interdisciplinary Research Group focused on the teaching of reading and writing.

6. Each degree program has been worked out between the two awarding departments. They determine together the requirements and the sequence of the courses on each side.

7. These cases should not be viewed as equally egregious. The Dickinson State audit found clear evidence of academic fraud, while the *New York Times* article mainly raised concerns about internal quality control procedures at Empire State. However, both situations captured the media spotlight in close proximity to each other and brought new attention to the question of what role systems should play in the internationalization activities of their constituent campuses.

## REFERENCES

Back, K. (2012). SUNY's strategic role in international education. In W. B. Leslie, J. B. Clark, & K. P. O'Brien (Eds.), *SUNY at sixty* (pp. 256–267). Albany: State University of New York Press.

Boatright, K. J. (1999). Many voices, one choice: Managing external affairs. In G. H. Gaither, (Ed.), *The multicampus system: Perspectives on practice and prospects* (pp. 21–39). Sterling, WV: Stylus Press.

Donovan, L. (2012, February 11). Violations found in Dickinson State University's foreign student program. *Bismarck Tribune*. Retrieved from http://bismarcktribune.com/news/state-and-regional/violations-found-in-dickinson-state-university-s-foreign-student-program/article_2a062be0-5455-11e1-8f8c-0019bb2963f4.html.

Gaither, G. H. (Ed.). (1999). *The multicampus system: Perspectives on practice and prospects*. Sterling, WV: Stylus Press.

Gerth, D. R. (2010). *The people's university: A history of the California State University*. Berkeley, CA: Berkeley Public Policy Press.

Guttenplan, D. D. (2012, March 12). An Albanian college, relying on U.S. cachet. *New York Times*. Retrieved from http://query.nytimes.com/gst/fullpage.html?res=9402E6DF1F3AF933A1575 0C0A9649D8B63.

Hendrickson, R. M., Lane, J. E., Harris, J. T., & Dorman, R. H. (2012). *Academic leadership and governance of higher education: A guide for trustees, leaders, and aspiring leaders of two- and four-year institutions*. Henderson, VA: Stylus Press.

Johnstone, D. B. (1999). Management and leadership challenges of multicampus systems. In G. H. Gaither (Ed.), *The multicampus system: Perspectives on practice and prospects* (pp. XX–XX). Sterling, WV: Stylus Press.

Knight, J. (2003). Updated internationalization definition. *International Higher Education, 33*, 2–3.

Lane, J. E. (2012). Higher education and international relations: A (very) brief overview of governmental strategies. White Paper presented at the Collaborative on Higher Education and International Relations Colloquium, Albany, New York.

Lane, J. E. (2013). Why governments should care about the internationalization of higher education. In M. Larinova & O. Perfilieva (Eds.), *Rationales for internationalization* (pp. 139–160). Moscow: Logos Publishing House. [Published in Russian.]

Lane, J. E., & Kinser, K. (Eds.). (2011). *Multi-national colleges and universities: Leadership, administration, and governance of international branch campuses*. San Francisco, CA: Jossey-Bass.

Lane, J. E., & Owens, T. (2012). The international dimensions of economic development. In J. E. Lane & D. B. Johnstone (Eds.), *Colleges and universities as economic drivers: Measuring and building success* (pp. 205–238). Albany: State University of New York Press.

Lee, E. C., & Bowen, F. M. (1971). *The multi-campus university: A study of academic governance*. New York, NY: McGraw-Hill.

Lee, E. C., & Bowen, F. M. (1975). *Managing multi-campus systems: Effective administration in an unsteady state*. San Francisco, CA: Jossey-Bass.

Lee, E. C., & Bowen, F. (1999). Introduction. In G. H. Gaither (Ed.), *The multicampus system: Perspectives on practice and prospects* (pp. ix–xvii). Sterling, WV: Stylus Press.

McGuinness, A. C. (1991). *Perspectives on the current status of and emerging policy issues for public multicampus higher education systems* (AGB Occasional Paper No. 3). Washington, DC: Association of Governing Boards of Universities and Colleges.

McGuinness, A. C., Epper, R. M., & Arrendono, S. (1994). *State postsecondary education structures handbook*. Denver, CO: Education Commission of the States.

Norris, D. M. (1999). Systemwide strategic planning in the knowledge age. In G. H. Gaither (Ed.), *The multicampus system: Perspectives on practice and prospects* (pp. 98–110). Sterling, WV: Stylus Press.

Richardson, R. C., Jr., Bracco, K. R., Callan, P. M., & Finney, J. E. (1999). *Designing state higher education systems for a new century*. Phoenix, AZ: Oryx Press.

Richardson, R. C., Jr., & Martinez, M. (2009). *Policy and performance in American higher education: An examination of cases across state systems*. Baltimore, MD: Johns Hopkins University Press.

State University of New York. (2012). *Delivering on our promise: The power of SUNY*. Albany, NY: Author.

University of North Carolina. (2007). University of North Carolina Tower Commission Report. Chapel Hill, NC: Author.

Weaver, J. (2012, September 4). Federal judge rules state cannot treat some Florida students as non-residents and charge higher tuition. *Miami Herald*. Retrieved from http://www.miamiherald.com/2012/09/04/v-fullstory/2984156/judge-fla-cannot-charge-students.html

# 13

## HIGHER EDUCATION SYSTEMS IN AN ERA OF PUBLIC ENGAGEMENT

*An Organizational Learning Perspective*

DAVID J. WEERTS

ABSTRACT

The higher education landscape is changing as economic, political, and technological forces reshape purposes, policies, and practices in higher education. In this context, a national movement has emerged to reenvision the civic roles and responsibilities of colleges and universities. This chapter explores how traditional missions, roles, and structures of higher education systems might be redesigned to facilitate public engagement among campuses and statewide partners. An organizational learning model is advanced, shifting systems from their traditional roles as regulators and assessors to serving as a resource, coach, and catalyst in leading a public agenda for higher education. In making this transition, the rational and strategic models that have characterized systems in the past are fortified by flexible holographic designs that support innovation and responsiveness to changing state needs. A case example of the State University System of Florida is analyzed through the organizational learning perspective.

Public colleges and universities are facing uncertain times as economic, political, and technological forces reshape purposes, policies, and practices in higher education. On the financial front, mountains of commentaries, reports, and scholarly articles have documented the relative decline in state support for public colleges and universities over the past 30 years. While state spending on higher education increased by $10.5 billion in absolute terms from 1990 to 2010, in relative terms, state funding of higher education declined. Real funding per public full-time equivalent (FTE) student dropped by 26.1% from 1990–1991 to 2009–2010 (Quinterno, 2012).

Alongside these financial changes is increased scrutiny about performance and affordability of colleges and universities, fueled by growing skepticism about the ability and interest among institutions to control costs (Immerwahr, Johnson, Ott, & Rochkind, 2010). In this context, disruptive start-up organizations are challenging traditional models of higher education and promise to create more efficient, accessible systems to address the country's growing workforce needs (Christensen, Horn, Soares, & Caldera, 2011).

The preceding paragraphs provide a glimpse into how the higher education landscape is shifting in fundamental ways, reflecting a rapidly changing world with new needs and challenges. These challenges present an opportunity to ask larger questions about the role of higher education systems in this emerging context. The purpose of this chapter is to pose these larger questions and examine how higher education systems might be redesigned to leverage the unique assets of colleges and universities to address the most pressing needs of their states. In doing so, this chapter challenges long-standing assumptions that have guided higher education systems in the past, offering a new model to help systems better address statewide priorities.

This chapter is organized into four sections. First, the chapter begins with a brief critique of higher education systems, discussing the limits of their current roles, structures, and practices. Second, the civic engagement movement in higher education is introduced as a framework to reconsider purposes, philosophies, and practices of higher education systems in response to these limitations. Third, the concept of organizational learning is advanced as a means to reorganize higher education systems in relation to the civic engagement framework. Finally, the chapter concludes with a case example of how these concepts might be applied in a statewide context.

## THE CHANGE IMPERATIVE: HIGHER EDUCATION
## IN A TIME OF TRANSITION

In his informative chapter, "The States and Higher Education," National Center for Higher Education Management Systems (NCHEMS) senior policy analyst Aims McGuinness (2011) explained that state-level governing boards and systems were historically focused on rational planning, which emphasized centralized control, regulation, and maintaining institutional capacity. Among the limits of this model, one-size-fits-all policies were developed that impeded institutional efforts to address unique regional needs of states.

Over the last two decades, systems have become more strategic—a move that corresponds with the rise of the accountability agenda, which emphasizes the needs of clients (students/learners, employers)—and new management tools to achieve desired ends (McGuinness, 2011). Systems have further evolved with a focus on developing a *public agenda* for their states, with the main purpose being to align higher education with state educational, social, and economic needs (see Lane, 2008; Davies, 2006). These statewide agendas have primarily focused on producing qualified graduates commensurate with state workforce needs.

Despite their evolution in design and function since the 1960s, higher education systems continue to be plagued by many intractable problems. State structures, regulatory procedures, and politics continue to create barriers to collaboration to address common issues. Furthermore, turnover of system leadership is high, and deficits in analytic capabilities preclude data-driven decision making. Above all, boards are still stuck in the regulatory practices developed in the 1970s and misguidedly focus their efforts on coordinating institutions rather than leading a public agenda for higher education (McGuinness, 2011). As such, "there is 'no one at home' when it comes to the responsibility to articulate and defend basic public purposes [of higher education]" (McGuinness, 2011, p. 164). McGuinness summarized his concerns about systems and their capability to meet new demands and leadership imperatives in the future:

Many of the state structures formed for other purposes in an earlier time cannot be expected to make the transition to new missions and modes of leadership. New thinking is needed about the ways states can shape decision-making structures and policies designed explicitly for new missions and functions. Crafting new alternatives must be a shared responsibility of both higher education and state leaders. (p. 165)

Inherent in McGuinness's (2011) provocative chapter is a challenge for educational leaders, policy makers, and scholars to disrupt prevailing assumptions about the purposes, functions, and value of higher education systems. This enterprise requires policy makers and system leaders to reframe guiding questions about the purposes of systems in relation to the rapidly changing needs of our society. To make such a leap, it is necessary to explore briefly the current narratives that guide the work of higher education systems.

A review of the top policy issues facing higher education today reveals that productivity (degree production and cost) and college completion remain the most salient policy objectives among lawmakers. Governance reform in relationship to these goals is a top priority (American Association of State Colleges and Universities, 2012). Commensurate with these objectives, systems are designed with the primary aim of helping member institutions produce more degrees in the most efficient manner. While such goals have merit, adhering exclusively to these objectives impedes the ability of leaders to think differently about decision-making structures and policies relative to statewide needs and challenges.

If defending the basic public purposes of higher education is to become a primary contribution of systems, policy makers and leaders must ask new, bold questions that interrogate the core purposes of higher education in a democratic society. Thus, instead of asking, "How can our higher education system help colleges produce more degrees in the most efficient manner?" broader questions must be asked, such as, "What are the most pressing needs, challenges, and opportunities facing our communities, nation, and society as a whole? What are the roles of higher education systems in supporting campuses to be instruments in addressing these challenges and opportunities? How might systems be redesigned to become brokers, catalysts, and agents in meeting these needs and opportunities?" Guided by these larger questions, the next section introduces the civic movement in higher education as a lens for envisioning new scenarios and reframing purposes, structures, and practices of higher education systems.

## THE CIVIC ENGAGEMENT MOVEMENT
## IN HIGHER EDUCATION

The growth and momentum of the civic movement in higher education over the past two decades provides important insights into how higher education systems might evolve in the future. During the 1980s, several factors coalesced to launch a national conversation about the civic roles of colleges and universities. Throughout this era, colleges and universities had increasing difficulty in explaining themselves to external audiences because they had drifted in character and mission (Thelin, 2004). Once viewed as the answer to poverty, racism, and other social ills, higher education had come to be viewed as wasteful, overpriced, and failing to deliver on its promises (St. John & Parsons, 2004). Furthermore, students were increasingly regarded as customers, and their overall levels of volunteerism and civic involvement diminished. An emphasis on earnings—the private benefits of higher education—defined the primary value of going to college (Hartley, 2009).

In an attempt to reverse these trends, dozens of initiatives were launched by networks of higher education practitioners and scholars to reclaim the civic missions of colleges and universities. Among them, Campus Compact, a coalition of campuses supporting the civic roles of higher education, was launched by three presidents in 1985. As of 2008, Campus Compact had grown to over 1,100 members, representing a quarter of all higher education institutions (Hartley, 2009). Fueling this civic resurgence were several reports and scholarly works that declared civic engagement to be a salient feature of 21st-century higher education. Within the land-grant institutions, the Kellogg Commission on the Future of State and Land-Grant Universities called on public research universities to become more productively engaged with the communities that they serve (Kellogg Commission, 1999) while the American Association of State Colleges and Universities (AACSU) challenged regional institutions to step forward as "stewards of place" (American Association of State Colleges and

Universities, 2002). *Scholarship Reconsidered* (Boyer, 1990), *Scholarship Assessed* (Glassick, Huber, & Maeroff, 1997), and *Making the Case for Professional Service* (Lynton, 1995) remain influential works that paved the way for rethinking how academic work might be more intimately connected with societal needs (Knox, 2001).

As the movement has grown, educational leaders, practitioners, and scholars have framed the civic responsibilities of colleges in nuanced ways. Many have focused on educating for democracy, which primarily aims to prepare students for participation in a democratic society (see Hartley, 2009). This view is illustrated in a recent report commissioned by the U.S. Department of Education, *A Crucible Moment: College Learning and Democracy's Future*, which largely focused on how students are educated in relation to civic competencies and attitudes (Association of American Colleges and Universities, 2012). Other leaders have taken a broader institutional view, exploring how civic engagement might be embedded in teaching, research, and service on campuses (see Fitzgerald, Burak, & Seifer, 2010; Furco, 2010). Within this perspective, a growing number of urban colleges and universities have embraced their roles as "anchor institutions" by leveraging their unique assets to promote economic development in their communities. The University of Pennsylvania is an example of an institution that has embraced this role, transforming itself in response to the social and economic needs of West Philadelphia (Rodin, 2007).

Leaders in the field often refer to such work as "community" or "public" engagement, which is defined by the Carnegie Foundation for the Advancement of Teaching (n.d.) as the "collaboration between institutions of higher education and their larger communities (local, regional/state, national, global) for the mutually beneficial exchange of knowledge and resources in a context of partnership and reciprocity." The phrase *public engagement* is distinctive from traditional definitions of service and outreach, which traditionally emphasize a "one-way" approach to delivering knowledge and service to the public. Instead, engagement emphasizes a "two-way" approach in which institutions and community partners collaborate to develop and apply knowledge to address societal needs (Weerts & Sandmann, 2008).

Public engagement provides a compelling new lens to look at the role of systems, since the approach advances the goals of policy makers, systems, and institutions. For example, research has suggested that students participating in engaged teaching and learning experiences such as service-learning programs are more likely to persist in and graduate from college (Astin & Sax, 1998; Roose et al., 1997). Furthermore, studies have shown that community-based organizations value the labor and resources provided by student service learners (Bloudin & Perry, 2009) along with the fresh perspectives, skills, commitment, and energy that they provide (Gelmon, Holland, & Shinnamon, 1998; Vernon & Ward, 1999). Faculty involved in community partnerships are also valued as they contribute expertise, leverage grant opportunities, provide access to facilities, and serve on advisory boards (Leiderman, Furco, Zapf, & Goss, 2003).

In the realm of research, engagement as a mode of inquiry also enhances the quality and utility of scholarship. Specifically, involving stakeholders in developing directions for research helps scholars develop important lines of inquiry that may not have been considered in a traditional setting. Stakeholder input challenges researchers to think differently about traditional theoretical frameworks and interpretation of their findings. As such, engaged scholarship provides scholars with expanded opportunities to test theory with practice, resulting in improved quality of work and greater likelihood of developing innovative solutions to societal problems (see Peters, Jordan, Adamek, & Alter, 2005). When designed properly, scholarship embedded in community issues is equally as rigorous and high quality as traditional research (Boyer, 1996).

Public engagement also expands opportunities for resource generation among public and private sources. One study, for example, showed that campuses that received larger than expected levels of state appropriations during the 1990s had developed a positive perception with state officials related to their commitment to service and outreach (Weerts & Ronca, 2006). A recent follow-up study supported these findings, suggesting that institutions that commit to "boots on the ground" engagement with community and industry leaders can mobilize political forces to support their campuses financially (Weerts, 2010). In the domain of private support, engagement also has the potential to attract private investment in higher education. Strickland's (2007) historical analysis of giving to higher education revealed that today's transformational donors are interested in building communities, not institutions as they did in the past. Rather, today's donors invest in issues and expect results (Grace & Wendroff, 2001), which provides engaged institutions with increased opportunities to raise private support in relation to public interests (Weerts, 2007).

Due to these promising outcomes emanating from the civic movement, there is significant momentum for public engagement across the nation. In 2006, the Carnegie Foundation created an elective classification system recognizing campuses by their commitment to community/public engagement via curricular and community partnerships (Carnegie Foundation, n.d.). The work of the Carnegie Foundation has brought national attention to engagement and has served to legitimize this work nationwide. Furthermore, regional accreditation bodies are increasingly supportive of public engagement and are beginning to include indicators of engagement in their assessments of institutional quality (Sandmann, Williams, & Abrams, 2009). Collectively, all these forces are revitalizing the civic missions of colleges and universities.

## HIGHER EDUCATION SYSTEMS IN AN ERA OF PUBLIC ENGAGEMENT

As the preceding discussion illustrates, several entities are coalescing to redesign reward systems, organizational structures, and teaching and learning strategies to reflect the values and philosophy of public engagement. These collaborative efforts show several promising results related to college completion, positive changes in communities, and enhanced revenue opportunities for colleges and universities. Noticeably absent in this national movement is a discussion about the role that higher education systems might play to facilitate this progress. Even the "public agenda" language that emerged in the 1990s focused almost exclusively on degree production in relation to workforce needs (see Davies, 2006). While this aim of systems is important, such a narrow conceptualization ignores higher education's larger role in improving our democracy and quality of life, which is central to the goals of engagement.

In broadening our view of systems through the lens of public engagement, several questions must be considered: What role, if any, might higher education systems play in facilitating engagement among communities and institutions? What might an "engaged" higher education system look like in structure and practice? What challenges and opportunities may exist for higher education systems that become brokers and catalysts for campus-community engagement?

## DIFFERENT PHILOSOPHY, DIFFERENT STRUCTURE

Envisioning higher education systems through the lens of engagement requires thinking about them in fundamentally different ways. First, higher education systems must be reconceptualized as open systems that are energized and nourished by their environment (see Scott, 1992). This perspective is a significant departure from the past, since state-level governing boards and systems have historically functioned as hierarchical, closed systems. Closed systems are typically insulated and detached from outside influences, which limits their ability to respond to stakeholder feedback and emerging needs. Today, the vestiges of these structural elements create problems for designing dynamic, two-way relationships with communities (McGuinness, 2011).

Second, the philosophy of engagement represents a significant shift in philosophy about the purposes of the academy and its relationship to the public. Traditionally, higher education was founded on the idea that knowledge was produced by the university and disseminated to users—primarily students and the public at large (Roper & Hirth, 2005). From this view, knowledge was largely viewed as a commodity that could be transferred from a knowledge producer to a user (National Center for the Dissemination of Disability Research, 1996). Higher education systems were built on this model, since they largely served to facilitate the delivery of knowledge from institutions to students. Systems that have become more strategic over time still frame learners as clients to serve rather than partners in discovery to address public problems. This view limits higher education to a one-way dissemination paradigm.

Moving toward a two-way philosophy of public engagement shifts this perspective considerably. Unlike the one-way dissemination paradigm, the two-way paradigm anchors engagement in the notion that the knowledge process is local, complex, and dynamic, not produced exclusively by experts in the academy. From this view, learning and systemic change takes place in a context where knowledge is applied (Hood, 2002). To summarize, higher education as a sector has historically been designed to fill students with knowledge ("filling an empty vessel" metaphor). Alternatively, engagement focuses on colleges and universities that create shared venues for faculty, students, and stakeholders to address public problems ("community of learners" metaphor). Hutchinson and Huberman's (1993) work illustrates how the conceptualizations of knowledge flow from inside to outside the academy in the context of science education.[1]

Finally, the engagement philosophy challenges the notion that simply producing more graduates more efficiently will sufficiently fulfill the wishes of policy makers and the general public. Instead, the engagement perspective emphasizes that systemic change in states and communities remains the salient interest of lawmakers and the public. This view is supported in St. John and Parsons's (2004) book, *Public Funding of Higher Education: Changing Contexts and New Rationales*. In short, the authors point out that throughout the 1960s, higher education was uniformly viewed as the key to individual prosperity, strong communities, and strong economies. However, this view is no longer widely accepted since inequality and other social and economic problems persist in the wake of significant investment in higher education. Acknowledging the new politics of higher education, the engagement model provides a contemporary framework for systems to broaden their focus on leading broad-based community change rather than solely increasing degree production toward these ends.

## SYSTEMS RECONSIDERED: PUBLIC ENGAGEMENT AND EMERGING ROLES FOR HIGHER EDUCATION SYSTEMS

The prior sections articulated the many challenges and opportunities associated with adopting an engagement model within today's higher education systems. For systems to make this transition, I posit that systems must move from the rational/strategic organizational model to an organizational learning model. Embedded in an open-systems view, the central premise of the organizational learning perspective is that organizations must go beyond being *adaptive* in responding to trends. Rather, they must be *generative* in creating new contexts and opportunities in which the organization will thrive. Central to these ideas are the concepts of single- and double-loop learning developed by Argyris and Schön (1978). Briefly summarized, single-loop learning refers to responding to problems within a given set of established norms, while double-loop learning addresses problems in ways that challenge underlying norms, policies, and objectives. Consequently, double-loop learning requires scanning changes in the environment to envision new patterns and opportunities. Double-loop thinking is where innovation occurs (Senge, 1990).

The organizational learning perspective applies well to thinking about higher education systems through the lens of public engagement. This perspective illuminates the fact that systems are currently entrenched in single-loop patterns. With efficiency and degree production as the salient purposes of today's higher education systems, systems almost exclusively focus their efforts on improving completion rates, facilitating transfer, and eliminating duplication among campuses. Moving to a double-loop perspective would challenge system leaders to create innovative strategies that align knowledge enterprises to create a better future for the state. In this realm, the central role of higher education systems leaders would be to create avenues for generative thinking and action related to a public agenda for their states, broadly defined. It is in this larger context that degree production and college performance would be processed and evaluated. Reorienting systems in this fashion would disrupt underlying norms, policies, and objectives that may thwart the emergence of new ways of thinking in relation to state goals. Put simply, systems as learning organizations could create new contexts and opportunities in which colleges and universities could contribute to their states.

## LEADING A STATEWIDE PUBLIC AGENDA

McGuinness (2011) lamented that higher education systems are erroneously focused on coordinating the efforts of institutions instead of leading a public agenda on behalf of their states. In an organizational learning model, a central focus of higher education systems would be to lead and steward a public agenda for higher education. Beyond coordinating and monitoring the performance of campuses, systems would help build capacity for public engagement among campuses and stakeholders. In doing so, they would support institutional efforts to advance engaged teaching, research, and service in relation to a statewide agenda.

A central part of the organizational learning model is its emphasis on shared leadership and accountability. In this model, system leaders would span boundaries to create mutually beneficial relationships among higher education institutions and across the private and public sectors to work on common problems. Nongovernmental organizations and mixed public/private providers could also assume leadership roles as they relate to addressing economic, social, and educational needs of their region. The overall emphasis for systems would be on creating new platforms for their institutions to serve the public. In this way, system staff would take more deliberate roles in breaking down boundaries among campuses, communities, and private/public partners to build collective action on behalf of their states.

Consistent with tenets of learning organizations, system leaders and staff would move beyond their current role as performance evaluators and play new roles as resources, coaches, and facilitators. System leaders would be charged with building unity and support around a public agenda for the state that mirrors the central role of learning organization leaders who build cohesion around a shared purpose (Morgan, 2006).

In facilitating multisector work around a public agenda, system leaders could be guided by the Smart Change framework developed by Baer, Duin, and Ramaley (2008). In short, the authors advocated for creating a "culture of inquiry" where stakeholders share insights within and among various communities of practice. In such a setting, change agents can come from anywhere and all are empowered to be part of the process (Baer, Duin, & Ramaley, 2008). The authors summarized how such integration can result in transformation at multiple levels:

> Transformative change requires a value-added definition of integrative engagement. At an individual level, this means identifying and assessing how involved one is in learning. At

an organizational level, this means identifying and assessing how we work together and the extent to which we share expectations, goals, resources, and risk and benefit with other participants. And at a community level, this means identifying and assessing how well we use campus and community resources to achieve the mission of a campus and to build and support strong, democratic communities. (p. 11)

In practical terms, a central role of system leaders in the organizational learning model is to build capacity for public engagement among campuses and stakeholders. Specific strategies may include convening public forums, providing professional development for collaborators, facilitating the development of cross-sector networks and teams, and supporting data collection and analysis for the learning teams.

## LEARNING ORGANIZATION STRUCTURES

Moving toward an organizational learning philosophy would require a different way to structure higher education systems. As discussed in McGuinness (2011), current structures were built on rational models that focus on enforcing regulations, performance reporting, and overall compliance with existing rules. From an organizational learning perspective, higher education systems must adopt more flexible, nimble structures that generate new opportunities in an ever-changing environment.

Holographic designs offer a new model for structuring higher education systems within the organizational learning view. Such designs allow organizations to reorganize as they learn to meet challenges posed by new demands. These designs reflect attributes of the human brain as they are flexible, resilient, and inventive (Morgan, 2006). Holographic designs have several salient features. First, they call for some overlap in skills and knowledge in the organization. This orientation is in contrast to rational models that have specialized parts connected to a hierarchy. In holographic designs, deliberately assembling teams with different skill sets allows the organization to meet the changing demands of the environment. Such systems are self-regulating and continually engaged in generative learning.

When functioning properly, these organizations are able to find novel and progressive solutions to complex problems (Morgan, 2006).

The application of holographic designs to the present analysis suggests that systems might create semi-autonomous "para-structures" that function for the sole purpose of leading and sustaining a public agenda. While the rational and strategic functions of systems would remain to monitor performance among institutions, a salient feature of "engaged" systems would be their expanded roles as learning organizations. As such, holographic structures can help to break down barriers between campuses and stakeholder groups to create new contexts for learning in response to state problems.

A key benefit of holographic systems is that they would allow the system to self-organize in relation to the emerging needs of the state.

Table 13.1. Evolving Model for Higher Education Systems

| Rational Perspective | Strategic Perspective | Organizational Learning Perspective |
|---|---|---|
| *Single-loop learning.* Focuses on regulating current system (retain status quo) | *Single-loop learning.* Focuses on strategic directions to improve institutional performance (improve current system) | *Double-loop learning.* Focuses on disrupting assumptions and purposes of current system (innovation: envision new models to better serve public agenda) |
| Rational planning for static institutional models | Strategic planning for dynamic market models | Generative multi-stakeholder platforms to facilitate learning, planning, and design around state needs (and subsequent role of higher education) |
| A focus on providers, mainly public institutions | A focus on clients, including students/learners, employers, and governments | A focus on sustaining cross-sector learning communities to address common problems for which higher education may contribute |
| Service areas defined by geographic boundaries of the state and monopolistic markets | Service areas defined by the needs of clients without regard to geographic boundaries | Problem contexts and settings defined through generative process facilitated by system leaders |
| Clients served by a single provider, a public university (knowledge dissemination model) | Clients served by multiple providers, with students enrolling simultaneously with two or more institutions (knowledge dissemination model) | Learning community comprised of public/private colleges, nonprofit organizations, private industries collectively serving state needs in relation to a public agenda |

With boundaries being more porous, systems could improve their capacity to tap resources and knowledge from outside the system. For example, in their research on university-community engagement, Bringle and Hatcher (2000) found that creating inclusive governing structures is one bridging strategy that institutions employ to facilitate meaningful exchanges with community partners. In these arrangements, community participation in shared governance, shared staff positions, and committee work is continually negotiated and restructured among partners. Effective university-community partnerships in these settings require a high degree of trust and development of sustained relationships (Maurrasse, 2001; Moely & Miron, 2005; Sandmann & Simon, 1999; Walshok, 1999; Ward, 1996; Zlotkowski, 1998). Systems could benefit from the same sets of principles

Table 13.1. (*continued*)

| Rational Perspective | Strategic Perspective | Organizational Learning Perspective |
|---|---|---|
| Tendency toward centralized control and regulations through tightly defined institutional missions, financial accountability, and retrospective reporting | More decentralized governance and management using policy tools to stimulate desired response (e.g., incentives, performance funding, consumer information) | Holographic design: whole built into the parts creating capacity to self-organize, create connectivity, and generalize/specialize around current and emerging state needs |
| Policies and regulations to limit competition and unnecessary duplication | Policies to "enter the market on behalf of the public" and to channel competitive forces toward public purposes | Policies to induce multisector educational collaborations around state and community needs |
| Quality defined primarily in terms of resources (inputs such as faculty credentials or library resources) as established within tertiary education | Quality defined in terms of outcomes, performance, and competence defined by multiple clients (students/learners, employers, governments) | Quality defined in terms of capacity building, economic, educational, social, and other systemic changes defined by state stakeholders. |
| Policies and services developed and carried out primarily through public agencies and public institutions | Increased use of nongovernmental organizations and mixed public/private providers to meet public/client needs (e.g., developing curricula and learning modules, providing student services, assessing competencies, providing quality assurance) | Collaboration with nongovernmental organizations and mixed public/private providers to develop/provide access to learning experiences in relation to a public agenda |

in developing their structures in response to state and community needs.

Adopting a learning organization perspective would increase the value of systems in significant ways. Instead of maintaining their status quo roles in coordinating institutions and monitoring performance, they would expand their roles as a resource, coach, and catalyst in leading and stewarding a public agenda. To make this paradigmatic shift, system leaders and staff must possess the requisite skill sets to rethink their traditional roles and lead collaborative ventures around common problems. Table 13.1 illustrates how the learning organization perspective relates to earlier models discussed in McGuiness (2011).

## CASE EXAMPLE: ENGAGEMENT AND THE STATE UNIVERSITY SYSTEM OF FLORIDA (SUSF)

To elaborate further on the attributes of the organizational learning model, I conclude this chapter with an analysis of community engagement efforts within the State University System of Florida (SUSF). Since the SUSF has explicitly included community engagement as a priority within its strategic plan, the organizational learning model illustrates how engagement could facilitate the system's progress in meeting this objective.

The Florida Board of Governors was established in 2002 to "operate regulate, control, and be fully responsible for the management of the whole university system" (State University System of Florida Board of Governors, 2011, p. 5). The board has authority over the state's 11 public universities, and the SUSF coordinates the unique educational, research, and service missions of these 11 institutions. On November 10, 2011, the board approved a strategic plan to guide the work of the SUSF from 2012–2025. The central components of the plan call for excellence, productivity, and strategic priorities around four distinctive areas: teaching and learning, scholarship, research and innovation, and community and business engagement (State University System of Florida Board of Governors, 2011).

The community and business engagement portion of the plan was discussed as a component of the systems's "tripartite mission" to "reach out and engage with Florida's communities and businesses"

(State University System of Florida Board of Governors, 2011, p. 18). The plan called for each institution to achieve the Carnegie Foundation community engagement classification by 2025. To gauge progress on these goals, the plan identified four performance indicators: percentage of students participating in community and business activities, enrollment in professional and continuing education courses, percent of baccalaureate graduates continuing their education or employment in Florida, and number of institutions achieving Carnegie's engagement classification.

Analysis of the SUSF's approach to the promotion of public engagement among its campuses reveals that the system is guided by a rational/strategic structure and approach to leadership. Specifically, SUSF's role in advancing engagement is largely focused on setting performance indicators and reporting results relative to those indicators. The focus of the plan is on clients (enrollment in continuing education, student participation in service) with quality of engagement defined as percentage of increases in institutional partnerships and curricular changes (as required by the Carnegie classification).

Within this paradigm, SUSF's approach to supporting engagement reflects a single-loop learning pattern. Simply put, the central strategy in SUSF's plan is to induce its 11 public institutions to increase their number of engagement-related activities. Furthermore, these activities largely reflect a one-way dissemination focus related to increasing program offerings and enrollment. Such an approach might be critiqued as a proxy for assessing quality and outcomes of engagement-related activities.

A final observation is that the strategic plan framed community and business partnerships as being a distinct and exclusive component of a "tripartite mission." Doing so disconnects engagement from separately listed goals of teaching and learning, scholarship, research, and innovation. In this way, engagement is viewed as rounding out the core functions of Florida's universities but not central to it.

## LEADING A PUBLIC AGENDA IN FLORIDA: AN ORGANIZATIONAL LEARNING PERSPECTIVE

SUSF's strategy to promote community engagement among Florida's 11 universities would look significantly different through an organizational learning perspective. Instead of monitoring performance around engagement, the SUSF would reconfigure itself as a resource, coach, and catalyst to support engagement on its campuses as it relates to a statewide public agenda.

Overall, the leadership, structure, and strategies to facilitate engagement would focus on creating new contexts and opportunities to improve the quality of life for Floridians. In developing a public agenda for the state, system leaders would be charged with convening multi-stakeholder forums to discuss state needs and the role of various entities in collectively serving these needs (e.g., public/private colleges, nonprofit organizations, private industries). In this model, a primary role of SUSF leaders would be to build unity and support around a statewide agenda for Florida.

Central to the development of the public agenda is the double-loop learning process, whereby system leaders and staff could engage stakeholders in collaborative learning, planning, and design in relation to a public agenda. Employing a holographic design, the SUSF could create a semi-autonomous para-structure with the ability to self-organize, create connectivity, and adapt quickly to emerging state needs. Within this para-structure, staff would assume roles as boundary spanners in convening public forums, facilitating the development of cross-sector networks and teams, providing professional development for collaborators, and supporting data collection and analysis for the learning teams. As in the Smart Change framework (Baer, Duin, & Ramaley, 2008), system leaders would seek to create a culture of inquiry within these teams. In this creative context, system staff could play key roles in leveraging public and private support in relation to the public agenda, creating policies to induce multisector collaboration around this work. Quality would be assessed in relation to capacity building in communities and economic, social, and other systemic changes defined by stakeholders.

Finally, central to the system's role would be the promotion of community and business partnerships as embedded in other strategic priorities related to teaching and learning, scholarship, research, and innovation. Thus, instead of being viewed as a separate component of the tripartite mission, engagement would be cast as a strategy to accomplish the other priorities.

For example, if a component of Florida's public agenda focused on environmental stewardship, SUSF staff could help their campuses to create opportunities for service learning, community-based

## Table 13.2. Advancing Community Engagement in Florida: Two Perspectives

| Rational/Strategic Perspective (current) | Organizational Learning Perspective (proposed) |
|---|---|
| *Single-loop learning*: Focuses on improving institutional performance around established modes of service and engagement (improve current system) | *Double-loop learning*: Focuses on disrupting assumptions and envisioning new scenarios to better address needs of Floridians (innovation: new models to serve public agenda) |
| *System as monitor and assessor*: A focus on providers, mainly public institutions to serve clients relative to community and business engagement needs (students/learners, employers); system as monitor and performance assessor | *System as leading engagement*: A focus on leading and sustaining generative, cross-sector learning communities to address common problems for which higher education is one contributor; system as resource, coach, catalyst, and convener |
| *Activity focused—serving clients*: Focus on serving the needs of clients by increasing the amount of engagement-related activity among institutions; engagement goals realized via bolstering enrollment in continuing education and community-related activity among students and faculty | *Problem focused—engaging a learning community around public problems*: Focus is on understanding problem contexts and sustaining leadership and action around a public agenda; learning community comprised of public/private colleges, nonprofit organizations, private industries collectively serve state need |
| *Bureaucratic design*: Decentralized governance, primarily monitoring performance of Florida's 11 public universities in increasing engagement-related activity (reporting to Board of Governors) | *Holographic design*: Para-structure within SUSF to promote connectivity around a public agenda for Florida; structure creates porous boundaries for broad stakeholder engagement (reporting to learning community and Board of Governors) |
| *Policy framework*: Policies to channel competitive forces toward public purposes | *Policy framework*: Policies to induce multi-sector educational collaborations around state and community needs |
| *Engagement as a goal*: Engagement defined in strategic plan as an exclusive goal to bolster partnerships and interactions with state stakeholders; engagement viewed as separate from other goals related to teaching and learning, scholarship, research, and innovation (framed as third component of tripartite mission) | *Engagement as a strategy to accomplish goals*: Engagement defined in strategic plan as a strategy to achieve goals related to teaching and learning, scholarship, research, and innovation; engagement framed as a means to strengthen degree production, reputation of programs, quality of scholarship, commercialization of research, and external funding opportunities (disrupts traditional concept of tripartite mission) |
| *Levels of engagement as quality indicator*: Quality defined in terms of productivity—the number of engagement-related activities serving community and business partners in Florida; quality linked to resources focused on engagement (inputs from students, continuing education programs, etc.) and its development of the workforce | *Systemic change as quality indicator*: Quality defined in terms of outcomes—extent of capacity building, economic, educational, social, and other systemic changes in Florida as defined by state stakeholders |

research, and other means to address environmental concerns in Florida. Doing so would help achieve the state's strategic goals in teaching, research, scholarship, and innovation.

Key to their leadership role, the SUSF could help institutions find their niche in serving the public agenda through their distinctive scholarly and curricular offerings. In this way, state flagship universities, regional institutions, and community colleges could showcase their unique collaborations and contributions. Table 13.2 illustrates how the organizational learning perspective contrasts from the rational/strategic perspective in promoting engagement in Florida.

In sum, the case example of the State University System of Florida illustrates one way that public engagement and organizational learning could become guiding principles in redesigning higher education systems to better serve state needs. Another example of how organizational learning theory relates to systems is visible in the North Dakota Higher Education Roundtable, housed in the North Dakota University System. As discussed in a comprehensive study by Lane (2008), the forum was launched in 1999 to convene key stakeholders around the needs of North Dakota and the role of higher education relative to these needs. Lane (2008) suggested that the roundtable has been successful since the needs of North Dakota are the salient driver of the agenda, with higher education framed as an instrument to address these needs. Strong leadership, effective use of data, private sector engagement, diverse membership, a focus on planning, and clear responsibilities are among the keys to its success. While current leadership transitions will test the sustainability of the roundtable, it provides an example of how learning organization and public engagement concepts can inform the development of a public agenda for higher education.

## CONCLUSION

As referenced earlier in this chapter, the state relations and policy analysis team from the American Association of State Colleges and Universities (AASCU) declared that governance reform is among the top state higher education policy issues in 2012. According to these analysts, state lawmakers are contemplating reducing or eliminating boards to save costs, and in their place, provide institutions more flexibility in exchange for agreed-upon measures of performance (AASCU, 2012). These trends reflect the proclivity of state leaders to engage in single-loop thinking, tweaking current governance/system models without considering how to make them more valuable to the state. In general, current trends undermine the value of systems in their roles as guardians of public interests.

Responding to these concerns, this chapter illustrates that public engagement is gaining momentum on campuses and can achieve many critical goals of state policy makers related to college completion, research, and innovation. The organizational learning model proposed in this chapter provides new ways of creating "value-added" systems as entities that create new opportunities and contexts to serve state needs. In creating this public value, three practical strategies might be employed among leaders who wish to create engaged higher education systems. First, leaders must develop a culture that supports continuous learning focused on changing state needs and opportunities. Toward this end, leaders must reward and improve capacity for inquiry around statewide needs. Second, leaders must help their staff develop new skills, knowledge, and competencies to lead a statewide public agenda to which higher education is just one contributor. As system personnel assume new roles as resources, coaches, and facilitators, they must be prepared to take on new challenges and identify emerging opportunities. Third, system leaders must develop structures that support innovation and emerging roles of system staff. As discussed in this chapter, holographic designs hold promise in developing nimble systems responsive to changing state needs.

While there are many promising aspects of this new model, it is not without its challenges. In his classic book on organizational theory, Morgan (2006) discussed the challenges of moving to an organizational learning model. Most significant is that the approach undermines the regulatory culture of many organizations and requires sharing power among a semi-autonomous group of actors. This shift is significant for systems that have historically operated as closed entities. In addition, the adjustment is a cultural one, which emphasizes independence, collaboration over competition, openness over closedness, and democratic inquiry. Self-criticism and reflective improvement are inherent in this culture (Morgan, 2006). In this context, ambiguity is commonplace, which contrasts rational and strategic forms of management and evaluation. As Baer and her colleagues (2008) explained:

> There are no clear answers and with every solution tried, the organization learns and adapts, and becomes more ready for the next challenge. This requires constant expansion of the core capacities of the organization across all levels and units. It involves working together differently and in a more systemic fashion. Value is added as relationships, collaboration and partnerships leverage outcomes, product quality or time to completion of tasks. (p. 12)

In closing, the future is uncertain for higher education systems as they navigate a changing economic, political, and technological landscape. New ways of thinking are needed to reframe systems beyond their traditional roles in coordinating institutions and monitoring their performance around a limited set of outcomes. As Ernest Boyer (1996), former president of the Carnegie Foundation for the Advancement of Teaching said, "I have a growing conviction that what is needed [for higher education] is not just more programs, but a larger purpose, a larger sense of mission, a larger clarity of direction in the nation's life" (p. 20). Systems must find their place in leading a new conversation about the larger purposes of higher education in society. Engaged systems could support this important role in significant ways.

## NOTE

1. See Weerts and Sandmann (2008) for a complete discussion about knowledge flow related to engagement.

## REFERENCES

American Association of State Colleges and Universities. (2002). *Stepping forward as stewards of place*. Washington, DC: Author.

American Association of State Colleges and Universities. (2012). *Top 10 state higher education policy issues for 2012.* Washington, DC: Author.

Argyris, C., & Schön, D. (1978). *Organizational learning: A theory of action perspective.* Reading, MA: Addison-Wesley.

Association of American Colleges and Universities. (2012). *A crucible moment: College learning and democracy's future.* Report of the National Task Force on Civic Learning and Democratic Engagement. Washington, DC: Author.

Astin, A. W., & Sax, L. J. (1998). How undergraduates are affected by service participation. *Journal of College Student Development, 39*(3), 251–263.

Baer, L. L., Duin, A. H., & Ramaley, J. (2008). Smart change. *Planning for Higher Education, 36* (2), 5–16.

Bloudin, D. D., & Perry, E. M. (2009). Whom does service learning really serve? Community-based organizations' perspectives on service learning. *Teaching Sociology, 37*(2), 120–135.

Boyer, E. L. (1990). *Scholarship reconsidered.* Princeton, NJ: Carnegie Foundation for the Advancement of Teaching.

Boyer, E. L. (1996). The scholarship of engagement. *Journal of Higher Education Outreach and Engagement, 1*(1), 11–20.

Bringle, R. G., & Hatcher, J. A. (2000). Institutionalization of service learning in higher education. *Journal of Higher Education, 71*(3), 273–290.

Carnegie Foundation for the Advancement of Teaching. (n.d.). *Classification description.* Retrieved from http://classifications.carnegiefoundation.org/descriptions/community_engagement.php.

Christensen, C. M., Horn, M. B., Soares, L., & Caldera, L. (2011). *Disrupting college: How innovation can deliver quality and affordability to postsecondary education.* Washington, DC: Center for American Progress.

Davies, G. K. (2006). Setting a public agenda for higher education in the states: Lessons learned from the National Collaborative for Higher Education Policy. Retrieved from http://www.higheredu-cation.org/reports/public_agenda/public_agenda.pdf.

Fitzgerald, H. E., Burak, C., & Seifer, L. (2010). *Handbook of engaged scholarship: Contemporary landscapes, future directions: Volume 1: Institutional change.* East Lansing: Michigan State University Press.

Furco, A. (2010). The engaged campus: Toward a comprehensive approach to public engagement. *British Journal of Educational Sciences*, 58(4), 375–390.

Gelmon, S. B., Holland, B. A., & Shinnamon, A. F. (1998). *Health professions schools in service to the nation: Final evaluation report*. San Francisco, CA: Community Campus Partnerships for Health.

Glassick, D. C., Huber, M. T., & Maeroff, G. I. (1997). *Scholarship assessed: Evaluation of the professorate*. San Francisco, CA: Jossey-Bass.

Grace, K. S., & Wendroff, A. L. (2001). *High impact philanthropy: How donors, boards, and nonprofit organizations can transform communities*. New York, NY: Wiley.

Hartley, M. (2009). Reclaiming the democratic purpose of American higher education: Tracing the trajectory of the civic engagement movement. *Learning and Teaching*, 2(3), 11–30.

Hood, P. (2002). *Perspectives on knowledge utilization in education*. San Francisco, CA: WestEd.

Hutchinson, J., & Huberman, M., (1993). *Knowledge dissemination and use in science and mathematics education: A literature review*. Washington, DC: National Science Foundation.

Immerwahr, J., Johnson, J., Ott, A., & Rochkind, J. (2010). *Squeeze play 2010: Continued public anxiety on cost, higher judgments on how colleges are run*. San Jose, CA: National Center for Public Policy and Higher Education.

Kellogg Commission on the Future of State and Land-Grant Universities. (1999). Returning to our roots: The engaged institution. Retrieved from Association of Public and Land-Grant Universities website: http://www.aplu.org/NetCommunity/Document.Doc?id=183.

Knox, A. B. (2001). Assessing university faculty outreach performance. *College Teaching*, 49(2), 71–74.

Lane, J. (2008). *Sustaining a public agenda for higher education: A case study of the North Dakota Higher Education Roundtable*. Boulder, CO: Western Interstate Commission for Higher Education.

Leiderman, S., Furco, A., Zapf., J., & Goss, M. (2003). *Building partnerships with college campuses: Community perspectives*. Washington, DC: Council of Independent Colleges.

Lynton, E. A. (1995). *Making the case for professional service.* Washington, DC: American Association for Higher Education.

Maurrasse, D. J. (2001). *Beyond the campus: How colleges and universities form partnerships with their communities.* New York, NY: Routledge.

McGuinness, A. C., Jr. (2011). The states and higher education. In P. G. Altbach, P. J. Gumport, & R. O. Berdahl (Eds.), *American higher education in the 21st century: Social, political, and economic challenges* (3rd ed., pp. 139–167). Baltimore, MD: Johns Hopkins University Press.

Moley, B. E., & Miron, D. (2005). College students' preferred approaches to community service: Charity and change paradigms. In S. Root, J. Callahan, & S. H. Billig (Eds.), *Improving service learning practice: Research on models to enhance impacts.* Greenwich, CT: Information Age Publishing.

Morgan, G. (2006). *Images of organization* (updated ed.). London: Sage.

National Center for the Dissemination of Disability Research. (1996). *A review of the literature on dissemination and knowledge utilization.* Austin, TX: Southwest Educational Development Laboratory.

National Center for Public Policy and Higher Education. (2008). *Measuring up 2008: The national report card on higher education.* San Jose: Author.

Peters, S. J., Jordan, N. R., Adamek, M., & Alter, T. R. (2005). *Engaging campus and community: The practice of public scholarship in the state and land-grant university system.* Dayton, OH: Kettering Foundation Press.

Quinterno, J. (March, 2012). *The great cost shift: How higher education cuts undermine the future middle class.* Retrieved from Demos website: http://www.demos.org/publication/great-cost-shift-how-higher-education-cuts-undermine-future-middle-class.

Rodin, J. (2007). *The university and urban renewal: Out of the ivory tower and into the streets.* Philadelphia: University of Pennsylvania Press.

Roose, D., Daphne, J., Miller, A. G., Norris, W., Peacock, R., White, C., & White, G. (1997). *Black student retention study: Oberlin College.* Unpublished manuscript, Oberlin College.

Roper, C. D., & Hirth, M. A. (2005). A history of change in the third mission of higher education: The evolution of one-way service to interactive engagement. *Journal of Higher Education Outreach and Engagement, 10*(3), 3–21.

Sandmann, L. R., & Simon, L. (1999). Fostering community guardianship: Serving children and families though community-university partnership. In T. Chibucos & R. Lerner (Eds.), *Serving children and families through community-university partnerships: Success stories* (pp. 211–216). Norwell, MA: Springer.

Sandmann, L., Williams, J., & Abrams, E. (2009). Higher education community engagement and accreditation: Becoming bedfellows through interpretive strategies. *Planning in Higher Education, 37*(3), 15–27.

Scott, W. R. (1992). *Organizations: Rational, natural, and open systems.* Englewood Cliffs, NJ: Prentice Hall.

Senge, P. M. (1990). *The fifth discipline: The art and practice of the learning organization.* New York, NY: Doubleday.

State University System of Florida Board of Governors. (2011). Strategic plan 2012–2025. Retrieved from State University System of Florida Board of Governors website: http://www.flbog.edu/pressroom/_doc/2011-11-28_Strategic_Plan_2012-2025_FINAL.PDF.

St. John, E. P., & Parsons, M. D. (2004). *Public financing of higher education: Changing contexts and new rationales.* Baltimore, MD: Johns Hopkins University Press.

Strickland, S. (2007). Partners in writing and rewriting history: Philanthropy and higher education. *International Journal of Educational Advancement, 7*(2), 104–116. doi:10.1057/palgrave.ijea.2150051.

Thelin, J. (2004). *A history of American higher education.* Baltimore, MD: Johns Hopkins University Press.

Vernon, A., & Ward, K. (1999). Campus and community partnerships: Assessing impacts and strengthening connections. *Michigan Journal of Community Service Learning, 6*, 30–37.

Walshok, M. L. (1999). Strategies for building the infrastructure that supports the engaged campus. In R. G. Bingle, R. Games, & E. A. Malloy (Eds.), *Colleges and universities as citizens* (pp. 74–95). Boston, MA: Allyn & Bacon.

Ward, K. (1996). Service learning and student volunteerism: Reflections on institutional commitment. *Michigan Journal of Community Service Learning, 3*, 55–65.

Weerts, D. J. (2007). Transforming campuses and communities through public engagement: Emerging roles for institutional advancement. *International Journal of Educational Advancement*, 7(2), 79–103. doi:10.1057/palgrave.ijea.2150055.

Weerts, D. J. (2010). Can community engagement leverage state appropriations for higher education? Paper presented at the annual meeting for the Association for the Study of Higher Education, Indianapolis, IN.

Weerts, D. J., & Ronca, J. M. (2006). Examining differences in state support for higher education: A comparative study of state appropriations for research I universities. *Journal of Higher Education*, 77(6), 935–965. doi: 10.1353/jhe.2006.0054.

Weerts, D. J., & Sandmann, L. R. (2008). Building a two-way street: Challenges and opportunities for community engagement at research universities. *Review of Higher Education*, 32(1), 73–106. doi: 10.1353/rhe.0.0027.

Zlotkowski, E. (Ed.). (1998). *Successful service-learning programs: New models of excellence in higher education*. Bolton, MA: Anker.

JAN M. IGNASH has served in state-level positions in four states: Florida, Washington, Illinois, and Michigan. She is currently the vice chancellor for academic and student affairs with the Florida Board of Governors. She joined the board in 2012 after having served as deputy director for policy planning and research with the Washington Higher Education Coordinating Board. Between 1994 and 1999, Dr. Ignash served as an assistant director for academic affairs with the Illinois Board of Higher Education. She began her career at the state level in the 1980s, working as a project coordinator on grant-funded initiatives with the Michigan Department of Education. In both Florida and Washington, she has served in leadership roles in those states' strategic master planning and accountability initiatives as well as policy and program issues central to academic and student affairs. Dr. Ignash has taught at both undergraduate and graduate levels, earning tenure at the University of South Florida in 2004. Dr. Ignash was awarded a Ph.D. in Education from UCLA and master's and bachelor's degrees from Michigan State University.

D. BRUCE JOHNSTONE is distinguished service professor of Higher and Comparative Education Emeritus at the State University of New York at Buffalo and director of the International Comparative Higher Education Finance and Accessibility Project. His principal scholarship is in higher education finance, governance, and policy formation in both domestic and international comparative higher education contexts. He is the author of many books, monographs, articles, and chapters on these topics and is coeditor, with Jason Lane, of the

SUNY series Critical Issues in Higher Education, of which this is the second volume. Johnstone has held posts of vice president for administration at the University of Pennsylvania, president of the State University College at Buffalo, and chancellor of the State University of New York System, the latter from 1988 to 1994. He holds bachelor's and master's degrees from Harvard and a PhD from the University of Minnesota.

C. JUDSON KING is provost and senior vice president of academic affairs, emeritus of the University of California, having served as provost from 1995 until 2004. He was previously provost of Professional Schools and Colleges and dean of the College of Chemistry on the Berkeley campus, and now directs the Center for Studies in Higher Education (http://cshe.berkeley.edu/) at Berkeley. He is also Professor Emeritus of Chemical and Biomolecular Engineering, having researched and published extensively in that field during his 50-year Berkeley career, including authoring a widely used textbook, *Separation Processes* (1971, 1980). He is a member of the National Academy of Engineering and has received various awards from the American Institute of Chemical Engineers, the American Society for Engineering Education, the American Chemical Society, the Council for Chemical Research, and the Yale Science and Engineering Association. He has been chair of the Board of the American University of Armenia Corporation (1995–2006, 2009–2012), vice chair and chair of the California Association for Research in Astronomy [Keck Telescopes] (2000–2006), member (1995–2004) and chair (2001–2004) of the California Council on Science and Technology, and interim director (2007–2009) of the Phoebe A. Hearst Museum of Anthropology on the Berkeley campus.

JASON E. LANE is the Associate Provost for the State University of New York (SUNY) and deputy director for research at the Nelson A. Rockefeller Institute of Government, SUNY's public policy think tank. He is also an associate professor of educational policy, senior researcher at the Institute for Global Education Policy Studies, and codirector of the Cross-Border Education Research Team (C-BERT) at SUNY-Albany. His research focuses on the organization and leadership of higher education institutions as well as their relationship to governments. Most recently he has been studying the globalization of higher education, with a specific interest in the emergence of the multi-national university and cross-border higher education. Lane has written numerous articles, book chapters, and policy reports and authored or edited seven books, including *Multi-National Colleges and Universities: Leadership and Administration of International Branch Campuses* (Jossey-Bass, 2011, with Kevin Kinser), *Academic Leadership and Governance of Higher Education* (Stylus Press, 2012, with Robert Hendrickson, James Harris, and Rick Dorman), and *Colleges and Universities as Economic Drivers* (SUNY Press, 2012, with Bruce Johnstone). He has served on the boards of the Comparative and International Education Society (CIES), Council for International Higher Education (CIHE), and the Gulf Comparative Education Society (GCES).

KATHARINE C. LYALL is president emeritus of the University of Wisconsin System where she served from 1992 to 2004. During her years as president, she regularly taught freshman economics. Prior to her service in Wisconsin, she held faculty positions at Syracuse University and Johns Hopkins University. She served as deputy assistant secretary at the U.S. Department of Housing and Urban Development in the Carter administration. Earlier in her career, she worked at the Chase Manhattan Bank on Wall Street doing trust fund investment analyses. She holds a BA and PhD in Economics from Cornell University and an MBA from New York University. She lives in Madison, Wisconsin and Menlo Park, California.

MARIO MARTINEZ is a professor of higher education at the University of Nevada, Las Vegas. Mario's research addresses state-level higher education policy, competency modeling, and most recently, innovation and change in higher education. He has worked on projects for Lumina, Gates, and Public Agenda, as a complement to his research.

AIMS C. MCGUINNESS JR. is a senior associate with the National Center for Higher Education Management Systems (NCHEMS), a private nonprofit policy center in Boulder, Colorado. At NCHEMS, he specializes in state governance and coordination of higher education; strategic planning and restructuring higher education systems;

roles and responsibilities of public institutional and multi-campus system governing boards; and international comparison of education reform. Prior to joining NCHEMS in 1993, he was director of higher education policy at the Education Commission of the States (ECS). Before joining ECS in 1975, was executive assistant to the chancellor of the University of Maine System. Over the past 35 years, McGuinness has advised many of the states that have conducted major studies of their higher education systems and undertaken higher education reforms. Recent and ongoing projects (conducted through NCHEMS) include advising the states of Arkansas, California, Colorado, Kentucky, Louisiana, Massachusetts, Mississippi, Oregon, Texas, Washington, and Wisconsin on governance and other higher education reforms. McGuinness is active at the international level in conducting policy reviews and advising governments on higher education policy, primarily through the Organisation for Economic Co-operation and Development (OECD) and the World Bank, including work in the Baltic States (Estonia, Latvia, and Lithuania), the Dominican Republic, Egypt, Greece, India, Israel, Ireland, Korea, Japan, Malaysia, the Russian Federation, and Turkey.

DAVID F. SHAFFER is a senior fellow at the Nelson A. Rockefeller Institute of Government, University at Albany, State University of New York. His research focuses on economic development, higher education, and workforce development. At the institute he has, among other things, coauthored *A New Paradigm for Economic Development: How Higher Education Institutions Are Working to Revitalize Their Regional and State Economies* (March 2010, with David J. Wright); and *How SUNY Matters: Economic Impacts of the State University of New York* (June 2011, with Rachel M. Teaman and David J. Wright). He has written about state government and public policy since 1973, first as a reporter for the Associated Press, and, from 1980–2008, on the staff of the Business Council of New York State, Inc. From 1993–2008, he was president of the Public Policy Institute, the council's research affiliate. He holds degrees in political science from Duke University (BA, 1970) and from Rockefeller College at the University at Albany (MA, 1972).

BRANDY SMITH is a post-doctoral scholar for the Association for the Study of Higher Education. She has consulted on projects funded by Lumina and Gates, and her research primarily focuses on organizational change within higher education settings and diffusion of educational innovations within state policy, postsecondary system, and institutional levels.

DAVID J. WEERTS is associate professor and director of the Jandris Center for Innovative Higher Education in the Department of Organizational Leadership, Policy and Development at the University of Minnesota-Twin Cities. Weerts's teaching and scholarly interests include state financing of higher education, university-community engagement, and alumni giving, advocacy, and volunteerism. His research on these topics appears in leading higher education journals including *The Journal of Higher Education, Research in Higher Education*, and the *Review of Higher Education*. In addition, Weerts has eight years of experience in university advancement and has held major gifts officer positions at the University of Wisconsin Foundation and University of Minnesota Foundation. He holds a PhD in higher education from the University of Wisconsin-Madison.

JANE V. WELLMAN is the executive director of the National Association of System Heads, the association of the chief executives of the 52 colleges and university systems of public higher education in the United States and Puerto Rico. Previously, she served as executive director of Delta Cost Project, a nonprofit research and policy organization focused on ways to improve public transparency about higher education finance, including comparative data on cost metrics. Wellman is widely recognized for her 30 years of work in public policy and higher education at both the state and federal levels, and for her particular expertise in state fiscal policy, cost analysis, strategic planning, state and federal regulation of higher education, accountability metrics and performance reporting, and quality control—including accreditation. She served as a senior associate with the Institute for Higher Education Policy, vice president for government relations with the National Association of Independent Colleges and Universities, deputy director of the California Postsecondary Education Commission, and staff director of the California Assembly Ways and Means Committee. Until 2012, Wellman also sat on the Association of American Colleges and Universities' board of directors, and was a member of the board of trustees for Argosy University.

NANCY L. ZIMPHER became the 12th chancellor of the State University of New York, the nation's largest comprehensive system of higher education, in June 2009. A nationally recognized leader in education, Chancellor Zimpher spearheaded and launched a new strategic plan for SUNY in her first year as chancellor. The central goal of the plan, called *The Power of SUNY*, is to harness the university's potential to drive economic revitalization and create a better future for every community across New York. Chancellor Zimpher is active in numerous state and national education organizations and is a leader in the areas of teacher preparation, urban education, and university-community engagement. As cofounder of Strive, a community-based cradle-to-career collaborative, Chancellor Zimpher has been instrumental in creating a national network of innovative systemic partnerships that holistically address challenges across the education pipeline. She has authored or coauthored numerous books, monographs, and academic journal articles on teacher education, urban education, academic leadership, and school/university partnerships. Chancellor Zimpher currently serves as chair of the Board of Governors of the New York Academy of Sciences and of CEOs for Cities. From 2005 to 2011, she chaired the national Coalition of Urban Serving Universities. She also recently co-chaired NCATE's blue-ribbon panel on transforming teacher preparation. She previously served as president of the University of Cincinnati, chancellor of the University of Wisconsin-Milwaukee, executive dean of the Professional Colleges, and dean of the College of Education at Ohio State University. She holds a bachelor's degree in English Education and Speech, a master's degree in English Literature, and a PhD in Teacher Education and Higher Education Administration, all from Ohio State University.

# INDEX

academic affairs
 roles of system-level officers in, 218–29
 steering of, 229–31
 system role in, 215–16
academic drift, 83
academic freedom, 78, 132–33
Adner, R., 171–72
Advanced Placement credits, 180
Albania, 276
Alfred University, 160–61
Alssid, J. L., 240, 250
Alter, J., 221–22
American Association of State Colleges and Universities (AACSU), 287, 302–3
Argyris, C., 293
Arizona, 52, 182, 184–85
Arkansas, 62
audit function, 104, 163
 for international programs, 276
autonomy, for universities, 78–82
 limits to, 90–94

Baer, L. L., 294–95, 304
Barak, R. J., 220, 222, 230
Bennis, W. G., 171
Beyle, T., 184
Boatright, K. J., 265
Boston Foundation, 250
Bowen, F. M., 15, 47, 203, 204, 264–65
Boyer, Ernest, 304

Bracco, K. R., 216
Bringle, R. G., 297
Brubacher, J. S., 14
budgeting, 115–16, 163
Buffalo, University at (SUNY), 35
Burke, W. W., 172
Burke-Litwiln Causal Model of Organizational Performance and Change, 172

California, 53
California, University of, 47, 118, 166–67n6
 campus-level boards for, 203, 209n3
 financing plan in, 140, 153
 international programs of, 263
 Regents for, 155, 158, 164
 state support for, 151
California State University (CSU), 8–10, 47, 164
 international programs of, 263, 271–72, 277
Callan, P. M., 58, 216
Campus Compact, 287
Cantor, M. C., 174
Carnegie Foundation for the Advancement of Teaching, 288, 290, 299
Carnevale, Anthony, 247
Christensen, C. M., 172
City University of New York (CUNY), 52–53, 175
civic engagement movement, 287–90
Clark, B. R., 217

317

Clemson University, 166n4
Cohen, A. R., 14
Coleman, J. S., 185
collective bargaining, 104–5
Collins, J., 32–33
Colorado, 60, 240, 274
community colleges, 37–38, 220
    acceptance of degrees issued by,
        88–89
    bachelor's degrees offered by, 83
    four-year programs in, 228
    future of, 252–55
    in Georgia, 244–46
    in Massachusetts, 249–52
    in North Carolina, 238–44
    system approaches to workforce
        development in, 240–41
    transfers from, 94, 120–21
    in Virginia, 246–49
    workforce development in, 237
Connecticut, 63–64
consolidated systems, 47, 48
Cornell University, 158, 160, 166n5
Courant, P. N., 174
Creamer, Elizabeth, 249
credit requirements, 120
    Advanced Placement for, 180
Cresswell, J. W., 15
Cuomo, Andrew, 4
Curriculum Improvement Process (CIP),
    243

Dahl, R. A., 47
data management and analysis, 225–26
Delaware, 66n5, 158, 166n4
Dewey, Thomas E., 29
Dickinson State University, 276, 280n7
double-loop learning, 293, 300
Duin, A. H., 294–95

Education, U.S. Department of,
    21–22n2, 288
Education Commission of the States,
    56, 246, 248
education partnerships, 154

Empire State College, 276, 280n7
employees
    benefits for, 119–20
    as state employees, 195
endowments, 139, 160
    governance and, 165
enrollment
    fiscal context of, 106
    governance and, 164
    strategic management of, 37
    undergraduate admissions, 84
ethical issues, 132–33

faculty
    in community colleges curriculum
        development, 243
    employee benefits for, 119–20
    policies for appointment and tenure
        for, 93–94
    in public engagement model, 289
    See also employees
Fain, P., 238
federal government. See United States
financial aid, 153
financing of higher education systems,
    101–2
    decline in state support for, 284
    facets of, 102–5
    fiscal context of, 105–12
    governance and, 150
    responses to changes in, 112–22,
        129–31
    stabilizing, 138–40
    state control in, 196
Finney, J. E., 216
flagship systems, 8, 47
    autonomy in, 18, 114
    campus leadership in, 134
    funding for, 136–37
    governing boards for, 96, 137–38
Florida, 221, 226–27
Florida, State University System of
    (SUSF)
    campus-level boards in, 158, 204,
        209n4

community engagement in, 298–99
governance in, 61
international students in, 277
organizational learning perspective
    in, 299–302
program review in, 223–24
Fogel, D. M., 32
for-profit educational institutions, 119
Friedman, T. L., 41–42
fundraising, 154

Gade, M. L., 15
Gaither, G. H., 15–16, 265
Garland, J. C., 157, 158
Garrett, R. L., 247, 254, 255n1
Georgia, 186
    community colleges in, 244–46, 253
Georgia, University System of, 51, 118
    study abroad programs of, 271, 272
G.I. Bill (U.S., 1944), 231
Gladwell, M., 185
globalization of higher education,
    261–63, 265
    administrative offices for, 266–77
Goldberg, M., 240, 250
Goldenberg, J., 185
Gonzalez, J., 247
governance, 149–50, 201–3
    alternative funding and, 152–55
    alternative structures for, 157–61
    changes in, 150–52, 285–86
    of community colleges, 242–44,
        247–50
    effectiveness in, 205–9
    evaluating approaches to, 161–62
    existing structures for, 155–57
    institutional authority in, 201–3
    local boards for, 162–65, 203–4
    in Oregon, 198–200
    restructuring systems for, 195–96
    state context for, 193–95
    steering function in, 217–18, 229–31
    system-level academic officers in,
        218–29
    in Wisconsin, 196–98

governing boards, 140–41
    for flagship institutions, 96, 137–38
governors, 183–84
Grady, J., 251
Graham, Robert, 61
Great Recession, 63–64, 151
Guerber, S., 50

Hatcher, J. A., 297
Henry, T. C., 15
Herstam, Chris, 182
Herstam Plan, 182, 184–85
Higher Education Act (U.S., 1965), 231
higher education systems
    change imperative in, 285–87
    changing roles of, 131–36
    civic engagement movement in,
        287–90
    definition of, 8
    as postsecondary systems, 170, 174
    public engagement in, 290–93
    *See also* public higher education
        systems
Hoenk, M., 238
holographic designs, 295–96
Huberman, M., 292
Hutchinson, J., 292

Idaho, 49–50
Ignash, Jan M., 19–20, 215–32
Illinois, 60, 223
income-contingent financing, 139–40
Independent Commission on the Future
    of the State University of New
    York, 55
Indiana, Western Governors University
    in, 178, 187
innovations, 171–72, 177–83
Institutional Management in Higher
    Education (IMHE), 274
insurance, for international programs
    and students, 276–77
internationalization of higher educa-
    tion, 261–63, 265
    administrative offices for, 266–77

international programs, 39, 263, 270
policing of, 275–77

Jacobson, D., 221–22
Jaggars, Shanna Smith, 238, 254
Johnstone, D. Bruce, 75–98

Kaine, Thomas, 248, 253
Kania, J., 41
Kansas, 50
Katz, E., 185
Kellogg Commission on the Future of
State and Land-Grant Universities,
287
Kentucky, 62
Kerr, Clark, 52, 54–56, 65n4, 203,
209n3
King, C. Judson, 18, 149–65
Kitzhaber, 200
knowledge, transfers of, 291
Kramer, M., 41

Lane, Jason E., 3–21, 302
on globalization strategies, 261–78
Lariviere, Richard, 139, 199
leadership, 134–35
learning model. See organizational
learning model
Lee, E. C., 15, 47, 203, 204, 264–65
Lincoln, Abraham, 29, 33
Louisiana, 62, 63, 175, 179, 185–86
Lumina Foundation, 227, 230–31
Lyall, Katharine C., 18, 127–44

Maine, 65n3, 204
Maine, University of, 118–20
international programs of, 272
market forces, 217
Martin, Carolyn "Biddy," 196-197
Martinez, Mario, 18–19, 169–89
Maryland, University System of, 54,
121, 179
local governing boards in, 204
Massachusetts, 54, 175
community colleges in, 249–54

local governing boards in, 204
Massachusetts, University of, 274
MassINC (think tank), 250–51
massive open online courses (MOOCs),
152
Mazursky, D., 185
McDonnell, Robert, 248–49
McGuinness, Aims C., Jr., 17, 19, 21,
293, 295
on academic affairs, 219
on changes in governance, 285–86
on future of higher education sys-
tems, 16
on history of higher education sys-
tems, 13, 45–64
on state context, 193–209
on systems, 264
McNelly, Jennifer, 238
Menzel, H., 185
Michigan, 151, 228
Millett, J. D., 14
Minnesota, 62, 221–22
Missouri, University of, 13, 22n4
Montana, 48–49, 62
Morgan, G., 303
Morrill, Justin, 29–30
Morrill Land-Grant Acts (U.S.; 1862,
1890), 29–30, 33, 40, 42, 151, 231
Morrissey, Sharon, 243
Murray, Therese, 251

National Association of System Heads
(NASH), 8, 64–65n1
National Center for Educational Statis-
tics, 228
National Center for Public Policy and
Higher Education, 59
National Governors Association, 56,
115
NCR Corporation, 246
Nebraska, University of, 119–20
Nevada, 186
New Badger Partnership (Wisconsin),
196, 208
Newby, Sir Howard, 127, 130

New Jersey, 55, 61, 186
New York, State University of. *See* State
University of New York
New York State, 155, 175
Statutory Colleges and Schools in,
160–61
Superstorm Sandy damage to, 4
North Carolina, 53, 158
community colleges in, 238–44,
253–55
North Carolina, University of, 118, 163
local governing boards in, 204
state regulatory control over, 195
study abroad programs of, 271
North Dakota, 51, 155, 276, 302
North Dakota Higher Education
Roundtable, 302
not-for-credit courses, 241–42
Nottis, D. M., 265
NYS 2100 Commission, 4–5

Observatory for Boarderless Higher
Education, 273–74
O'Donnell, K., 225, 227
Ohio, 158, 180, 184, 185
Oregon
centralization in, 51
financing in, 113–14, 139
governance in, 65n3
local boards in, 204
state regulatory control in, 195,
198–200
strategic directions for, 207, 208
study abroad programs of, 263, 272
organizational change, 172
organizational learning model, 292–94
in Florida, 299–302
obstacles to, 303–4
structures for, 295–98

Parsons, M. D., 292
Patrick, Deval, 251–53
Pennsylvania, 54, 121, 158, 178–79
local governing boards in, 204
Pennsylvania, University of, 288

Pennsylvania State University, 22n3
performance, 176
Perkins, J. A., 79
Pfeffer, J., 186
planning, 224–25
international, 269–70
postsecondary systems, 170, 174–77
Povar, Elizabeth, 247–48
*Power of SUNY* (strategic plan), 31,
274
pre-college education, 39–40
private universities
boards for, 156
conversion of public universities to,
160
productivity, 120–22
program approvals, 219–24
program reviews, 222
Progressive Era, 48–50
public engagement, 288–89
in Florida, 298–99
in higher education systems, 290–93
public higher education systems
alternatives to, 94–98
autonomy and authority in, 76–82
changes in financing of, 101–22
definition of, 8
as ecosystem, 169–70, 173–74
governance of, 155–65
tensions within, 82–90

Quick Start programs (Georgia),
245–46, 253

Ramaley, J., 294–95
rational tuition, 87, 99n3
Reilly, Kevin, 197, 198
research ventures, 154
resource allocation, 34
Rhode Island, 11–12, 180
Richardson, R. C., Jr., 216, 217, 231
Rockefeller, Nelson A., 29
Rogers, E. M., 172, 187
Roskens, R. W., 15
Rudy, W., 14

Safman, P., 222
St. John, E. P., 292
Schneider, J., 240, 250
Schön, D., 293
senior colleges
    acceptance of community colleges'
        degrees by, 88–89
    transfers from community colleges
        to, 94
Shaffer, David F., 20, 237–55
silos, 246
single-loop learning, 293
Smith, Brandy, 18–19, 169–89
Solomon, S., 185
South Carolina, 158
South Dakota, 49, 183, 187
South Korea, 263
states
    community colleges supported by,
        242
    constitutional powers of, 78
    decline in support for public higher
        education in, 284
    funding of public higher education
        systems by, 150, 151
    globalization of higher education
        and, 262
    higher education systems of, 7–8
    in public higher education ecosys-
        tems, 175–76
    regulatory control of university sys-
        tems by, 195–96
State University of New York (SUNY),
    30–31, 175
    collaboration among campuses of,
        182–84
    community colleges of, 37–38
    as comprehensive system, 10
    creation and history of, 12, 29, 52
    globalism of, 38–39
    Independent Commission on the
        Future of SUNY, 55
    international offices of, 274–75
    international programs of, 276
    local governing boards in, 204
    master plan for, 207

NYS 2100 Commission and, 4–5, 19
research funding for, 105
resource allocation within, 34
shared services within, 34–36
state regulatory control over, 195
Statutory Colleges and Schools under,
    161
strategic plan of, 20, 31–32
student mobility in, 36–37
study abroad programs of, 263,
    271–73
systemness of, 5–6, 27
strategic planning, 224–25
Strickland, S., 289
students
    admission decisions on, 84–86
    competition for, 194
    financial aid for, 153
    in governance, 156
    income-contingent financing by,
        139–40
    international exchanges of, 270–73,
        277
    international recruitment of, 274
    mobility of, 36–37
    in public engagement model, 289
    strategic enrollment management of,
        37
    tuition and fees paid by, 86–88
    See also tuition and fees
study abroad programs, 263, 270–73
Superstorm Sandy, 3–4
sustainability, 135–36
systemness, 5-6; 27-44
    definition of, 27
    in globalization, 263
    of SUNY, 5–6, 29
    shared services, 34-36
    student mobility, 36
    workforce development, 240, 253,
        255
systems, knowledge about, 12–17

technology, 141–43
Templin, Robert G., Jr., 247
Tennessee, 53

Texas, 54, 175
Western Governors University in, 178
Texas, University of, 121
Thelin, J. R., 13–14
transfer students, 36, 89, 94, 120–21
tuition and fees, 86–88, 93, 194
dependency on, 107–10
federal role in assistance for, 112
in financing higher education systems, 104, 153
in governance, 163–64
income-contingent financing of, 139–40
retained at campus level, 112
two-year institutions, 220
*See also* community colleges

United States
commitment to higher education by federal government, 231
higher education of population of, 133–34
student debt financing by, 140
training programs funded by, 246
tuition assistance from federal government, 112
University of. *See under main part of name*
Utah, 158, 204, 220–21
program review in, 222–23

Vermont, 66n5, 158, 166n4
Virginia, 151
community colleges in, 240, 246–49, 253
Virginia, University of, 152
Vos, J., 221–22

Walker Scott, 197
Wallace, J., 221

Washington (state), 180
accountability in, 228
program review in, 224
Western Governors University in, 178, 187
Weerts, David J., 20–21
on public engagement in higher education systems, 283–304
Wellman, Jane, 17–18, 225–26
on financial issues in higher education systems, 101–22
Western Governors University (WGU), 178, 184, 187
West Virginia, 60, 62
Wildavaky, A., 224
Williams, G. L., 217
Wisconsin, 112, 181
state regulatory control in, 195–96
strategic directions for, 207, 208
Wisconsin, University of
autonomy of UW-Madision within, 181, 196–98
centralization in, 53
local governing boards in, 204
Wisconsin Idea in, 12, 20–21
Wisconsin Idea Partnership, 197–98
workforce development, in community colleges, 237–41
future of, 252–55
in Georgia, 244–46
in Massachusetts, 249–52
in North Carolina, 241–44
system approach to, 240–41
in Virginia, 246–49
Workforce Strategy Center (WSC), 248–51
Wyoming, 66n5

Yale University, 119

Zimpher, Nancy L., 5, 17, 27–42

Made in the USA
Lexington, KY
22 October 2013